Praise for *A Revelation to the Church*

"One thing we all agree on is that Jesus is indeed coming back again…which we are all looking forward to. In fact the darker our world becomes the more we find ourselves praying, 'Lord haste the day!' But the how's, when's and what happens before his final return to establish his Kingdom have for centuries been points of theological and exegetical interest. And, sadly, varying points of view have often divided followers of Christ into eschatological camps that look more like warrior groups than irenic discussions."

"What I love about Stephen's book is not only the thorough treatment of biblical texts that support his view of the end times but the charitable spirit in which it is written. Anyone seeking clarity in mind and spirit about the drama of end times will need to read this book! It will ramp up your anticipation of that great and long awaited day!"

—Dr. Joseph M. Stowell
President
Cornerstone University

"Stephen Popp is a careful and courageous reader of the biblical text. He bravely puts aside his own preconceptions and follows the book of Revelation wherever he believes it leads. The result is wise, godly counsel for Christians living in the last days. Regardless of your view of the end times, you will find in this book a thoroughly researched, meticulously argued, timely word."

—Michael Wittmer
Professor of Systematic & Historical Theology
Grand Rapids Theological Seminary

"Through a careful, scholarly analysis of Revelation, Stephen provides a needed balance to the other more technical approaches and an apt answer to the practical question, 'What does all this mean for us?' I strongly recommend that one read this book as part of studying the book of Revelation. It will greatly aid you in your understanding of God's plan not just for some distant future time, but indeed for the present as well."

—Andrew Smith
Associate Professor of New Testament
Cornerstone University

"Stephen Popp's *A Revelation to the Church* offers a thoughtful approach to the book of Revelation. His work reminds us that Revelation is not about creating timelines of end-time events but advising Christians how to live in light of these events. I recommend the book to be read with an open mind, a prayerful spirit, and an obedient will."

—Dr. Jim Lacy
Director of Church Health
Converge MidAmerica, Michigan

"Stephen's heart and goal are evident both in the structure and content of *A Revelation to the Church*. This work sets out to offer meaningful and understandable biblical exegesis through engaging, sweeping biblical themes while not getting caught up in constructing tight timeframes. The end result is a persuasive call to the church to exercise joyous and faithful obedience to the God Who Is!"

—Jeffrey Halsted, Ph.D.
Senior Pastor
Calvary Baptist Church

A Revelation to the Church

To the Church

A Call for the Endurance and Faith of the Saints

Stephen Popp

Foreword by Andrew Smith

Copyright © 2016 by Stephen Popp

A Revelation to the Church
A Call for the Endurance and Faith of the Saints
by Stephen Popp

Back cover photo is courtesy of Ryan Prins Photography and Cornerstone University.

Printed in the United States of America.

ISBN 9781498474948

All rights reserved solely by the author. The author guarantees all contents are original and do not infringe upon the legal rights of any other person or work. No part of this book may be reproduced in any form without the permission of the author. The views expressed in this book are not necessarily those of the publisher.

Unless otherwise indicated, Scripture quotations taken from the English Standard Version (ESV). Copyright © 2001 by Crossway, a publishing ministry of Good News Publishers. Used by permission. All rights reserved.

www.xulonpress.com

Dedicated to

*Joshua, Jonathan, Jennifer, and Jessica
In hopes that each will believe in Jesus Christ,
Hear the words of this prophecy, and
Be clothed with fine linen, white and pure.*

Contents

Foreword by Andrew Smith   *xi*
Preface   *xiii*
Acknowledgements   *xv*

Part One: Preliminaries   1

Establishes the foundational premise that the book of Revelation was written to, for, and about the church

    Introduction   2
    The Primary Thesis   6
    To the Church   7
    The Whole Church   10
    The Whole Book   14
    For the Church   18
    About the Church   24
    Purpose of Revelation   34
    Summary   36

Part Two: Commentary   37

Walks through the book of Revelation and fleshes out the premise that Revelation was written to, for, and about the church

    Introduction   38
    Prologue (Rev. 1)   40
    The Seven Messages (Rev. 2-3)   47
    The Throne Room of God (Rev. 4-5)   51
    The Seven Seals (Rev. 6)   56
    The Two Visions of the Church (Rev. 7)   60

A Revelation to the Church

The Seven Trumpets (Rev. 8-9)	64
The Seven Thunders (Rev. 10)	67
The Two Witnesses (Rev. 11:1-14)	68
The Seventh Trumpet (Rev. 11:15-19)	70
The Woman, the Dragon, and Her Children (Rev. 12)	71
The Two Beasts (Rev. 13)	78
The Church with Christ (Rev. 14:1-5)	81
The Message of the Three Angels (Rev. 14:6-13)	83
The Harvest of the Earth (Rev. 14:14-20)	85
The Angels with the Last Plagues (Rev. 15)	87
The Seven Bowls (Rev. 16)	89
The Prostitute and the Beast (Rev. 17)	93
The Fall of Babylon (Rev. 18-19:10)	98
The Rider on the White Horse (Rev. 19:11-21)	102
The Thousand Years (Rev. 20)	105
All Things New (Rev. 21-22:5)	108
The Epilogue (Rev. 22:6-21)	118

Part Three: Confessions   121

Exposes the weaknesses of our theology that denies the premise that Revelation was written to, for, and about the church

Introduction	122
Exegetical Weakness	124
Hermeneutical Weakness	130
Structural Weakness	134
Historical Weakness	140
Theological Weakness	143
Second Chances	145
Purgatory	152
Escapism	155
Impersonal Gospel Agents	160
Abandoned Christians	164

Contents

Israel and the Church	168
God's Wrath and the Church	175
Logical Weakness	180
Literary Weakness	184
Moral Weakness	188
Pastoral Weakness	190

Part Four: Application — 193

Specifies how we, as members of the church, may receive the blessing promised to those who read and obey the message of Revelation

Introduction	194
Hear the Words	196
Believe in Jesus Christ	204
Separate Yourselves	215
Worship God	226
Take Your Stand	234
Hold to the Testimony	243
Endure to the End	255
Glory in the Cross	261
Notes	267

Foreword by Andrew Smith
ΑΩ

Like many others in our tradition, I grew up in a church that was what I term "lovingly legalistic." As strange, and even as oxymoronic, as that sounds, it is true. It was a church that was deeply and profoundly concerned about evangelizing and discipling the "next generation" of believers. Such things as the use of tobacco, the consumption of alcohol, and even attending the movie theater or using playing cards were considered patently unchristian. This was all done out of a pure heart, for they truly believed that avoiding such "vices" was a vital part of one's spiritual growth.

One doctrinal issue that was part of this Christian setting was a belief not only in premillennialism (the teaching that Christ would reign on earth for a literal thousand years as mentioned in Revelation 20:1-7), but also pretribulationalism (the teaching that God would remove the church from the earth before the tribulation, so that God could deal with Israel in the final stages of his salvific plan as laid out in Daniel 9:24-27). It always struck me as fascinating that such a doctrine, which was formulated only some 200 years ago, could become a test of fellowship among fundamentalists who rallied around the foundational teachings of the Christian faith.

As I grew older, I soon discovered that passages such as 1 Thessalonians 4:13-18 and Revelation 4:1 do not support pre-tribulational theology, but they in fact teach something quite different. 1 Thessalonians 4:13-18 assures believers that they, whether alive or asleep, will always be "with the Lord," not that they will be taken out of the world for any kind of tribulation period; and Revelation 4:1

A Revelation to the Church

depicts John, not the church or as a representative of the church, being caught up to heaven in his vision, where he sees things from the perspective of God's throne.

It also became clear that the entire book of Revelation does not teach a sort of escapism or avoidance of persecution for those who are faithful to Jesus Christ. Quite the contrary, Revelation speaks of two cities: Babylon—whose first century incarnation was the Roman Empire with its Imperial Cult and persecution of the church—and the New Jerusalem—which is clearly a term describing those whose faith is in the finished work of the Lamb. The book of Revelation calls upon the church to be faithful and not to give in to the demands of Babylon. If they did this, they could be assured that, current persecution and even martyrdom notwithstanding, they would one day dwell with Jesus in the new heaven and new earth.

Stephen's work is both scholarly and pastoral. It unites and addresses the concerns of both the academy and the assembly. Through a careful, scholarly analysis of Revelation, it gives assurance that, even in these challenging last days, we can be sure that our "King of kings and Lord of lords" will indeed triumph over the dragon, the beast, and the false prophet. We can be sure that when Babylon is finally fallen, Jesus will dwell with us as we live in our resurrected bodies on a glorified new earth.

I have taught the book of Revelation some six times during my thirty-plus years on the faculty of Cornerstone University. I have found Stephen Popp's work to be biblical and timely. I have asked him if I may use this book the next time I teach the course in the spring of 2017. I strongly recommend that one read this book carefully and prayerfully as part of studying the book of Revelation. It will greatly aid you in your understanding of God's plan not just for some distant future time, but indeed for the present as well.

—Andrew Smith
Associate Professor of New Testament
Cornerstone University

Preface
ΑΩ

I am not a prophet, nor the son of a prophet (Amos 7:14). I simply declare what I believe is clear in Scripture: the book of Revelation was written to, for, and about the church. This is not a popular view, for many evangelicals believe the church will be taken away prior to the tribulation. This is not a pleasant view, for this means that the church will go through the tribulation. Yet, the biblical text leads the reader to this view; and to the extent that we correctly read, understand, and apply the Word of God, there is peace and safety.

Although I am not a prophet, at times I feel like a prophet. The prophet Jeremiah, for instance, lived during a period of time when false prophets abounded. These false prophets were not seeking out, listening to, and declaring the Word of God. They were proclaiming peace and safety when, in fact, war and destruction were around the corner. They had crafted lies in their heart and developed a theology which taught people that Jerusalem, the city of God, was impregnable. This theology offered hope to the people, morale to the troops, and confidence to the king.

Jeremiah, in stark contrast, faithfully sought out, listened to, and proclaimed the Word of God. Jeremiah had gone back to and poured over the covenant that God had made with his people. In the book of Deuteronomy, God had promised abundant blessings to the Hebrew nation if they obeyed him, but he promised to bring judgment upon the nation if they turned away from him. Jeremiah then applied the Word of God to his own generation. Since the people had broken the covenant, God's curse was upon them. Babylon would soon overtake Jerusalem, if they did not repent.

By likening myself to Jeremiah, I am not claiming to have a corner on the truth, nor am I declaring that others who disagree with me are false prophets. I am simply questioning a popular theology that promises peace and safety, when, in fact, the book of Revelation warns of trials and tribulation. I feel like a lone voice, calling people back to the biblical text and challenging our commonly held beliefs about the end times. I am proclaiming a view that calls people to believe in Jesus Christ and to prepare for his soon return.

I submit my writing to the church—to whom, for whom, and about whom the book of Revelation was written. Consider my words. See whether they are true. And if so, prepare yourselves for things to come, for the time is near.

Acknowledgements
ΑΩ

The apostle Paul reminds us not to think of ourselves more highly than we ought to think, but to think of ourselves with sober judgment and to recognize that God has given each of us different gifts and abilities according to his grace (Rom. 12:3-8). To this end, I want to acknowledge those people who have played a special role in the publication of this book.

I want to thank Karen Stadt and Karen Hall for their willingness to proofread the manuscript during the final stages. While I accept the responsibility for any remaining grammatical or spelling errors, their careful reading of the text has greatly improved the final product. Karen Stadt is a longtime friend and neighbor who has been ray of sunshine to our family, and Karen Hall is my beloved sister who exemplifies what it means to be a Christian in the home and in the workplace.

I want to thank Mark Popp and Cindy Wiltheiss for their continual source of encouragement. My brother Mark purposefully lives out the Bible in daily life and basks in the grace of God. Every time we spoke on the phone, he consistently prompted me, "I am still waiting for your book." Cindy Wiltheiss, the Director of Food Services at Cornerstone University, hardly needs any introduction, for her passion for ministry and excitement for people are unmatched. Every time she stopped by my office, she would ask, "How is your book coming along?"

I want to thank Priscilla Popp, Andy Smith, and Brian Holda for their mutual interest in the topic. Having led me to Christ at an early age, my mother, Priscilla, is the reason for my salvation. As a layperson in the church, she has served as a sounding board for many of my thoughts. Andy Smith is a longtime, respected faculty member at

Introduction
AΩ

The end of the world is coming sooner than we'd like to think. People will be proclaiming "peace and safety," and then the end will come (1 Thess. 5:3). Unfortunately, those who are proclaiming "peace and safety" are from our own circles. Many conservative, evangelical theologians, preachers, and teachers have popularized a view of the end times that has lulled the church into thinking that there is "peace and safety" when, in fact, "sudden destruction" is coming. What is more, we have accepted this view without "examining the Scriptures" to see if these things are so (Acts 17:11).

This view is called pretribulationalism, and it teaches that the next major event on God's timeline of future events is the rapture of the church. All those who have placed their faith in Jesus Christ, whether dead or alive, will be "caught up together...in the clouds to meet the Lord in the air, and so we will always be with the Lord" (1 Thess. 4:17). No other prophetic event must take place before the rapture; all remaining prophecy will be fulfilled after the rapture. Once Christians have been removed from the earth, the rest of humanity will be thrown into the most tumultuous period of time the world has ever seen (Matt. 24:21).

This view of the end times has dulled our senses and made us indifferent toward the future. This view has taught us that there is nothing for which we need to be watching. There is nothing for which we need to be preparing. This view has taught us that, while we may experience some difficulties in this life, the state of the world will not deteriorate much while we are on the earth. Life will generally continue on as we know it until we meet Jesus in the clouds. We will be removed from the earth before the social order collapses and gives

Introduction

rise to the Antichrist (1 John 2:18, 22; 4:2-3; 2 John 1:7; 2 Thess. 2:3-4; Rev. 13:1-4).

This view of the end times is dangerous, for it leaves us ill-prepared for the future. All three synoptic Gospels record Jesus' warning: "See that no one leads you astray. For many will come in my name, saying, 'I am the Christ,' and they will lead many astray" (Matt. 24:4-5; cf. Mark 13:5-6; Luke 21:8-9). Jesus forewarned us so that we may be on the lookout for false christs and not be deceived by them. To the extent that we are not watching, we will be susceptible to deception. If we are not paying attention, we may unwittingly follow the Antichrist and share in his judgment rather than in God's blessing.

The day of the Lord will overtake unbelievers like a thief in the night; however, that day should not take us by surprise. The apostle Paul wrote, "But you are not in darkness, brothers, for that day to surprise you like a thief. For you are all children of light, children of the day. We are not of the night or of the darkness" (1 Thess. 5:4-5). That day should not surprise us because the Lord has given us signs for which we can and should be looking. When we see these signs, we need to respond in the way that the Lord has instructed us.

The most important step we should take now to prepare for the Lord's coming is to pursue holiness. We need to "set [our] minds on things that are above, not on things that are on earth" (Col. 3:1-2). Sin, by its nature, preoccupies our minds and hearts; it prevents us from being alert. Sin steals our affection for the Lord; it keeps us from thinking about his will. If we are caught up in sin, we will not delight in the study of God's Word. Instead, we will be thinking about evil continually. And, when we are forced to choose between them, we will choose sin over the Lord.

Eschatology, the study of end times, should affect how we live in the present. If we don't pursue holiness now, then we won't pursue holiness in the future. If we don't stand for what is right in the present, then we won't stand for what is right when life gets tough. If we begin to think "Christ won't come today" or "I'll get my life straightened out later," then sudden destruction will overtake us. We will be consumed by the comforts of this life and the pleasures of sin instead of the coming judgment of God and the redemption of this world.

A Revelation to the Church

The coming of Christ will be like the coming of the flood in the days of Noah. During the days of Noah, people were going about their normal lives. They were "eating and drinking, marrying and giving in marriage, until the day when Noah entered the ark" (Matt. 24:38). They were completely unaware of the imminent danger, until the floodwaters came and swept them away.

We would be amiss to think that God did not warn Noah's generation about the coming flood. Noah spent one hundred years building an enormous boat on dry ground! His construction project both forewarned and condemned the world (Heb. 11:7; cf. 1 Peter 3:18-20; 2 Peter 2:5), yet they did not repent or believe. People were caught off guard because they disregarded the warning signs. They were completely fixated on their own wickedness (Gen. 6:5). Let us not follow the pattern of the ancient world which failed to see what was coming because of its gross immorality. Instead, since we have the hope of Christ's coming, let us purify ourselves as he is pure (1 John 3:2-3).

To be sure, our salvation is not based on our works. At the same time, Scripture places a high expectation on the believer. We are not what we used to be. We are a changed people. We should therefore live like it. If we walk in the Spirit, we may be confident that we belong to God. If we follow our sinful nature, Scripture does not give us any assurance that we are a genuine believer. Quite the contrary, Scripture says, "Those who do such things will not inherit the kingdom of God" (Gal 5:21; cf. 1 Cor. 6:9-10; Eph. 5:5). Instead, "their portion will be in the lake that burns with fire and sulfur, which is the second death" (Rev. 21:8).

I am convinced that, if we love God with all of our being and love our neighbors as ourselves, the deception of the Antichrist will be self-evident. Without studying a single word of prophecy, we will refuse the mark of the Antichrist on the grounds that it is contrary to who God is and what he has commanded. If we are in the practice of discerning right from wrong, we will recognize the mark of the Beast for what is—evil—and, if we are in the practice of doing what is right, we will oppose it.

Choosing to live a holy life is more important than being able to understand biblical prophecy. We need to devote ourselves *now* to what is right and good. We need to put away *now* what is wrong and evil. We need to decide *now* whose side we are on. We need to make *his* will the pattern of our lives. This is our number one priority as we prepare for Christ's coming.

The Primary Thesis

The book of Revelation was written to, for, and about the church.

To the Church
AΩ

The Audience Identified

The book of Revelation was written to the seven churches that are in Asia. The prologue expressly identifies the churches as the intended recipient of Revelation. In the prologue, the apostle John greeted the seven churches that are in Asia. By so doing, John identified himself as the author of Revelation and the seven churches as the recipient of Revelation.

> John *to the seven churches* that are in Asia: Grace to you and peace from him who is and who was and who is to come, and from the seven spirits who are before his throne, and from Jesus Christ the faithful witness, the firstborn of the dead, and the ruler of kings on earth. Rev. 1:4-5 (italics mine)

Knowing the intended recipient of Revelation should affect the way we read the book of Revelation. Since the book of Revelation was written to the churches, the rest of Revelation must be read from this perspective. Our interpretation of the book should recognize the relevancy to the churches; otherwise, it is not supported by the biblical text. Any interpretation that minimizes the relevancy to the churches should be suspect of error.

The Audience Further Defined

The opening vision of Christ expressly identifies the churches as the intended recipient of Revelation. While in exile on the island called Patmos, the apostle John had a vision of the glorified Christ. While

John was in the Spirit, Jesus Christ commanded John, "Write what you see in a book and send it to the seven churches, to Ephesus and to Smyrna and to Pergamum and to Thyatira and to Sardis and to Philadelphia and to Laodicea" (Rev. 1:11).

This verse repeats and elaborates upon what has already been stated in the prologue. This verse repeats the point that the book of Revelation was written to the churches, for Jesus commanded John to write what he saw and send it to the churches. This verse also elaborates upon this point, for it lists the seven churches by name. The seven churches are Ephesus, Smyrna, Pergamum, Thyatira, Sardis, Philadelphia, and Laodicea.

This is the second time the book of Revelation expressly identifies the churches as the intended recipient of Revelation. I emphasize this point because it speaks against the prevailing interpretation of the book that says Revelation 4-19, which speaks of the tribulation, has no bearing on the churches. As I said before, our interpretation of the book should recognize the relevancy to the churches; otherwise, it is not supported by the biblical text.

The Audience Individually Addressed

The seven messages of Christ expressly identify the churches as the intended recipient of Revelation. In Revelation 2-3, Jesus commanded the apostle John to record a unique message for each of the seven churches. Before delivering each message, Jesus first identified the church to which he was speaking. In so doing, Jesus reinforced again and again the intended recipient of Revelation.

> To the angel *of the church* in Ephesus write... Rev. 2:1 (italics mine)

> And to the angel *of the church* in Smyrna write... Rev. 2:8 (italics mine)

> And to the angel *of the church* in Pergamum write... Rev. 2:12 (italics mine)

> And to the angel *of the church* in Thyatira write.... Rev. 2:18 (italics mine)

And to the angel *of the church* in Sardis write.... Rev. 3:1 (italics mine)

And to the angel *of the church* in Philadelphia write.... Rev. 3:7 (italics mine)

And to the angel *of the church* in Laodicea write.... Rev. 3:14 (italics mine)

Revelation 2-3 identifies the recipient of Revelation seven more times as the text moves from church to church. These messages not only provide the names of the seven churches, but they also demonstrate the relevancy of Revelation to the churches. Jesus spoke both words of commendation and words of condemnation. Jesus spoke both words of hope and words of rebuke. In these messages, Jesus demonstrated his passion for the churches. As we read through these messages, we cannot deny the clear truth that the book of Revelation was written to the churches.

The Audience Identified, Again

The epilogue of Revelation expressly identifies the churches as the intended recipient of Revelation.

In a personal letter, it is only necessary to identify the intended recipient once. "Dear Lori" is sufficient for my wife to recognize that the whole letter was written to her. The same is true of biblical books. The book of Revelation identified its intended recipient in the prologue. That was sufficient. Yet, the book of Revelation repeated its intended recipient in the opening vision of Christ and seven more times as Jesus addressed each of the seven churches.

The book of Revelation goes even further. After twenty-two chapters of heavenly visions, troubling sights, and deafening sounds, the reader may conceivably lose sight of the fact that Revelation was written to the churches. Lest anyone forget to whom the book was written, the epilogue reminds the reader that this prophecy was expressly written to the churches. Jesus himself closed the book by saying, "I, Jesus, have sent my angel to testify to you about these things *for the churches*" (Rev. 22:16, italics mine).

Clearly, the book of Revelation was written to the churches.

The Whole Church
ΑΩ

In the previous chapter, we established the point that the book of Revelation was written to the churches. In this chapter, we would like to show that the book of Revelation was written not just to the seven churches that are in Asia but to the whole church. What was spoken to seven churches in a particular region was intended for the church throughout the world. What was spoken to seven churches at a particular point in time was intended for the church throughout time.

The Significance of Seven

Numbers play a symbolic role throughout the Bible, especially in apocalyptic literature, as in the book of Revelation. While the book of Revelation singles out and individually addresses seven particular churches, we should not think the message of the book is somehow limited to these churches. On the contrary, we recognize the significance of the fact that God picked seven churches. The number seven represents "wholeness" and "completeness." The selection of seven churches underscores the applicability of the book to the church at large.

These seven churches represent the universal church. The characteristics we see in these churches are characteristics we see in all congregations: some of these churches were zealous, some of them were apathetic, and some were lukewarm. The issues faced by these churches are issues faced by all congregations: some of these churches faced internal problems (problems of sexual immorality, socio-economic injustices, and false teaching) and others faced external pressures (hostility from the Jewish community and/or the

The Whole Church

Roman authorities). All, though, shared a common confession in Jesus Christ.

As we read through the messages recorded in Revelation 2-3, we can hear Christ speaking to our churches today. These characteristics (zeal, apathy, and tepidity) still describe our churches, and these problems (sexual immorality, socio-economic injustices, false teaching, and oppressive governance) still plague our churches. These similarities show that the book of Revelation was written to us. These ancient churches represent our churches, and these early Christians represent us contemporary Christians.

"He Who Has an Ear"

In Revelation 2-3, Christ individually addressed seven particular churches. After delivering his words of commendation and/or condemnation, Christ wrapped up each message with the exhortation, "He who has an ear, let him hear what the Spirit says to the churches." This statement appears in each of the seven messages: to Ephesus (Rev. 2:7), to Smyrna (Rev. 2:11), to Pergamum (Rev. 2:17), to Thyatira (Rev. 2:29), to Sardis (Rev. 3:6), to Philadelphia (Rev. 3:13), and to Laodicea (Rev. 3:22).

The phrase "he who has an ear" demonstrates that these messages were not limited to these particular churches. Although Jesus in every case spoke to an identified assembly, the message went beyond that group of believers. The message was for anyone who was willing to listen. Jesus invited anyone "who has an ear" to hear what the Spirit was communicating to the seven churches. Jesus encouraged everyone, even those who were not members of these churches, to listen in and to benefit from these messages. He has given everyone, the church at large, permission to eavesdrop and to learn from these seven congregations.

What is true of the seven messages contained in Revelation 2-3 is true of the entire book. The open invitation to "anyone who has an ear" appears again in Revelation 13:9. This occurrence is significant in that it falls outside the seven messages contained in Revelation 2-3. It sits in the middle of the book. As each message contained in Revelation 2-3 was addressed to a particular church and open to anyone who was willing to listen, so the book as a whole was

The Whole Book
ΑΩ

In the previous chapter, we have shown that the book of Revelation was written explicitly to seven churches and implicitly to the whole church. In this chapter, I would like to show that the whole book of Revelation was given to the church.

This statement is significant when we consider what many of us have been taught. In our evangelical circles, it is commonly taught that God speaks to the church in Revelation 1-3, and he speaks about the nation of Israel in Revelation 4-19. However, such a division is manufactured and unnatural to the book itself. The whole book of Revelation, including Revelation 4-19, was given to the church.

Revelation Is a Prophetic Book

The opening verse of Revelation identifies the book as a message of "things that must soon take place" (Rev. 1:1). This is a fitting identification as most of the book describes future events. Although the first three chapters of Revelation describe the way things are now, the body of the book—the remaining nineteen chapters—describe the way things will be. For this reason, the book of Revelation repeatedly calls itself a prophetic book.

> Blessed is the one who reads aloud *the words of this prophecy*, and blessed are those who hear, and who keep what is written in it, for the time is near. Rev. 1:3 (italics mine)

> Blessed is the one who keeps *the words of the prophecy* of this book. Rev. 22:7 (italics mine)

The Whole Book

> And [the angel] said to me, "Do not seal up *the words of the prophecy* of this book, for the time is near." Rev. 22:10 (italics mine)

> I warn everyone who hears *the words of the prophecy* of this book: if anyone adds to them, God will add to him the plagues described in this book, and if anyone takes away from *the words of the book of this prophecy,* God will take away his share in the tree of life and in the holy city, which are described in this book. Rev. 22:18-19 (italics mine)

Everyone readily acknowledges that Revelation 1-3 relate to the church. In these chapters, Christ speaks about the present state of affairs ("the things...that are"). However, many of us do not think that Revelation 4-19 relate to the church. In these chapters, Christ speaks about future events ("the things...that are to take place after this"). In our evangelical circles, we commonly believe that these chapters relate to the nation of Israel. This, however, runs against the point that God gave a prophetic book to the church.

How can we say God gave a prophetic book to the church and then say the prophetic portions of the book do not relate to the church? This is like handing a hymnal to a man and telling him to disregard all the songs it contains, or giving a cookbook to a woman and telling her to ignore all the recipes it includes. A hymnal, by definition, contains songs. A cookbook, by definition, includes recipes.

If we say that Revelation 1-3 was given to the church, how much more should we say that Revelation 4-19 was given to the church! After all, Revelation is a prophetic book, and the bulk of the prophecy appears in Revelation 4-19. If we acknowledge that God has described the present state of affairs to the church, how much more should we acknowledge that God has revealed the future state of affairs to the church!

Revelation Is One Book

The book of Revelation is one, undivided book. Jesus Christ commanded the apostle John, "Write what you see in a book and send it to the seven churches" (Rev. 1:11). Notice that the word "book" is singular. Jesus told John to write a [singular] book and to send that [one] book to the seven churches. Although Jesus individually addressed the seven churches that are in Asia, each church received more than the few verses that were specifically directed to them. They received a copy of the whole book.

Ephesus, for instance, did not receive a one-page letter consisting of eight verses. No, the church at Ephesus received a complete copy of Revelation. Yes, eight verses were specifically addressed to them; however, these verses do not stand alone but find their context in the larger work. God expected the church at Ephesus to read and pay attention to all 404 verses found in the book (Rev. 1:3; 22:7, 10, 18-19).

If each of the seven churches received a copy of the whole book, how can we split up the contents of Revelation and assign different audiences to different sections of the book? How can we say, for instance, Revelation 1-3 is for the church, but Revelation 4-19 is for the nation of Israel? The book of Revelation is a single book with a single audience, the church.

Revelation Is a Literary Work

The book of Revelation is a single piece of literature. As such, many themes weave their way through the pages of the book and bind them into a cohesive whole. The primary themes are persecution, judgment, and deliverance. These themes will be explored at length in the chapter entitled "About the Church." For now, it is sufficient to say that these themes recur throughout the book of Revelation and bridge the theological breaks we have arbitrarily made in the biblical text.

In addition, there are many secondary themes that likewise span the breadth of Revelation. They include imminence (see chapter entitled "For the Church" in Part One), hearing (see chapter entitled "Hear the Words" in Part Four), the people of God vs. the inhabitants of the earth (see chapter entitled "Believe in Jesus Christ" in Part Four), moral purity (see chapter entitled "Separate Yourselves" in Part Four), worship of God and of the Lamb (see chapter entitled "Worship God" in Part Four), the testimony of Jesus (see chapter entitled "Hold to the Testimony" in Part Four), and endurance (see chapter entitled "Endure to the End" in Part Four).

All of these themes demonstrate the literary unity of the book. Like glue, they bind the pages of the book together into a collective whole.

We cannot take a penknife and slice the book apart without doing significant damage to the book. We cannot cut off one section (Revelation 1-3) and give it to the church, and cut off another section (Revelation 4-19) and give it to Israel. The whole book belongs to the church.

For the Church
ΑΩ

The book of Revelation was not only addressed to the church, but it was written for the benefit of the church.

The Imminence of the Future

Revelation 1:3 pronounces a blessing on those who read, hear, and obey the message of Revelation. Revelation 1:3 reads, "Blessed is the one who reads aloud the words of this prophecy, and blessed are those who hear, and who keep what is written in it, for the time is near."

The last five words of this blessing ("for the time is near") explain the reason why the readers of Revelation would receive a blessing. The events described in the book of Revelation were imminent: they were at the door; they would begin at any moment.

This perspective of Revelation is consistent with all biblical prophecy. The prophets of the Bible often viewed the future in two dimensions—having height and width but no depth. The immediate and the distant were often blurred together. There was no dimension of time. For this reason, though some two thousand years have passed, the time for the fulfillment of these things was near.

The following passages from the book of Revelation highlight the imminence of the things to come.

> The revelation of Jesus Christ, which God gave him to show to his servants *the things that must soon take place.* Rev. 1:1 (italics mine)
>
> *Behold, he is coming* with the clouds, and every eye will see him, even those who pierced him, and all tribes of the

earth will wail on account of him. Even so. Amen. Rev. 1:7 (italics mine)

Remember therefore from where you have fallen; repent, and do the works you did at first. If not, *I will come* to you and remove your lampstand from its place, unless you repent. Rev. 2:5 (italics mine)

Therefore repent. If not, *I will come to you soon* and war against them with the sword of my mouth. Rev. 2:16 (italics mine)

I do not lay on you any other burden. Only hold fast what you have *until I come.* Rev. 2:24-25 (italics mine) [Here John anticipates the church will remain until the coming of Jesus Christ. Since Christ's coming is placed at the end of the tribulation (Rev. 19:11-16), this verse demonstrates that John expected the church to live through the tribulation.]

Remember, then, what you received and heard. Keep it, and repent. If you will not wake up, *I will come like a thief,* and you will not know at what hour *I will come against you.* Rev. 3:3 (italics mine)

I am coming soon. Hold fast what you have, so that no one may seize your crown. Rev. 3:11 (italics mine)

[The souls under the altar] cried out with a loud voice, "O Sovereign Lord, holy and true, how long before you will judge and avenge our blood on those who dwell on the earth?" Then they were...told to rest *a little longer*, until the number of their fellow servants and their brothers should be complete. Rev. 6:10-11 (italics mine)

And the angel whom I saw standing on the sea and on the land raised his right hand to heaven and swore by him who lives forever and ever...that *there would be no more delay,* but that in the days of the trumpet call to be sounded by the seventh angel, the mystery of God would be fulfilled, just as he announced to his servants the prophets. Rev. 10:5-7 (italics mine)

The second woe has passed; behold, *the third woe is soon to come.* Rev. 11:14 (italics mine)

And I heard a loud voice in heaven, saying, "Now the salvation and the power and *the kingdom of our God and the authority of his Christ have come,* for the accuser of our brothers has been thrown down, who accuses them day and night before our God." Rev. 12:10 (italics mine)

"Therefore, rejoice, O heavens and you who dwell in them! But woe to you, O earth and sea, for the devil has come down to you in great wrath, because he knows that *his time is short!*" Rev. 12:12 (italics mine)

And he said with a loud voice, "Fear God and give him glory, because *the hour of his judgment has come,* and worship him who made heaven and earth, the sea and the springs of water." Rev. 14:7 (italics mine)

And another angel came out of the temple, calling with a loud voice to him who sat on the cloud, "Put in your sickle, and reap, for *the hour to reap has come,* for the harvest of the earth is fully ripe." Rev. 14:15 (italics mine)

Behold, I am coming like a thief! Blessed is the one who stays awake, keeping his garments on, that he may not go about naked and be seen exposed! Rev. 16:15 (italics mine) [Here we find a parenthetical comment to the recipients (i.e. the church) to prepare themselves for the things to come, particularly the coming of Christ.]

Let us rejoice and exult and give him the glory, for *the marriage of the Lamb has come,* and his Bride has made herself ready. Rev. 19:7 (italics mine)

And *behold, I am coming soon.* Blessed is the one who keeps the words of the prophecy of this book. Rev. 22:7 (italics mine)

And he said to me, "Do not seal up the words of the prophecy of this book, for *the time is near.* Rev. 22:10 (italics mine) [Unlike the angel who told Daniel in the Old Testament to "Go your way...for the words are shut up and sealed until the time of the end" (Dan. 12:9), the angel tells John the opposite. From John's perspective, the end is here!]

Behold, I am coming soon, bringing my recompense with me, to repay each one for what he has done. Rev. 22:12 (italics mine)

The Spirit and the Bride say, *"Come."* And let the one who hears say, *"Come."* And let the one who is thirsty come; let the one who desires take the water of life without price. Rev. 22:17 (italics mine)

[The Lord Jesus] who testifies to these things says, *"Surely I am coming soon."* Amen. Come, Lord Jesus! Rev. 22:20 (italics mine)

The Relevancy of This Prophecy

The imminence of the future explains why readers would benefit from reading the book of Revelation. The imminence of the future assumes that the people reading the book will live to see what is prophesied in the book. The words of this prophecy would therefore have immediate relevancy for the readers. It will tell them what to expect, how to respond, and what will be the end of all things.

The book of Revelation predicts the rise of a world leader who will defy God and persecute Christians. This prophecy would enable the readers to anticipate these events and to find encouragement during this tumultuous period of time. This prophecy does not expect another generation of people to come and go; rather, the book anticipates that its readers will see the fulfillment of these events. The readers will need the insight and encouragement that the book of Revelation offers.

Who were the readers?

The apostle John would have only understood these words to apply to the church, to whom the book was addressed and of which he was a part. The church were the recipients of this prophecy. The church would live through the events described in this book. The church would need to hear the words of this prophecy. The church would benefit from reading and applying the message contained in this book. In short, the book of Revelation was written for the benefit of the church.

The Exiled Apostle

The aged apostle John identified himself with his readers who would be persecuted for their faith. At the time John received his revelation, John was sitting in exile on the island of Patmos because of the word of God and the testimony of Jesus. For this reason, he called himself a "partner in the tribulation" and a "fellow servant with you...who hold to the testimony of Jesus."

Consider the following verses:

> I, John, *your brother and partner in the tribulation* and the kingdom and the patient endurance that are in Jesus, was on the island called Patmos on account of the word of God and the testimony of Jesus. Rev. 1:9 (italics mine)

> Then I fell down at [the angel's] feet to worship him, but he said to me, "You must not do that! I am a fellow servant *with you and your brothers who hold to the testimony of Jesus.* Worship God." Rev. 19:10 (italics mine)

> I, John, am the one who heard and saw these things. And when I heard and saw them, I fell down to worship at the feet of the angel who showed them to me, but he said to me, "You must not do that! I am a fellow servant *with you and your brothers the prophets, and with those who keep the words of this book.* Worship God." Rev. 22:8-9 (italics mine)

Like his readers, the apostle John saw himself standing on the threshold of things to come. The apostle John did not expect deliverance, for he nowhere spoke about the rapture of the church. Rather, John expected that his faith would continue to be tested until Christ came, an event that he described after the tribulation (Rev.

19:11-16). John's present situation was only a foretaste of further persecution, not simply for himself, but for all of his readers.

The Blessing for Us

The book of Revelation offers a blessing to us if we read, hear, and obey its message (Rev. 1:3). Why? Because the time is near. The prophetic events described in the book would soon start, and we would be pulled into the drama. The message of the book would therefore have immediate relevancy for us.

While much time has passed since the writing of Revelation, there is coming a generation that will live through the events described in the book. Every generation that comes and goes is that much closer to the fulfillment of the prophetic events. We may indeed be that generation.

If we interpret the book as dealing with some other group of people, then there is no relevancy for us. On the other hand, if we recognize that the book was written for the church, then it will shape the way we live in the days ahead. Do we want to ignore this blessing, or do we want to be the recipients of it?

About the Church
ΑΩ

The book of Revelation was not only addressed to the church and written for the benefit of the church, it also talks about the church throughout its pages. The book of Revelation reveals the future state of the church both on earth and in heaven.

The Church Is Not Mentioned
In our evangelical circles, people will argue that the church will not be present on earth during the tribulation because Revelation 4-19, which describes the tribulation, does not use the word "church." The apostle John frequently employed the word "church" in the first three chapters of Revelation. In these chapters, the word "church" appears nineteen times (Rev. 1:4, 11, 20; 2:1, 7-8, 11-12, 17-18, 23, 29; 3:1, 6-7, 13-14, 22). As soon as we come to Revelation 4, the word "church" suddenly disappears from the text. The word does not appear again until the final chapter of the book. There it is used once more (Rev. 22:16).

The Church Is Mentioned
Despite what is commonly taught, the book of Revelation talks about the church throughout its pages. Admittedly, the specific word "church" only appears once after chapter 3; however, the apostle John employs many other words to refer to the membership of the church.

The book of Revelation repeatedly talks about the "apostles" (Rev. 2:2; 18:20; 21:14), "prophets" (Rev. 10:7; 11:10, 18; 16:6; 18:20, 24; 22:6, 9), "priests" (Rev. 1:6; 5:10; 20:6), "saints" (Rev. 5:8; 8:3, 4; 11:18; 13:7, 10; 14:12; 16:6; 17:6; 18:20, 24; 19:8; 20:9), "brothers" (Rev. 1:9; 6:11; 12:10; 19:10; 22:9), and "servants" (Rev. 1:1; 2:20;

6:11; 7:3; 10:7; 11:18; 15:3; 19:2, 5, 10; 22:3, 6, 9). All of these groups refer to subsets of the church and demonstrate the presence of the church on earth during the tribulation.

And that's not all.

This list can be expanded to include the "souls" of the martyrs (Rev. 6:9; 20:4), the saved of the "nations" (5:9; 7:9; 15:3-4; 21:24, 26; 22:2), those who have been "redeemed" (Rev. 5:9; 14:3-4), those who have been "called" (17:14; 19:9), those who have been "chosen" (Rev. 17:14), those who are "faithful" (Rev. 2:10, 13; 17:14), those who are "holy" (Rev. 18:20; 20:6; 22:6, 11), and those who will share "in the first resurrection" (Rev. 20:6). Without a doubt, the church is talked about throughout the book of Revelation.

The Story of the Church

The book of Revelation tells the story of the church in three progressive, yet interwoven, movements. After being introduced in Revelation 1-3, the church is persecuted in Revelation 4-13. This is the first movement. The church is avenged in Revelation 14-18. This is the second movement. And the church is delivered in Revelation 19-22. This is the third movement. While each movement highlights a particular theme—specifically, the theme of persecution, the theme of judgment, and the theme of victory—each theme weaves its way through the whole book of Revelation as it tells the unifying story of the church.

Persecution

Persecution is a theme that weaves its way through the story of Revelation.

The apostle John is introduced as "your brother and partner in the tribulation and the kingdom and the patient endurance that are in Jesus" (Rev. 1:9). Furthermore, he was "on the island called Patmos on account of the word of God and the testimony of Jesus" (Rev. 1:9).

To the church in Ephesus, Jesus says, "I know your works, your toil and your patient endurance" (Rev. 2:2). To the church in Smyrna, Jesus says, "I know your tribulation...and the slander of those who say that they are Jews and are not" (Rev. 2:9). To the church in Pergamum, Jesus says, "I know where you dwell, where Satan's throne is. Yet you hold fast my name, and you did not deny my faith even in the days of Antipas my faithful witness, who was killed among you" (Rev. 2:13).

In heaven, John sees "under the altar the souls of those who had been slain for the word of God and for the witness they had borne" (Rev. 6:9). They cried out, "How long before you will judge and avenge our blood on those who dwell on the earth?" (Rev. 6:10).

One of the elders explains the identity of the great multitude to John: "These are the ones coming out of the great tribulation. They have washed their robes and made them white in the blood of the Lamb" (Rev. 7:14).

God will raise up two witnesses to prophesy against the Beast that rises from the bottomless pit. Though for a time, they will be supernaturally protected. The Beast "will make war on them and conquer them and kill them" (Rev. 11:7). For three and a half days, people will "gaze at their dead bodies and…rejoice over them and make merry and exchange presents" (Rev. 11:9-10).

The dragon tries to devour the male child of the woman clothed with the sun (Rev. 12:4). Unsuccessful, the dragon pursues the woman who is supernaturally protected in the wilderness for 1,260 days (Rev. 12:5-6). In heaven, Michael and his angels fight against the dragon and his angels (Rev. 12:7). Although thrown out of heaven, the dragon is enraged. Knowing his time is short, he goes off "to make war on the rest of [the woman's] offspring, on those who keep the commandments of God and hold to the testimony of Jesus" (Rev. 12:17).

Chapter 13 describes the Beast rising out of the sea, commonly known as the Antichrist (1 John 2:18, 22; 4:2-3; 2 John 1:7), and the Beast rising out of the earth, commonly known as the False Prophet (Rev. 16:13; 19:20; 20:10). The Antichrist will open his mouth and utter blasphemies against God, and the False Prophet will force everyone to worship the Beast. "All who dwell on earth will worship it, everyone whose name has not been written before the foundation of the world in the book of life" (Rev. 13:8). Those who do not worship the Beast—namely, the saints—will be taken to captivity and slain with the sword (Rev. 13:10). For this reason, Revelation calls "for the endurance and faith of the saints" (Rev. 13:10).

About the Church

After the three angels deliver their messages of judgment against the inhabitants of the earth who worship the Beast and/or receive his mark, there is "a call for the endurance of the saints, those who keep the commandments of God and their faith in Jesus" (Rev. 14:12).

During the outpouring of the seven bowls, God's wrath is justified on the basis of the Antichrist's treatment of God's people. "Just are you, O Holy One, who is and who was, for you brought these judgments. For they have shed the blood of saints and prophets, and you have given them blood to drink. It is what they deserve!" (Rev. 16:5-6).

Babylon is described as "the great, mother of prostitutes and of earth's abominations" and as "the woman, drunk with the blood of the saints, the blood of the martyrs of Jesus" (Rev. 17:5, 6). A voice from heaven declares, "Pay her back as she herself has paid back others, and repay her double for her deeds; mix a double portion for her in the cup she mixed" (Rev. 18:6). In her was found "the blood of prophets and of saints, and of all who have been slain on the earth" (Rev. 18:24). With her judgment, God has avenged "the blood of his servants" (Rev. 19:2).

The nations will gather at Armageddon (Rev. 16:16) and "make war on the Lamb" (Rev. 17:14). This war will be waged against the one sitting on the white horse and against his army (Rev. 19:19). After the thousand years are ended, the nations will once again gather for battle and surround "the camp of the saints and the beloved city" (Rev. 20:7-9).

During the millennium, those who reign with Christ will bear the evidence of their martyrdom (Rev. 20:4).

On the new earth, God "will wipe away every tear from [the eyes of those who were persecuted], and death shall be no more, neither shall there be mourning, nor crying, nor pain anymore, for the former things have passed away" (Rev. 21:4). All those who cause pain in this life— "murderers, the sexually immoral, sorcerers, idolaters, and all liars"—will be assigned a portion in the lake of fire (Rev. 21:8). They will be shut out from the New Jerusalem and denied access to the Tree of Life (Rev. 22:15). "No longer will there be anything accursed," and God's servants will be able to worship him freely (Rev. 22:3).

Thus, the angel who spoke to John concludes, "Let the evildoer still do evil, and the filthy still be filthy, and the righteous still do right, and the holy still be holy" (Rev. 22:11).

Clearly, the theme of persecution weaves its way through the pages of Revelation as it tells the unifying story of the church.

Judgment

Judgment is a theme that weaves its way through the story of Revelation.

Revelation begins with a vision of Christ, whose "eyes were like a flame of fire" and from whose "mouth came a sharp two-edged sword" (Rev. 1:14, 16).

To the church in Pergamum, Jesus warns, "Therefore repent. If not, I will come to you soon and war against them with the sword of my mouth" (Rev. 2:16). To the church in Thyatira, Jesus says, "Behold, I will throw [Jezebel] onto a sickbed, and those who commit adultery with her I will throw into great tribulation" (Rev. 2:21-22). To the church in Philadelphia, Jesus says, "Behold, I will make those of the synagogue of Satan who say that they are Jews and are not...come and bow down before your feet" (Rev. 3:9).

In heaven, the Lamb tears the seven seals of the scroll. With the opening of the seals comes war (Rev. 6:1-2), death (Rev. 6:3-4), famine (Rev. 6:5-6), and pestilence (Rev. 6:7-8). The final seal triggers a great earthquake, cosmic disturbances, and sheer panic (Rev. 6:12-15). People cry out to the mountains and rocks, "Fall on us and hide us from the face of him who is seated on the throne, and from the wrath of the Lamb" (Rev. 6:16).

As the 144,000 servants of God are sealed, an angel calls to the four angels who had been given power to harm earth and sea, "Do not harm the earth or the sea or the trees, until we have sealed the servants of our God" (Rev. 7:2-3).

With the blowing of the trumpets comes horrific judgments on the trees and grasses; on the oceans and its creatures; on the fresh water sources and its consumers; and on the sun, moon, and stars (Rev. 8:6-13). The final three trumpets solicit a dire proclamation, "Woe, woe, woe to those who dwell on the earth, at the blasts of the other trumpets that the three angels are about to blow!" (Rev. 8:13).

Tormented with pain, people will seek death but not find it (Rev. 9:6). Fire, smoke, and sulfur will wipe out a third of mankind (Rev. 9:18).

When God raises the two prophets whom the Antichrist had killed, a great earthquake shakes the earth, a tenth of the city of Jerusalem falls, and seven thousand people are killed (Rev. 11:13).

The blowing of the seventh trumpet is accompanied by flashes of lightning, rumblings, peals of thunder, an earthquake, and heavy hail (Rev. 11:19).

The great dragon, that ancient serpent, who is called the devil or Satan, is thrown down to earth, and his angels with him (Rev. 12:9). He is enraged, "because he knows that his time is short" (Rev. 12:12). He will soon be bound for a thousand years (Rev. 20:1-3) and then thrown into the lake of fire (Rev. 20:10).

An angel flies overhead, proclaiming with a loud voice, "Fear God and give him glory, because the hour of his judgment has come" (Rev. 14:7). Another angel follows, saying, "Fallen, fallen is Babylon the great" (Rev. 14:8). And a third angel comes, saying, "If anyone worships the beast ...he also will drink the wine of God's wrath...he will be tormented with fire and sulfur...And the smoke of their torment goes up forever and ever, and they have no rest, day or night" (Rev. 14:9-11).

Seated on a cloud, one like a son of man swings his sickle across the earth, and the earth is reaped (Rev. 14:16). The clusters of grapes are thrown "into the great winepress of the wrath of God. And the winepress was trodden outside the city, and blood flowed from the winepress, as high as a horse's bridle, for 1,600 stadia" (Rev. 14:19-20).

Seven angels appear in heaven with seven plagues, "which are the last, for with them the wrath of God is finished" (Rev. 15:1). As each angel pours out his bowl, havoc ensues on earth: the inflicting of painful sores on man (Rev. 16:2), the turning of the sea into blood (Rev. 16:3), the turning of fresh waters into blood (Rev. 16:4), the scorching of people with fire (Rev. 16:8-9), the plunging of the world into darkness (Rev. 16:10-11), the paving of the way to Armageddon (Rev. 16:12-16), and the shaking of the earth and the collapse of Babylon (Rev. 16:17-21).

Babylon will "become a dwelling place for demons, a haunt for every unclean spirit, a haunt for every unclean bird, a haunt for every unclean and detestable beast" (Rev. 18:2). In a single hour judgment will come upon her (Rev. 18:10), and all her wealth will be laid waste (Rev. 18:17). No more will merchants purchase from her "gold, silver, jewels, pearls, fine linen, purple cloth, silk, scarlet cloth" (Rev. 18:12). No more will be heard in her "the sound of harpists and musicians, of flute players and trumpeters" (Rev. 18:22). She will be decimated (Rev. 19:3).

Though the nations make war on the Lamb, "the Lamb will conquer them" (Rev. 17:14). Christ will ride in conquest on a white horse, and he "will tread the winepress of the fury of the wrath of God the Almighty" (Rev. 19:15). Ravenous birds will come "to eat the flesh of kings, the flesh of captains, the flesh of mighty men, the flesh of horses and their riders, and the flesh of all men, both free and slave, both small and great" (Rev. 19:17-18).

The Beast who had made war on the saints and the False Prophet who had deceived the earth are captured, and they are both thrown into the lake of fire that burns with sulfur (Rev. 19:20). The rest of mankind who had followed them "were slain by the sword that came from the mouth of him who was sitting on the horse, and all the birds were gorged with their flesh" (Rev. 19:21). And the dragon, that is, the devil, is seized, bound, and thrown into a bottomless pit for a thousand years (Rev. 20:1-3). Afterwards, he too will be "thrown into the lake of fire and sulfur where the beast and the false prophet were" (Rev. 20:10).

God will take his seat on the great white throne and judge the dead according to what they had done (Rev. 20:11-13). The cowardly, the faithless, the detestable, murderers, the sexually immoral, sorcerers, idolaters, and all liars will all be assigned a place "in the lake that burns with fire and sulfur, which is the second death" (Rev. 21:8). They will not enter the New Jerusalem or have access to the Tree of Life (Rev. 21:27; 22:3, 14-15).

Finally, the book ends with a warning of judgment against anyone who tampers with the message of Revelation. To anyone who adds to the prophecy of Revelation, God will add the plagues described in the book (Rev. 22:18). And to anyone who takes away from the prophecy of Revelation, God will take away his share in the Tree of Life and the Holy City described in the book (Rev. 22:19).

Clearly, the theme of judgment weaves its way through the pages of Revelation as it tells the unifying story of the church.

Victory

Victory is a theme that weaves its way through the story of Revelation.

The apostle John begins his book with a doxology: "To him who loves us and has freed us from our sins by his blood and made us a kingdom, priests to his God and Father, to him be glory and dominion forever and ever" (Rev. 1:5-6).

To the one who conquers, Jesus will "grant to eat of the tree of life" (Rev. 2:7). That person "will not be hurt by the second death" (Rev. 2:11). He will be given "a white stone, with a new name written on the stone that no one knows except the one who receives it" (Rev. 2:17). He will be given "the morning star" (Rev. 2:28) and be clothed "in white garments" (Rev. 3:5). His name will never be blotted out of the Book of Life; rather, Christ will "confess his name before my Father and before his angels" (Rev. 3:5). He will be made "a pillar in the temple of my God" (Rev. 3:12), and he will live in "the new Jerusalem, which comes down from my God out of heaven" (Rev. 3:12). And he will sit with Jesus on his throne, as Jesus conquered and sat on his throne (Rev. 3:21).

In heaven, the four living creatures and the twenty-four elders sing a new song about the Lamb: "Worthy are you...for you were slain, and by your blood you ransomed people for God from every tribe and language and people and nation, and you have made them a kingdom and priests to our God, and they shall reign on the earth" (Rev. 5:9-10).

Of the great multitude, one of the elders tells John, "They shall hunger no more, neither thirst anymore; the sun shall not strike them, nor any scorching heat. For the Lamb in the midst of the throne will be their shepherd, and he will guide them to springs of living water" (Rev. 7:16-17).

The two witnesses, whom the Antichrist had killed, God will raise to life and call to himself as their enemies look on (Rev. 11:11-12).

With the blowing of the seventh trumpet, the twenty-four elders declare that, though the nations have raged, the time has come for judging the dead and rewarding God's servants, the prophets and saints (Rev. 11:16-18).

When the dragon is thrown out of heaven, a loud voice proclaims, "Now the salvation and the power and the kingdom of our God and the authority of his Christ have come, for the accuser of our brothers has been thrown down...they have conquered him by the blood of the Lamb and by the word of their testimony" (Rev. 12:10-11).

John sees the Lamb, standing with the 144,000 servants of God, on Mount Zion. He also hears the sound of harps playing and voices singing a new song that only the 144,000 could learn. These "have been redeemed from mankind as firstfruits for God and the Lamb," and they "follow the Lamb wherever he goes" (Rev. 14:4-5).

After the three angels deliver their messages of judgment and the book of Revelation issues a call for the endurance of the saints, a voice from heaven declares, "Blessed are the dead who die in the Lord from now on...Blessed indeed...that they may rest from their labors, for their deeds follow them" (Rev. 14:13).

Though the nations make war on the Lamb, "the Lamb will conquer them, for he is Lord of lords and King of kings, and those with him are called and chosen and faithful" (Rev. 17:14).

With the destruction of Babylon, a great multitude in heaven cries out, "Hallelujah! Salvation and glory and power belong to our God, for his judgments are true and just" (Rev. 19:1). The twenty-four elders and the four living creatures echo, "Amen. Hallelujah!" (Rev. 19:4). A voice from the throne adds, "Praise our God, all you his servants, you who fear him, small and great" (Rev. 19:5). And the great multitude declares, "Hallelujah! For the Lord our God the Almighty reigns" (Rev. 19:6).

The bride who has clothed herself with fine linen, bright and pure, meets her groom (Rev. 19:7-8). The souls of those who had been beheaded for the testimony of Jesus come to life and reign with Christ for a thousand years (Rev. 20:4). And the first heaven and the first earth with all of its corruption pass away, and the new heaven and the new earth come (Rev. 21:1). God is "making all things new" (Rev. 21:5).

About the Church

Of the new earth, a loud voice from the throne declares, "Behold, the dwelling place of God is with man. He will dwell with them, and they will be his people, and God himself will be with them as their God" (Rev. 21:3). As it relates to man's hardships in the present life, God "will wipe away every tear from their eyes, and death shall be no more, neither shall there be mourning, nor crying, nor pain anymore, for the former things have passed away" (Rev. 21:4). As it relates to man's experience in the future life, "No longer will there be anything accursed, but the throne of God and of the Lamb will be in it, and his servants will worship him" (Rev. 22:3).

With the curse of sin removed and the victory won, people may once again eat from the Tree of Life and live in the very presence of God (Rev. 22:14).

Clearly, the theme of victory weaves its way through the pages of Revelation as it tells the unifying story of the church.

Purpose of Revelation
ΑΩ

The book of Revelation serves two purposes. First, it was written to prepare the church *for* the tribulation. Second, it was written to encourage the church *during* the tribulation. Let's look at each of these purposes in turn.

To Prepare the Church

In the Olivet Discourse, Jesus forewarned his disciples that "false christs and false prophets will arise and perform great signs and wonders, so as to lead astray, if possible, even the elect" (Matt. 24:24). Jesus told his disciples about these events before they occurred so that they would not be deceived. Jesus said, "So, if they say to you, 'Look, he is in the wilderness,' do not go out. If they say, 'Look, he is in the inner rooms,' do not believe it." (Matt. 24:26).

Jesus did not want his followers to be deceived. He did not want them to be in the dark. Jesus told them what was going to happen, so that they would not be caught off-guard but prepared for things to come. In like fashion, Jesus has revealed "the things that must soon take place" to the church so that she will be prepared. By giving the book of Revelation to the church, Jesus is seeking to prepare the church for this period of unprecedented persecution.

To Encourage the Church

The book of Revelation exhorts Christians to endure. During the tribulation, the faith of Christians will be put to the test. The Antichrist will do everything he can to make Christians deny their faith in Christ, and he will do everything he can to prevent people from coming to faith in Christ. "Revelation pictures a life and death struggle between

Christ and Antichrist for the hearts of men; and the conqueror is he who is unswervingly loyal to his Lord even though it costs him his life."[4] In this context, the book of Revelation serves as "a call for the endurance and faith of the saints" (Rev. 13:10; cf. 14:12).

The book of Revelation was written for such a time as this. The words of this prophecy instill hope in the heart of the believer. It assures Christians that God will care for his people despite what they may go through, and it assures Christians that Christ will ultimately triumph. Those who have done evil will be brought to justice, and those who have done good will be vindicated. Eternal life is presented both as a gift through the blood of the Lamb and as a reward to those who conquer.

May we heed the call and endure to the end!

Summary
ΑΩ

The book of Revelation was written to, for, and about the church.

The book of Revelation expressly identifies its recipient not just once, but on multiple occasions: in the prologue, in the opening vision of Christ, in the seven messages of Christ, and in the epilogue of the book.

The book of Revelation was written for the benefit of its readers. John anticipated the time when the church would be plunged into a period of unprecedented persecution. The church would therefore need the foresight and encouragement that the book offered, and the church would consequently be blessed if she read its message.

And, finally, the book of Revelation talks about the church throughout its pages as it describes the climactic struggle between the people of God and the forces of evil.

The intended audience of Revelation is so emphasized that one may begin to think that God anticipated a day when people would say this prophecy was not written to, for, and about the church. Knowing that the church would need this message in order to conquer, God seemingly underscored this point as if to counteract such thinking. It is bewildering that we have adopted a view of Revelation that has effectively taken the book out of the hands of the church.

Let us conform our thinking to the mind of God and accept the book of Revelation as a gift from God. God is preparing us for the future, and we will be blessed if we listen to him.

Part Two

Commentary

Introduction
ΑΩ

The purpose of this commentary is to walk through the book of Revelation and flesh out the premise that Revelation was written to, for, and about the church.

This commentary does not try to explain every verse in the book of Revelation. If you are interested in a verse-by-verse commentary, I would recommend either George Ladd's *A Commentary on the Revelation of John* or Robert H. Mounce's *The Book of Revelation*. While I may not agree with these authors on every point, they both share the perspective that the book of Revelation was written to, for, and about the church.

This commentary instead walks briskly through the book of Revelation and discusses the key ideas found in the text. It especially highlights those ideas that relate to the foundational premise that the book of Revelation was written to, for, and about the church. This brief, thematic commentary should provide the reader with a framework for further reading and study.

This commentary also has a pastoral intent. As each day passes, we are that much closer to the actual events predicted in the book of Revelation. There is coming a generation of Christians who will live through the tribulation. For these Christians, the book of Revelation will be particularly relevant. In light of this, I want to prepare the church for this day. I want to put the book of Revelation back into the hands of the church. This commentary therefore moves quickly from discussing the text to applying its message.

Before you read each chapter in this commentary, I would recommend that you first read the corresponding passage of Scripture. You will then have the biblical text in mind as you consider the ideas raised in this commentary. You may wish to re-read the biblical text after you have read these notes. This second reading will afford you an opportunity to evaluate what has been said and to discover even more about things to come.

Prologue (Rev. 1)
ΑΩ

The prologue introduces the book of Revelation. The author is Jesus Christ. The messenger is the apostle John. The recipients are the seven churches that are in Asia. And the content is the future.

The Title of the Book

The opening verse of Revelation entitles the book, "The revelation of Jesus Christ." The prepositional phrase "of Jesus Christ" may be understood in one of two ways: Jesus Christ may be the subject or the object of the revelation. If Jesus is the subject of the revelation, this title would indicate that Jesus is the one who has disclosed what we are about to read. In other words, Jesus Christ is the revelatory agent through whom God has given this book. We could thus render the title "The Revelation *from* Jesus Christ." On the other hand, if Jesus is the object of the revelation, this title would indicate that Jesus is the central focus of what we are about to read. In other words, Jesus Christ is the one being revealed in this book. We could thus render the title, "The Revelation *about* Jesus Christ."

While not everyone will agree with me, I believe Jesus Christ should be understood as the subject of the revelation. As such, the title of the book underscores the source of the revelation—Jesus Christ. These are not the words of an old, exiled, and deranged apostle; rather, these are the words of Jesus Christ, the One in whom we have believed and the One for whom we may be persecuted. The context makes this clear. The first two verses of Revelation not only state the title of the book, but they also detail the transmission of the message. Jesus Christ played a key role in the transmission of Revelation.

Prologue (Rev. 1)

Although the books of the Bible were physically written by a human author, we recognize that a divine Author stands behind all of Scripture. 2 Timothy 3:16 tells us, "All Scripture is breathed out by God;" and 2 Peter 1:21 adds, "no prophecy was ever produced by the will of man, but men spoke from God as they were carried along by the Holy Spirit." These familiar passages speak to the inspiration of Scripture; however, they do not speak to the transmission of Scripture.

Revelation 1:1-2 explains to us the process that God used to deliver his message to us.

> The revelation of Jesus Christ, which God gave him to show to his servants the things that must soon take place. He made it known by sending his angel to his servant John, who bore witness to the word of God and to the testimony of Jesus Christ, even to all that he saw.
>
> Rev. 1:1-2

Like a baton in a relay race, the message went from one person to another until it came to us. God entrusted this revelation to Jesus Christ. Jesus Christ in turn gave this revelation to an angel. The angel delivered this revelation to the apostle John. John wrote down what he heard and saw, and he distributed the book of Revelation to the seven churches. These verses highlight the source of the revelation. This revelation came from Jesus Christ and ultimately from God himself.

Figure 2: Transmission of Revelation

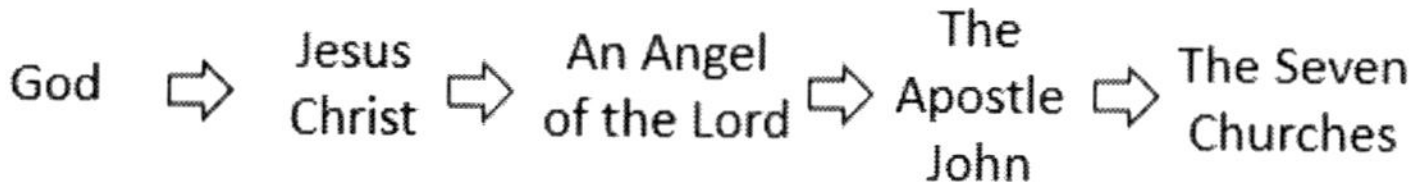

God ⇨ Jesus Christ ⇨ An Angel of the Lord ⇨ The Apostle John ⇨ The Seven Churches

Revelation 1:1-2 also reveals the subject of the book. Jesus gave this revelation with the express purpose "to show to his servants the things that must soon take place." Jesus Christ did not deliver this book with the purpose of telling people more about himself; rather, he delivered this book with the purpose of telling people about what is to come. Things to come, not Jesus Christ, is the subject of the book.

Consequently, the phrase "of Jesus Christ" should be understood as "*from* Jesus Christ" and not "*about* Jesus Christ."

Although the book of Revelation was written to tell us about things to come, we still learn a great deal about Jesus Christ from this prophecy. Future events, particularly those related to the end of the world, find their consummation in Jesus Christ. Christ's disciples understood this when they asked him, "What will be the sign of your coming and of the close of the age?" (Matt. 24:3). Christ's coming and the end of the world go hand-in-hand. It is impossible to talk about the one without talking about the other. After all, God is working toward this end: "to unite all things in [Christ], things in heaven and things on earth" (Eph. 1:10).

The Author Is Jesus Christ

The author of Revelation is Jesus Christ. Whereas the Gospels present Jesus in his humility, the book of Revelation presents Jesus in his glory. Whereas the Gospels emphasize the humanity of Christ, the book of Revelation emphasizes the divinity of Christ. Whereas the Gospels see Jesus as the world saw Jesus—a popular but controversial Jewish rabbi who died at the hands of the Romans—the book of Revelation sees Jesus as he truly is—the supreme Sovereign who not only created and redeemed humanity but rules over heaven and earth. Whereas the world believes Jesus was crucified under Pontius Pilate and is still in the grave, the church believes Jesus was raised from the dead and is now seated at the right hand of the throne of God (Acts 2:22-24, 32; 3:12-15; 4:10, 33; 5:30-32; 13:27-31; 17:2-3, 18; 23:6; 24:14-15, 21; 25:19; 26:6-8, 22-23). The resurrected and glorified Christ is the author of Revelation.

There is probably no greater vision of the glorified Christ than that captured by the pen of the apostle John:

> Then I turned to see the voice that was speaking to me, and on turning I saw seven golden lampstands, and in the midst of the lampstands one like a son of man, clothed with a long robe and with a golden sash around his chest. The hairs of his head were white, like white wool, like snow. His eyes were like a flame of fire, his feet were like burnished bronze, refined in a furnace, and his voice was

like the roar of many waters. In his right hand he held seven stars, from his mouth came a sharp two-edged sword, and his face was like the sun shining in full strength. Rev. 1:12-16

What a contrast from his humiliation! What a cause for our hope! What an impulse for exultation!

The book of Revelation captures for us a wonderful vision of our risen and glorified Savior. What we now know by faith, we will one day see with our eyes: Jesus in his glory. When Christ appears, our hope will be realized, our faith vindicated, and our perseverance rewarded. When Christ comes, he will come on the clouds of heaven with power and great glory (Matt. 24:30). The apostle John thus encourages us with these words, "Behold, he is coming with the clouds, and every eye will see him, even those who pierced him, and all tribes of the earth will wail on account of him" (Rev. 1:7).

The Messenger Is the Apostle John

The prologue of Revelation introduces us to the messenger of the book. John was a servant, a witness to the word of God. While John was a servant in the general sense that he carried out God's commands, he was more than that. He was a servant who had been uniquely commissioned by God to communicate his truth to God's people. He stood in a long line of prophets who had faithfully proclaimed "Thus says the Lord." We must not put ourselves in the same category as John. John held a unique office that we do not. God spoke directly to his servants the prophets, but he speaks indirectly to us through the prophets (Rev. 10:7; 11:18; 22:6).

Although John played a unique role in redemptive history, John identified himself with us. In Revelation 1:9, John called himself our "brother" and "partner." Like ourselves, John was born a sinner and in need of a Savior. He thus glorified Jesus Christ, "To him who loves us and has freed us from our sins by his blood...to him be glory and dominion forever and ever" (Rev. 1:4). Notice the first person, plural pronoun "us." John recognized that he was no different. He was in the same boat as his audience, and he praised Jesus Christ for the salvation that he made possible.

As John wrote about future persecution and hardship for the church, he himself was enduring persecution and hardship for his faith. John had been exiled to the island called Patmos, and the severity of his sentence evidences itself in his self-description. In Revelation 1:9, he called himself a "partner in the *tribulation* and the *kingdom* and the *patient endurance* that are in Jesus" (italics mine). His present situation was the source of much "tribulation" and required "patient endurance" to get through it. In the end, John would enjoy the "kingdom" with those reading his prophecy.

John was in this situation, not because he asked for it or deserved it, but because he had faithfully proclaimed the Word of God. John had not been arrogant or disrespectful to the authorities, nor had John committed some heinous crime against the state. John had been exiled "on account of the word of God and the testimony of Jesus" (Rev. 1:9). John had declared what he had heard, what he had seen, and what he had touched (1 John 1:1-3). John had declared the person of Jesus Christ and, for this, he had been exiled.

The Recipients Are the Seven Churches That Are in Asia

The recipients are the seven churches that are in Asia. Since we have covered this point at length in Part One, I will keep my comments brief here. The book of Revelation was addressed "to the seven churches that are in Asia" (Rev. 1:4). Revelation 1:11 identifies each of the seven churches: Ephesus, Smyrna, Pergamum, Thyatira, Sardis, Philadelphia, and Laodicea. The book of Revelation was written for the benefit of the churches. Revelation 1:3 pronounces a blessing on those who read, hear, and keep the words of this prophecy. Finally, the book of Revelation is about the churches.

The churches, like the apostle John, were being persecuted for their faith. John's self-description that he was a "partner in the tribulation" implies that the churches were likewise enduring hardship for their faith (Rev. 1:9). This book would instill hope as it revealed "the things that must soon take place." No matter how hard life would get, these churches were held securely in the right hand of Jesus Christ who would destroy all opposition with the word of his mouth (Rev. 1:16). These churches were not only a partner with John

Prologue (Rev. 1)

in the persecution but also in the victory. They were fellow citizens of Christ's kingdom which would come to earth (Rev. 1:9; 11:15)

The Content Is the Future

The book of Revelation is about the future. The opening verse of Revelation indicates the purpose of the book: God the Father gave this message to the Son "to show to his servants the things that must soon take place" (Rev. 1:1; cf. Rev. 4:1). Since the purpose of the book is to show the things that must soon take place, then the content of the book must be about the future. This explains why the book is oftentimes referred to as prophecy (Rev. 1:3; 22:7, 10, 18, 19).

Although the book of Revelation is about the future, it still had relevancy for the original readers and, if it had relevancy for the original readers, it also has relevancy for us today. The blessing pronounced in verse 3 makes this very clear: "Blessed is the one who reads aloud the words of this prophecy, and blessed are those who hear, and who keep what is written in it, for the time is near." The reason for its relevancy is given in the phrase, "for the time is near." For the prophet, the end is seen through the transparency of the present; the end is seen as imminent. While the content is the future, the future is now.

From his finite perspective, the apostle John presumed that he stood on the threshold of things to come. These prophetic events were about to commence; and he, along with his readers, would live through them. The book of Revelation would provide a "survivor's guide" to get them through the coming tribulation. They would be blessed if they listened to the guide; otherwise, they would flounder with the rest of the world.

Every generation that comes and goes must live with this same perspective. Although John's generation did not live to see these events, this does not mean that our generation will also come and go. This book of prophecy is a book of future history. These events will come to pass. One generation will live through what has been foretold. We may be that generation. If we are, the book of Revelation states we will be blessed if we read the words of this prophecy and keep the exhortations that are given in it.

Even if we are not the final generation, the book of Revelation still has relevancy for us. The book of Revelation records the final chapter in the world's history-long struggle between good and evil. While the ultimate fulfillment of Revelation may lie in the future, we are a part of this battle between good and evil now. The struggle of the church in the future is our struggle now. The victory of the church in the future is our victory now. As such, the book of Revelation is our hope, encouragement, and consolation.

In the Olivet Discourse, Jesus described the future by way of analogy. He compared the events leading up to the end of the world to the birth pains of a pregnant woman. During her pregnancy, a woman experiences many discomforts, ailments, and even false labor as she anticipates the birth of a child. As intense and disheartening as this can be, she is not in true labor. This is necessary preparation for true labor. Once true labor starts, there is no mistaking it for what has come before, and there is no turning back until the child is born.

In like manner, we are "pregnant" as we anticipate Christ's return. As we go through history, we will experience many discomforts, ailments, and even false labor. All of these experiences mimic the end of the world. As we get closer to the end, these occurrences will become more frequent and intense. The evil of our day may even convince us that we are the last generation of Christians, for the Bible affirms that many antichrists will come upon the scene. But the Bible also speaks of *the* Antichrist who will speak blasphemy against God, lead the world in unrestrained wickedness, and initiate unprecedented persecution against Christians (1 John 2:18, 22; 4:2-3; 2 John 1:7; 2 Thess. 2:3-4; Rev. 13:1-4). This is the true labor that will lead to the glorious appearing of our Lord and Savior.

No matter where we find ourselves in history, the book of Revelation is our story. It is God's ultimate judgment against all those who have committed evil and his ultimate vindication of all those who have pursued righteousness. The book of Revelation is our story, our exhortation to live godly, and our promise of ultimate victory regardless of what we may face in this life.

The Seven Messages (Rev. 2-3)
ΑΩ

Jesus Christ spoke a series of seven messages, each addressed to a particular congregation. These seven churches were all located in Asia Minor and existed during the end of the first century. These churches, while they may be pinpointed to a city on a map, represent the church worldwide. These churches, while they existed at a single point in history, represent the church throughout time. The characteristics of these churches characterize churches throughout the world, and the issues faced by these churches arise in every generation. These churches represent the universal church (see chapter entitled "The Whole Church" in Part One).

Each message begins by identifying the recipient of the message and by describing the originator of the message. The body of the message evaluates the state of the local body and includes words of commendation and/or condemnation. Each message closes with an exhortation to listen to what has been said and a promise to the one who conquers.

The Author

Jesus Christ is the author of the messages to the seven churches. He uniquely introduces himself at the beginning of each message. To the church in Ephesus, Jesus is the one "who holds the seven stars in his right hand, who walks among the seven golden lampstands" (Rev. 2:1). To the church in Smyrna, Jesus is "the first and the last, who died and came to life" (Rev. 2:8). To the church in Pergamum, he is the one "who has the sharp two-edged sword" (Rev. 2:12). To the church in Thyatira, he is "the Son of God, who has eyes like a flame of fire, and whose feet are like burnished bronze" (Rev. 2:18). To the church in

Sardis, he is the one "who has the seven spirits of God and the seven stars" (Rev. 3:1). To the church in Philadelphia, he is "the holy one, the true one, who has the key of David, who opens and no one will shut, who shuts and no one opens" (Rev. 3:7). To the church in Laodicea, he is "the Amen, the faithful and true witness, the beginning of God's creation" (Rev. 3:14).

The Exhortation

The exhortation to listen demonstrates that these seven churches represent the universal church. The phrase "he who has an ear" (Rev. 2:7, 11, 17, 29; 3:6, 13, 22) extends the message beyond the congregation to whom the message is addressed and to anyone who is willing to listen. Everyone, it is assumed, has ears to physically hear the message; but, not everyone combines what they hear with faith. The exhortation to hear goes beyond simply hearing but includes believing and obeying. The message is for anyone who is willing to respond obediently to what Christ is saying.

The recurring statement "hear what the Spirit says to the churches" (Rev. 2:7, 11, 17, 29; 3:6, 13, 22) also shows that these messages were not limited to seven historical churches. While the messages were addressed to specific churches, all are encouraged to listen in and "hear what the Spirit says to the churches." Again, anyone and everyone can benefit from the messages being communicated. These messages deal with issues that come up again and again in different places and times. We all would do well to spend time reflecting upon what has been communicated and to respond accordingly.

The Promise

Christ wrapped up each message by making a promise to the one who conquers. Although he employed different word pictures, Christ promised that the one who conquers will experience the splendor of eternal life. Eternal life is not only a gift from God, it is also a reward for godly living. These promises assure the one who conquers that the reward is well worth the sacrifice.

Listen to the various depictions of eternal life.

To the church in Ephesus, Christ says the one who conquers will have the right "to eat of the tree of life, which is in the paradise of God"

(Rev. 2:7). To the church in Smyrna, Christ says the one who conquers "will not be hurt by the second death" (Rev. 2:11). To the church in Pergamum, Christ says the one who conquers will be given "some of the hidden manna" and "a white stone, with a new name written on the stone that no one knows except the one who receives it" (Rev. 2:17). To the church in Thyatira, Christ says the one who conquers will receive "authority over the nations, and he will rule them with a rod of iron, as when earthen pots are broken in pieces" (Rev. 2:26-27). To the church in Sardis, Christ says the one who conquers will be clothed in white garments, will never be blotted out of the Book of Life, and will be confessed before God and his angels (Rev. 3:5). To the church in Philadelphia, Christ says the one who conquers will be made a permanent pillar in the temple of God. The name of Christ, and of his God, and of the New Jerusalem will be written on him (Rev. 3:12). And finally, to the church in Laodicea, Christ says the one who conquers will "sit with me on my throne, as I also conquered and sat down with my Father on his throne" (Rev. 3:21).

These promises should not be restricted to a certain class of believers (for instance, persecuted Christians); rather, these promises are the hope of every believer. Christians will not all face the same kind or degree of persecution, yet all Christians are called to conquer. Christianity is not simply a profession of faith at a point in time; Christianity is a walk of faith to the end. We all are called to maintain our profession of faith in Jesus Christ until our death or the Lord's return. In the mind of the apostle John, Christians are those who make it. They are the ones who endure to the end, the ones who conquer, and the ones who ultimately receive the reward.

Having said this, these promises are all the more precious to those who endure great hardship. Those who suffer for their faith eagerly anticipate the fulfillment of these promises. Those who enjoy relative ease are less inclined to look beyond this life. This is not to say we should go looking for trouble, or make life unnecessarily difficult on ourselves. It is simply stating that those who have it hard now tend to look ahead to something better.

If we want to kindle a love for Christ's return, we should lift up our eyes and look at the world around us. God never intended for hurricanes to destroy cities, earthquakes to level countries, and tsunamis to sweep away thousands. God never intended for terrorists to bomb subways, planes to fly through skyscrapers, and schoolchildren to gun down classmates. God never intended for extremists to govern countries, women to be subjugated, reporters to be beheaded, families to flee their homes, and millions to die of starvation and dysentery. God never intended for babies to die at birth, mothers to be diagnosed with cancer, adolescents to demand independence, and fathers to abandon families. As we consider the devastating effects of sin, we will eagerly long for Christ's return and, with it, the restoration of all creation.

The Throne Room of God
(Rev. 4-5)
ΑΩ

Jesus Christ has just finished describing "the things...that are" in Revelation 2-3. In the seven messages to the churches, Jesus evaluated the present state of the church. In some areas, the church was strong. In other areas, the church was weak, even at the point of death. At times, he commended the church with words of encouragement. At other times, he critiqued the church with loving words of rebuke. In every case, he called Christians to conquer. The blessings of eternal life await everyone who endures to the end.

Jesus Christ now moves on to disclose "the things...that are to take place after this." The prepositional phrase "after this" indicates a change in time, not a change in kind. The text does not support the view that God has moved his focus away from the church and back to the nation of Israel. To interpret the angel's exhortation to "Come up here" as an allusion to the rapture is to read one's theology into the text (Rev. 4:1). Indeed, there is a change. We are now looking at a future period of time; however, the text does not mention a change in audience. Jesus is still dealing with the church, though he is now talking about the future state of the church.

John's vision changes from Christ in his glory (Rev. 1:12-16) to God on his throne (Rev. 4:1-6). Revelation 4 captures John's vision of the throne room of God.

The Centrality of God

God is at the center of the scene, and everything else lies in relationship to the throne and him who sits on it. A rainbow *encircled the throne* (Rev. 4:3). Twenty-four elders, clothed in white, wearing gold crowns, sat on their thrones *around the throne* (Rev. 4:4). Flashes of lightning, rumblings, and peals of thunder emanated *from the throne* (Rev. 4:5). Seven torches of fire, representing the seven-fold spirit of God, burned *before the throne* (Rev. 4:5). A sea of glass lay like crystal *before the throne*. Four living creatures, full of eyes in front and behind, *surrounded the throne* (Rev. 4:6).

God is not only physically located at the center of the scene, but he is vocally declared to be the center of everyone's praise. God is thrice proclaimed holy because of his omnipotence and self-existence (Rev. 4:8). God is also pronounced worthy of praise, honor, and power because he both chose to create and did create everything that exists (Rev. 4:11).

The centrality of God offers encouragement to Christians who are going through suffering. When civil justice is perverted, political agendas are pushed, and human rights are violated, Christians can be assured that such behavior will not be overlooked. What we see is not all there is. There is a God who is enthroned in heaven and who sits at the center of the universe. The scales will be balanced, the innocent will be vindicated, and the wicked will be punished.

The Unity of The People of God

The twenty-four elders may likely represent the twelve tribes of Israel and the twelve apostles of Jesus. If this is the case, then believers of both dispensations—those living under the old covenant and those living under the new covenant—are represented in heaven. While the core of Christ's revelation focuses on and encourages the final generation of believers, we must understand that the book records the final chapters of human history. These final chapters wrap up everything that has taken place throughout the course of time. As such, the book of Revelation is a source of encouragement for believers of every generation.

The Theme of Redemption

The four living creatures and the twenty-four elders proclaim that Christ is worthy to open the scroll because of his redemptive work:

> Worthy are you to take the scroll and to open its seals, for you were slain, and by your blood you ransomed people for God from every tribe and language and people and

The Throne Room of God (Rev. 4-5)

nation, and you have made them a kingdom and priests to our God, and they shall reign on the earth. Rev. 5:9-10

This theme of redemption does not fit with our commonly accepted belief that Revelation 4-19 deals with Israel. The scroll yet unopened contains "the things...that are to take place after this." The scroll describes the events of the tribulation (Rev. 6:1-17). We have been taught that the tribulation is for Israel, not the church. If this is true, then why is the theme of the heavenly chorus about redemption instead of a reaffirmation of the Abrahamic covenant? Christ's redemption is the foundation of the church, whereas the Abrahamic promise is the foundation of Israel.

This proclamation of Christ's redemption only makes sense when we consider that "the things...that are to take place after this" pertain to the church. Christ appeared once to pay the penalty of sin, and he will appear again not to die but to bring salvation to those who eagerly long for his appearing (Heb. 9:28). Christ has secured the victory through his death, burial, and resurrection. Now he enacts the victory he has previously secured. Christ's death on the cross in the past is the basis for Christ's reign on the earth in the future.

John's Despair

John continues his vision of the throne room in chapter 5. In the hand of the One seated on the throne is a scroll (Rev. 5:1). This scroll contains "the things...that are to take place after this" (Rev. 1:19). However, no one is found worthy to open the seals, read the book, and bring about the consummation of history (Rev. 5:3). When John realizes this, he begins to weep (Rev. 5:4).

John's despair expresses the emotions of his reading audience. They are suffering hardship, undergoing persecution, and even facing martyrdom for their faith. In the midst of such adversity, it is difficult for anyone to see beyond their present circumstances. We feel as though there is no end in sight. There is no hope of relief. There is no reason to go on. As a result, we lose hope. We want to give up. We ask the hard questions of life: "Why is this happening to me?" "Where is God?" "Why doesn't God do anything?" "Does God hear?" "Does God care?"

An elder interrupts John's despair and points his attention to the Lion of the Tribe of Judah, the root of David (Rev. 5:5). Jesus Christ has conquered and is found worthy to break the seals and open the book. Because the God-man died on the cross for the sins of the world, he is qualified to bring history to a close. There will be an end to suffering. There is hope for relief. There is a reason to go on.

Hearing that Christ has conquered not only assures us that he is able to bring this world's story to a fitting conclusion, but it also assures us that we will be able to conquer in the here and now. Knowing that the decisive battle has already been won, we can be confident in the outcome of the minor skirmishes that are still taking place. Knowing that the One in whom we trust was able to conquer, we can be assured that he is able to strengthen those of us who are in the process of conquering. Christ's victory is our victory, and Christ's strength is our strength.

When John lifts his head and looks, he does not see a ferocious lion; rather, he sees a wounded Lamb (Rev. 5:6). Our deliverance will come from no other source than the One who was "pierced for our transgressions" and "crushed for our iniquities" (Isa. 53:5). More than simply identifying the Lamb, his wounds uniquely qualify him for the task at hand (Rev. 5:9). Since the Lamb has provided the means of our salvation, he is also able to bring about the fulfillment of our salvation. Jesus Christ is qualified for the task of bringing history to a close.

All of heaven above (Rev. 5:11-12) and creation below (Rev. 5:13) rejoice over the selection and qualification of the Lamb. And those closest to the throne—the four living creatures and the twenty-four elders—affirm this sentiment (Rev. 5:14).

There is coming a time of intense, systematic persecution against Christians. The book of Revelation was written to encourage these—and all—Christians to endure to the end. Those who have confessed Jesus as Lord may be tempted to judge Jesus as impotent because of their personal experience. Quite the contrary is true. Jesus Christ is the only one worthy to draw history to a close.

Revelation 5 affirms the worthiness of the Lamb in whom we have placed our trust. No matter how unsettled our faith is before we read this passage of Scripture, the only appropriate response after reading it is a renewed confidence that Jesus Christ will bring this persecution to an end.

The Seven Seals (Rev. 6)
ΑΩ

Preparatory Events

The Lamb opens the seven seals of the scroll one at a time. The seven seals describe events that will precede the end of the world. These events bring us to the end but are not the end itself. How do we know this?

First, the seals are on the outside of the scroll and prevent people from viewing the contents inside the scroll (Rev. 5:2). What is on the outside of the scroll may be clearly seen by all; however, what is on the inside of the scroll is only known to its maker, presumably God. What is evident to all is the present, but what is unknown is the future. The scroll contains the undisclosed will of God for the future.

Second, the souls under the altar cry out, "O Sovereign Lord, holy and true, how long before you will judge and avenge our blood on those who dwell on the earth?" (Rev. 6:10). This question presumes the wrath of God has not begun. The souls are told to "rest a little longer, until the number of their fellow servants and their brothers should be complete" (Rev. 6:11).

Third, the cosmic disturbances do not occur until the sixth seal. Cosmic disturbances signify the arrival of the eschatological day of the Lord. People from every socio-economic background will recognize this signal when it happens and cower in fear of God and the Lamb (Rev. 6:15-17). The first five seals precede the sun and moon turning black, the stars falling from the sky, and a worldwide earthquake.

Fourth, the opening of the seventh seal is the anticipatory and uneasy quiet before the storm (Rev. 8:1). In the quiet, the world braces itself for the unleashing of God's wrath, and heaven pauses silently to consider the vengeance of God before it actually happens.

The Seven Seals (Rev. 6)

The seven seals which describe war, disorder, famine, and death are like birth pains. They feel like and anticipate real labor, but they are not the real thing. Labor itself is clear and unmistakable. It is much more intense, regular and persistent. It does not go away until the end is accomplished. There is no relief until the newborn child is brought into the world.

Revelation 6:9-11 touches upon at least three topics: the unity of the people of God, the delay in God's wrath, and the prayers of the saints. Let's look at each of these in turn.

The Unity of the People of God

There is a relationship between the souls under the altar and those people who are going to die for their faith. The souls under the altar are those people who have already died for their faith—from the slaying of Abel, to the stoning of Stephen, to the martyrdom of Christians in our world today. This bloodshed is not over. There are still those who are going to die during the tribulation. These future martyrs will join those who have already died for their faith. All of these martyrs are classified together. There is no special category of believers, called "tribulational saints," which somehow exists apart from the church.

The outpouring of God's wrath is God's vengeance for all saints who have died for their faith. While the book of Revelation tells the story of the last generation of believers, it also records the consummation of history for all believers. Revelation tells how God balances the scales for all the injustices that have taken place throughout the course of human history—from the persecution of the early church under Nero, to the atrocities committed in Nazi Germany, to the unrestrained evil of the coming Antichrist.

The Delay in God's Wrath

The souls under the altar are told to wait for the onset of God's wrath until all their fellow servants have been killed. This text makes a clear distinction between the tribulation and the wrath of God. The tribulation is the unprecedented persecution of believers, and the wrath of God is the outpouring of God's judgment on the unbelieving world. The tribulation, the period of time in which Christians will be martyred, will precede the wrath of God, the period of time in which the blood of the martyrs will be avenged.

The delay in God's wrath fits well with the rest of the New Testament that teaches the church will be exempt from the coming wrath (Rom. 5:9; 1 Thess. 1:10; 5:9). All Christians who are going to die for their faith will rest from their labors and be safe in heaven before God signals the start of his wrath (Rev. 7:13-17). The present text, though, does not talk about those Christians who evade the aggression of the Antichrist and live to see the coming of Christ. How will God save these people from the coming wrath?

There are multiple ways by which God could save his people from the coming wrath. God could save his people by waiting until the last Christian dies before he unleashes his wrath, as the present text seems to indicate. Or, God could save his people by differentiating and protecting them from the effects of his wrath, as Revelation 7:1-8 seems to indicate. Or, God could save his people by removing them from the earth before he unleashes his wrath, as Revelation 14:14-16 seems to indicate. The text does not say.

The difficulty arises for us who want to place all these events on a nice, neat timeline. Revelation does not concern itself with chronology as much as with principles. The principle here is that God will save his people from the coming wrath. God's wrath is never intended for believers; rather, it is always directed against "those who dwell on the earth" (Rev. 3:10; 6:10; 8:13; 11:10, 18; 13:8, 14; 14:6; 17:8). Revelation uses this idiom to refer to everyone who stands opposed to God and his Christ, that is, "everyone whose name has not been written before the foundation of the world in the book of life" (Rev. 13:8).

The Prayers of the Saints

Revelation mentions "the prayers of the saints" three times (Rev. 5:8; 8:3-4); yet, these verses do not disclose the content of their prayers. The present passage fills in the gap.

The prayers of the souls under the altar echo the prayers of Christians who are facing martyrdom on earth. The Christians on earth are fervently praying to the One seated on the throne, "How long, O Sovereign Lord, before you will judge and avenge our blood on those who dwell on the earth?" The answer that God gives to the souls under the altar is the answer that God gives to the Christians on earth, "Rest a little longer, until the number of your fellow servants should be complete. Then, I will judge and avenge your blood on those who dwell on the earth."

God responds to the prayers of his saints. As we visualize the throne room in heaven, particularly as it is described in Revelation 8:1-5, we realize that the prayers of the saints permeate everything that happens in heaven. The prayers of the saints are described as smoke that rises from the altar and fills the room with its sweet aroma. Everyone, including God himself, breathes deeply of its fragrance. The prayers of the saints stimulate God to action. The prayers of the saints create the ambiance in which everything in heaven takes place.

God not only acts for his own glory, but he also acts for his people. God loves his people, and he demonstrates his love in that he hears and responds to their prayers. God will deliver his people and avenge their blood, but he will do so in his perfect timing. The book of Revelation, with its promise of deliverance and its assurance of justice, is the divine answer to the prayers of the saints.

The Two Visions of the Church (Rev. 7)

ΑΩ

The Church on Earth (Rev. 7:1-8)

While heaven and earth stop in anticipation of the wrath of God, which has been announced (Rev. 6:15-17) but has not yet commenced (Rev. 8:6), 144,000 people from the nation of Israel are given a seal on their foreheads. This sealing identifies these people as the "servants of our God" and protects them from the coming judgments (Rev. 7:3). The four angels who have been ordained to execute God's judgments are restrained from doing so until God's servants are clearly marked and distinguished from the rest of mankind. These 144,000 people will not be removed from the earth, but they will be supernaturally protected from God's judgments (Rev. 9:4).

The identification of the 144,000 people is a matter of interpretive debate. Are they the literal descendants of the tribes of Israel? Romans 11:25-31 seems to indicate that a time is coming when God will once again grant faith and salvation to the nation of Israel. Or, do the 144,000 people figuratively represent the church on earth? In which case, Revelation 7:1-8 describes the church on earth, and Revelation 7:9-17 describes the church in heaven.

A mediating position would propose that the 144,000 people are both Israelites and Christians. They are Israelites by physical birth, and they are Christians by spiritual birth. According to this view, the 144,000 servants of God are the believing remnant of Israel, a subset of the church. The apostle John would fall into this category, as would Peter and Paul. After all, the church is made up of both Israelite and Gentile believers (Eph. 2:11-22).

This mediating position has further support for the following reasons:

The Two Visions of the Church (Rev. 7)

First, the book of Revelation portrays the Jews as hardened to the gospel and as persecutors of the church. For instance, Jesus spoke these words to the church in Smyrna:

> "I know your tribulation and your poverty (but you are rich) and the slander of those who say that they are Jews and are not, but are a synagogue of Satan. Rev. 2:9

Similarly, Jesus spoke these words to the church in Philadelphia:

> "Behold, I will make those of the synagogue of Satan who say that they are Jews and are not, but lie—behold, I will make them come and bow down before your feet, and they will learn that I have loved you." Rev. 3:9

It is hard to imagine how the author of Revelation could take enemies of the cross and turn them into friends of God, unless they come to faith in Jesus Christ and become part of the church.

Second, the book of Revelation elsewhere talks about different subsets of people within the church. In Revelation 12, the apostle John describes how the dragon pursues the woman who gave birth to a male child. Unable to touch the woman (commonly understood to be the nation of Israel), the dragon pursues the rest of her offspring, those who keep the commandments of God. Apparently, during the tribulation, some saints are supernaturally protected (Jewish believers) while others are martyred (Gentile believers).

Finally, the 144,000 people have a notable seal of God's favor on their forehead. To receive God's favor, a person must place their faith in Jesus Christ, for there is no going back in revelatory history. While God spoke to people in different ways and at different times in the Old Testament economy, God has spoken to us in the present time through his Son (Heb. 1:1-4). To deny this revelation is to be an enemy of God, subject to damnation (Heb. 2:1-4). Since the 144,000 people know the favor of God, they must have placed their faith in Jesus Christ. In which case, they belong to the church.

The Church in Heaven (Rev. 7:9-17)

John's attention now turns from earth, where he saw the 144,000 servants of God, to heaven, where he sees an innumerable assembly from every nation. These people, clothed in white, are waving palm branches and praising the One who is seated on the throne and the Lamb who was slain. The theme of their doxology is God's salvation.

The salvation of which they sing may refer to their deliverance from sin, though their deliverance from the oppression of the Antichrist is more likely in view given the description of the group. The elder tells John that "these are the ones coming out of the great tribulation" (Rev. 7:14). These people escaped the tribulation not through natural death but through martyrdom. They not only resisted the Antichrist ("they...washed their robes"), but they gave up their lives for the cause of Christ ("...and made them white in the blood").

The single-hearted devotion of these people cost them their very lives. They chose to follow Christ rather than to be soiled by the immoral filth around them. These people fought the fight, stood their ground, and as a result were put to death. While unable to turn the tide of evil on earth, they are welcomed into God's throne room and assured of final rest. They have served the Lamb faithfully in hardship; now they will serve the Lamb in rest. Their hardship was temporal, but their rest is eternal.

> They shall hunger no more, neither thirst anymore;
>   the sun shall not strike them,
>   nor any scorching heat.
> For the Lamb in the midst of the throne will be their shepherd,
>   and he will guide them to springs of living water,
>   and God will wipe away every tear from their eyes.
>
> Rev. 7:16-17

This passage is the ultimate comfort for all of us who take a stand for what is right because of our faith in Jesus Christ. Our stand will invite opposition and, no doubt, result in suffering. We may go hungry. We may be thirsty. We may have to flee for our lives. We may have nowhere to sleep. We may have to endure scorching heat, drenching rain, chilling nights, and heavy dews. We may never again have somewhere to call home. Yet, if we endure, we can look forward to greater joys.

We will enter the presence of God, enjoy his abundant favor, and serve him unhindered forever. We will never again experience hardship. We will never again experience hunger. We will never again experience thirst. The elements of nature will never again beat down on us. All of the painful memories of this present life will be removed from us. God will dwell among us, the Lamb will shepherd us, and we will drink from the springs of living water.

The Seven Trumpets (Rev. 8-9)
ΑΩ

After a half hour of silence, seven angels are issued a trumpet. Before the first angel sounds his trumpet, John sees an angel offer incense upon a golden altar in the presence of God. The smoke rises from the altar and permeates the throne room, and the angel removes hot embers from the altar and casts them toward the earth.

The Efficacy of Prayer

This vision accentuates the efficacy of prayer for those who may feel their prayers are unheard and/or unanswered. During times of persecution, it's easy to think that God does not hear or care about us. Yet, this vision assures us that the very opposite is true. The prayers of the saints come before God and cause him to act (Rev. 8:3). The prayers of the saints fill the heavenly throne room and permeate everything that is done in heaven (Rev. 8:4). The prayers of the saints call God to deliver and vindicate his people. The prayers of the saints stand behind the sounding of the trumpets and the outpouring of God's wrath.

The First Four Trumpets

With God's people at rest in heaven and/or sealed on earth, the seven angels interrupt the silence with the blasts of their trumpets. With the sounding of the trumpets, destruction falls upon the earth. The first four trumpets scorch the vegetation of the earth, turn the oceans into blood, darken the sky, kill a third of all sea life, wreak havoc on the shipping industry, and pollute a third of the fresh water.

An Eagle's Message

As if this devastation were not severe enough, an eagle flies overhead warning the inhabitants of the earth about the next three trumpets. The judgments associated with the next three trumpets will be worse than the judgments associated with the first four trumpets.

"Those Who Dwell on the Earth"

The phrase "those who dwell on the earth" (Rev. 8:13) refers to those "whose names have not been written in the book of life" (Rev. 17:8). They are, in other words, unbelievers. They stand in contrast to "those people who...have the seal of God on their foreheads" (Rev. 9:4). The former come under God's judgments, while the latter are exempt from God's wrath. The former should fear God and give him glory, while the latter receive God's protection and enjoy his favor.

The Presence of Believers on Earth

In Revelation 9:3-4, God permits the locusts to torment "only those people who do not have the seal of God on their foreheads." This verse suggests that both believers (those who have the seal of God on their foreheads) and unbelievers (those who do not have the seal of God on their foreheads) will be on earth during the sounding of the seven trumpets.

This verse reminds us that God is able to save his people from his judgments without necessarily removing them from the place where his judgment falls (2 Peter 2:9). This was true of Noah and his family during the days of the flood (2 Peter 2:5). This was true of Lot and his daughters with the destruction of Sodom and Gomorrah (2 Peter 2:6-8). This was true of the Hebrew people during the plagues on Egypt (Ex. 8:21-23; 9:2-6, 25-26; 10:22-23; 11:6-7). And this will be true during the tribulation. God will pour out his judgments, yet he will miraculously preserve his people.

The Justice of God's Wrath

God is perfectly just in the outpouring of these plagues. God's actions are justified by the response of the unbelieving world. Even while those on earth are being punished for their idolatry and immorality, they still refuse to repent (Rev. 9:20-21; cf. Rev. 16:9, 11). Although God's judgment should drive them to their knees, they are instead hardened in their rebellion. In the words of John, "people loved the darkness rather than the light because their works were evil" (John 3:19). God "has endured with much patience vessels of wrath prepared for destruction, in order to make known the riches of his glory for vessels of mercy, which he has prepared beforehand for glory" (Rom. 9:22-23).

The Fifth Trumpet, the First Woe

The fifth trumpet releases an army of locusts from the depths of the earth. These locusts torment humankind for five months. The sting of their tails is like the sting of a scorpion. Although people will long for relief, they will not find it. The pain will be so excruciating that people would rather die than live with the searing pain. The horror of the woe is that even death will flee from them. Although they will prefer to die, they will not be permitted to die. They will be forced to endure this unrelenting, debilitating pain. This is the first woe.

The Sixth Trumpet, the Second Woe

The sixth trumpet releases four angels. These four angels have been ordained for mass slaughter. They have been prepared and ready to go but have been restrained until this moment. Loosed, they discharge their mission with swift action. They lead an army of two hundred million mounted troops and massacre a third of humanity. People are killed from the fire, smoke, and sulfur that pour out of the horses' mouths, and people are stung by the ends of horses' tails, which are like the heads of vipers. No one escapes unscathed. This is the second woe.

The Seven Thunders (Rev. 10)
ΑΩ

While the book of Revelation discloses many forthcoming events, much of the future remains a mystery. There are certain truths that God has made known to us, and there are other truths that he has chosen to keep hidden. In the words of Moses, "The secret things belong to the Lord our God, but the things that are revealed belong to us and to our children forever" (Deut. 29:29). Revelation 10 records some of these "secret things" that belong to God. For this reason, I will limit my comments and wait for God to reveal the rest at the time of his choosing.

John sees a strong angel, clothed in a cloud, encircled by a rainbow, straddling the earth and sea. This angel cries out with a loud voice, and seven thunders respond. John is about to write down what he sees, but a voice forbids him from doing so. John gets to see it, but we do not. The next group of Christians to see these events will be those Christians who live through the tribulation.

What can we know?

Thunder symbolically represents God's presence and/or his judgment. Apparently there is another series of seven judgments about which we do not know the details. As there are seven seals, seven trumpets, and seven bowls, so there are seven thunders. With the sounding of these thunders, the mystery of God, as announced to the prophets, is fulfilled (Rev. 10:5-7). The mystery of God is the arrival of Christ's kingdom on earth. This message will include an aspect of great joy but also an aspect of deep sorrow (Rev. 10:10). The message is sweet in that it describes the events that will lead to Christ's appearance, but it is bitter in that Christ's appearance will be preceded by great suffering.

The Two Witnesses (Rev. 11:1-14)
ΑΩ

During the tribulation, God will raise up two witnesses who will boldly speak out against the atrocities of the Antichrist. God will supernaturally protect these prophets from anyone who would seek to harm them, including the Antichrist. These two witnesses will be able to call down fire upon their enemies, to shut up the sky from raining, to turn bodies of water into blood, and to strike the earth with every kind of plague.

When the two witnesses have completed their work, God will allow the Antichrist to overpower and kill them. The Antichrist will deny them a proper burial, so that their corpses will be a spectacle for the whole world to see. The Antichrist will want the world to see that he is sovereign and that no one can oppose him. The death of these witnesses will mark a momentary victory for the Antichrist and a devastating loss for believers on earth.

The inhabitants of the earth will believe the lie. They are so distorted in their thinking that they will rejoice in the death of these prophets. They will turn the day of their deaths into a day of celebration, and they will exchange gifts with one another. These prophets, they reason, were the ones who have been responsible for the trouble in the world. The unbelieving population is unwilling to acknowledge that their idolatry and immorality is the cause of God's judgment in the world.

The two prophets are soon vindicated as God restores their lives and calls them to heaven. Shocked, people are overwhelmed with fear. That they "gave glory to the God of heaven" should not be understood to mean that they repented of their sin and confessed their faith in Jesus Christ; rather, they realized that they have been caught in their

The Two Witnesses (Rev. 11:1-14)

sin and will now have to pay the price (Rev. 11:13). They have killed God's prophets, and now God will avenge their deaths.

God vindicates his prophets. A tenth of the city is destroyed, and seven thousand people lose their lives.

With the second woe now complete, one woe yet remains (Rev. 11:14).

The Seventh Trumpet
(Rev. 11:15-19)
ΑΩ

The seventh trumpet announces the unmediated reign of Jesus Christ over the earth. The battle is nearly done, and the victory is sure. While one woe remains, the end of history is now in sight. Interestingly, the details of the third woe are not disclosed here. Instead, we read a broad stroke of what is yet to be accomplished: the nations will rage, God's wrath will be poured out, the dead will be judged, the saints will be rewarded, and those who destroy the earth will be destroyed.

The Woman, the Dragon, And Her Children (Rev. 12)
ΑΩ

Before John spells out the details of the final woe—a series of seven bowls (Rev. 15-16)—John looks up into the sky and sees a woman, clothed with the sun, standing on the moon, and encircled by twelve stars. In highly symbolic language, John rehearses the history-long struggle between God's people and his enemies. It all started in the garden of Eden.

The Biblical Story

In the garden of Eden, Satan entered a serpent, deceived Eve, and caused humanity's figurehead, Adam, to rebel against God. God consequently sentenced the serpent to crawl on the ground, the woman to bear children in pain, and the man to know back-breaking work. God promised a child to the woman who would ultimately crush Satan (Gen. 3:15). This promise of a coming child has been the hope of humanity, and we understand this child to be Jesus Christ.

On multiple occasions, Satan attempted to kill this child or at least to thwart God's plan for this child (Matt. 2:13-15; 4:5-6; Luke 4:28-30; John 6:14-15; 8:59). Satan's greatest attempt to foil God's plan was Christ's death on the cross. If Satan could but keep Christ in the grave, Satan would be the victor. Death, though, could not restrain Jesus. Jesus rose from the dead, ascended in the clouds to heaven, and sat down at the right hand of God. Unable to kill Jesus, Satan now seeks to destroy the woman and her other children (1 Peter 5:8).

The book of Revelation tells the end of the story. Satan is cast out of heaven and exiled to the earth. Knowing that his time is short, he will wreak havoc on the earth. After three and a half years, he will be bound for a thousand years and then loosed to lead one final rebellion against God. Ultimately, he will be thrown into the lake of fire. When that day comes, God's people will be able to enjoy eternal bliss with the accuser of the brothers out of the picture.

The Identification of the Characters

As we work through the details of Revelation 12, we are able to identify the Dragon and the male child with a high degree of certainty. Revelation 12:9 identifies for us the Dragon. He is none other than "that ancient serpent, who is called the devil and Satan, the deceiver of the whole world." And Revelation 12:5 identifies for us the male child. He is the "one who is to rule all the nations with a rod of iron."

Most commentators believe the male child refers to Jesus Christ. Not only does he now sit at the right hand of the throne of God, he will soon come back to earth as the victorious king and establish his visible, unmediated rule over the earth (Rev. 19:11-16). Revelation 19:15 says, "From his mouth comes a sharp sword with which to strike down the nations, and he will rule them with a rod of iron."

Some commentators suggest the male child refers to the church collectively, for the believer who conquers will receive "authority over the nations, and he will rule them with a rod of iron, as when earthen pots are broken in pieces" (Rev. 2:26-27). While Christians will rule with a rod of iron, our authority is a derived authority. It is dependent upon the reign of Christ (Rev. 3:21; 20:4).

Identifying the woman and the rest of her offspring is more difficult. Some commentators believe that the woman represents the nation of Israel and her children represent the church. Other commentators believe that the woman and her children both represent the church, albeit two different aspects or segments of the church.

This latter view has a number of variations. The woman could be the ideal church and her children, the empirical church. The woman could be the church in heaven and her children, the church on earth. The woman could be the church as a whole and her children, members in particular. The woman could be Jewish believers and her children, Gentile believers. The woman could be a particular community of believers and her children, believers throughout the world.

Let's explore the biblical support for the two primary positions.

The Woman, the Dragon, and Her Children (Rev. 12)

The Woman Is Israel, Her Children Are the Church

Revelation 12:1 describes the woman as "clothed with the sun, with the moon under her feet, and on her head a crown of twelve stars." This description takes us back to the first book of the Bible. The book of Genesis uses similar language in the Joseph narrative to describe Jacob's family. Joseph had a dream in which God foretold that he would someday have such great authority that even his parents and brothers would bow down to him. Joseph recounted the dream to his brothers: "Behold, I have dreamed another dream. Behold, the sun, the moon, and eleven stars were bowing down to me" (Gen. 37:9). They all understood that this dream referred to their family. The sun was their father, the moon was their mother, and the brothers were the eleven stars (Gen. 37:10). The book of Revelation picks up this imagery and uses it to identify the nation of Israel.

Revelation 12:5 says that the woman gave birth to the male child as well as to other children. Biblical history attests to the fact that Christianity is "of the Jews" (Matt. 2:2; 27:11, 29, 37; Mark 15:2, 9, 12, 18, 26; Luke 23:3, 37, 38; John 4:22; 18:33, 39; 19:3, 19, 21; Acts 10:39; Rom. 3:29; 9:24). The promise of the Messiah was given to the Jews (Gen. 12:1-3, 7; Ps. 2; Isa. 52:13-53:12; Mic. 5:2-5). Jesus was a Jew (Matt. 1:1-16), who was sent to the Jews (John 1:11-13), in order to save the Jews (Matt. 10:5-6, 23; 15:21-24). The book of Acts recounts the establishment of the church (Acts 2), how the salvation message advanced to the Gentiles, and how Christianity went from being a Jewish sect to a worldwide religion (Acts 9:13-15; 10:44-45; 11:1-8; 13:46-48; 15:1-31; 18:6; 21:18-26; 22:21; 26:12-23; 28:28-31). In effect, Israel not only provided the Messiah but "birthed" the church.

The difficulty with this position is that it breaks up the unity of the people of God. It imagines two distinct peoples of God: Israel (the physical descendants of Abraham) and the church (the spiritual descendants of Abraham).

This runs against the teaching of Jesus. Jesus taught that he was making one flock of believers out of Jews and Gentiles. He said, "I am the good shepherd. I know my own and my own know me...I have other sheep that are not of this fold. I must bring them also, and they will listen to my voice. So there will be one flock, one shepherd" (John

10:14-16). Jesus would accomplish this through his death, for he did not die "for the [Jewish] nation only, but also to gather into one the children of God who are scattered abroad" (John 11:52).

This also runs against the teaching of Paul. The apostle Paul taught that God has formed one people of God out of Jews and Gentiles. This union was no small task as the Jews had everything and the Gentiles had nothing. The Jews had "the adoption, the glory, the covenants, the giving of the law, the worship, and the promises" (Rom. 9:4), but the Gentiles were "separated from Christ, alienated from the commonwealth of Israel and strangers to the covenants of promise, having no hope and without God in the world" (Eph. 2:12). In spite of all this, Christ has broken down the dividing wall of hostility, and has brought us peace, and has created in himself one new body of believers (Eph. 2:13-16).

The Woman and Her Children Are the Church

As it can be stated that Jesus is born "of the Jews," it can also be advanced that Jesus Christ is the firstborn of the church (Rom. 8:29). Jesus is not the firstborn in the sense of physical descent but in terms of priority and supremacy. The church did not give birth to Jesus; rather, Jesus gave birth to the church (Matt. 16:18). When Jesus ascended to heaven and sat down at the right hand of God, he sent the Spirit on the day of Pentecost which resulted in the formation of the church (John 14:16-17, 25-26; 15:26-27; 16:7; Acts 1:7-8; 2:1-13, 37-41).

From this perspective, the woman represents the church and her firstborn is Jesus. As the firstborn of the church, Jesus is the head of the body (Eph. 1:22-23; Col. 1:18). He is the founder and perfecter of our faith (Heb. 12:1-2). He provides leadership to the church by appointing apostles, prophets, evangelists, pastors, and teachers (Eph. 4:11-13). He gave himself up for the church, that he might sanctify and cleanse her by the washing of the Word (Eph. 5:25-27; Col. 2:18-19). And, he is the image to which we are being conformed (Rom. 8:29; 1 John 3:2).

The rest of the woman's children also represent the church. The offspring of the woman are described as "those who keep the commandments of God and hold to the testimony of Jesus" (Rev. 12:7).

The Woman, the Dragon, and Her Children (Rev. 12)

Indeed, Christians are those who obey the commands of God (Matt. 5:17-19; 28:19-20; John 14:15) and place their faith in Jesus (John 3:16; 20:30-31; Rom. 10:9-10, 13). Furthermore, Christians are called children of God (John 1:12; 1 John 3:1), brothers of Jesus Christ (Rom. 8:29; Heb. 2:10-13), and co-heirs with Christ (Rom. 8:16-17).

The difficulty with this position is that there is a clear distinction between the woman and her children. The woman gives birth to her children. How can the church give birth to herself? The woman is supernaturally protected, and her children are pursued by the Antichrist. How can the church be unharmed on the one hand (that is, as the woman) and assaulted on the other (that is, as her children)? The woman and her children are clearly not the same people, and to view them as such presents a contradiction in the text. Any interpretation of the passage must do justice to this distinction.

Toward a Solution

The solution to the problem recognizes that the passage was written to, for, and about the church (a difficulty for the first position) and that there is some clear distinction between the woman and her children (a difficulty for the second position). I believe the answer lies in the fact that John was both an Israelite and a Christian. As such, he belonged to both Israel and the church. He saw the church not as a separate program from God's dealings with Israel but rather as a continuation of God's dealings with Israel. The woman, therefore, refers to Israelite believers, a subset of the church, and her children refers to Gentiles believers, a different subset of the church. The Israelite believers are supernaturally protected, and the Gentile believers are pursued by the Dragon.

The Primary Point

In any case, the primary point of the passage is clear. This passage provides an explanation for the intensity of the persecution against the church. Satan has been ousted from heaven, and he knows his time is short (Rev. 12:12). His days are numbered, and his doom is sure. Thus, he is going to wreak havoc while he can. The heavens can rejoice because Satan no longer has access into the throne room of God (Rev. 12:10-12); but the earth and sea should be afraid because Satan will not be holding anything back.

While we may think that no Christian can survive in this hostile environment, the text assures us that the opposite is true. The Antichrist may seek out, arrest, and put Christians to death; yet, he is not the victor. The goal of the Antichrist is to destroy the faith of Christians, but he will not succeed in this objective. Christians will cling firmly to their confession in Jesus Christ. In so doing, Christians will not simply survive; they will prevail. Revelation 12:11 declares, "And they have conquered him by the blood of the Lamb and by the word of their testimony, for they loved not their lives even unto death."

This verse encourages us to hold firmly to our faith, regardless of what may come against us. If we succeed in this one exhortation, we have won, even though it may have cost us our lives.

Martin Luther

Martin Luther captured the spiritual climate of the last days in his hymn, *A Mighty Fortress*. Armed with cruel hate, our ancient foe wanders the earth seeking to destroy our faith in Christ. If we had to fight this battle alone, we would surely lose, for Satan has no equal on earth. Our trust, though, is not in ourselves, but in Jesus Christ. Jesus only needs to say one word, and the battle will be over. People may threaten, torture, and even kill us; nonetheless, Jesus will win the battle, and his kingdom will be forever.

> A mighty fortress is our God
>   A bulwark never failing;
> Our helper He, amid the flood
>   Of mortal ills prevailing:
> For still our ancient foe
>   Doth seek to work us woe;
> His craft and power are great,
>   And, armed with cruel hate.
> On earth is not his equal.
>
> Did we in our own strength confide,
>   Our striving would be losing,
> Were not the right Man on our side,
>   The man of God's own choosing:

The Woman, the Dragon, and Her Children (Rev. 12)

Dost ask who that may be?
  Christ Jesus, it is He;
Lord Sabaoth His name,
  From age to age the same,
And He must win the battle.

And though this world, with devils filled,
  Should threaten to undo us,
We will not fear, for God hath willed
  His truth to triumph through us:
The Prince of Darkness grim,
  We tremble not for him;
His rage we can endure,
  For lo, his doom is sure;
One little word shall fell him.

That word above all earthly powers,
  No thanks to them, abideth;
The Spirit and the gifts are ours
  Through him who with us sideth:
Let goods and kindred go,
  This mortal life also;
The body they may kill:
  God's truth abideth still;
His kingdom is forever.

The Two Beasts (Rev. 13)
ΑΩ

Revelation 13 anticipates the coming of two powerful world leaders—the first, a political leader and the second, a religious leader.

A Political Leader, the Antichrist

The coming political leader will exert great authority. The text likens him to a leopard in speed, a bear in strength, and a lion in ferocity. He will masquerade as Jesus Christ. As Jesus Christ lived, was crucified, and rose again, so this leader will come to power, incur a mortal wound, and miraculously survive. Far from weakening his authority, this wound will only intensify his strength. He, and the world, will be convinced that he is indestructible, invincible, and divine. After all, no one could walk away from such a blow unscathed.

Emboldened by his uncanny survival, this political leader will make blasphemous statements, even proclaiming that he is God. He will call the world to worship him and create a totalitarian state over the whole world. He will expand his authority to control every aspect of people's lives, he will silence anyone who would oppose him, and he will use every medium available to advocate his agenda. He will slowly push the morals of society beyond its conscience and intentionally desensitize society to what is right and wrong. Individual opinion and conscience will give way to the values and ideals of the state.

This coming political leader will hold sway over every tribe and people and language and nation, except those whose names are written in the Book of Life (Rev. 13:7-8). Christians will recognize this leader for who he is and refuse to worship him. He is none other than the Antichrist, a man prophesied in Scripture and empowered by the

Devil. He may very well be the Devil incarnate. Christians will consequently become the target of his wrath. Revelation 13:7 says he is going "to make war on the saints and to conquer them." In other words, he will seek out, arrest, and put Christians to death.

When this systematic persecution begins, Christians may think they can bear no more, but more hardships come. Christians may think they can continue no longer, yet another day dawns. Christians may think it cannot get any worse, yet their suffering grows. Indeed, the tribulation will be the worst days for Christians to live, for the Devil knows his time is short and he will not be holding anything back. Christians will need to be wise, so that they are not deceived. Christians will need to exercise faith, so that they will stand. Christians will need to endure, so that they will be found faithful at the end.

A Religious Leader, the False Prophet

The coming religious leader will likewise exert great authority. He will speak for the Devil and use force, if necessary, to compel people to worship the Antichrist. He will perform great signs and wonders that cause people to stand in awe and follow him. As for those who would oppose him, he will call down fire from heaven to consume them. He will cause people to erect an image of the Antichrist. He will give life to this image and demand that everyone worship it. Those who do not, he will put to death. No one will stand in his way.

The False Prophet will require everyone to receive a physical mark on their hand and/or forehead. This mark will be necessary for commerce—buying groceries, purchasing a home, holding down a job, traveling from region to region, etc. Acceptance of this mark will signify absolute allegiance to the ideology of the Antichrist and clear, individual support of his programs. Refusal of this mark will keep people from getting the provisions they need to live. Christians will lose their positions of employment, be forced out of their homes, scavenge to find food to eat and water to drink, and take great risks to help others.

We do not want to receive this mark. While refusing the mark means losing everything in this life, accepting it means aligning ourselves with the Antichrist. This mark is not just about holding down a job, acquiring bread to eat, supporting a family, and enjoying the simple amenities of life. This mark is about turning against God and his Christ. This mark is about signing our life over to the Devil. By accepting this mark, we are putting our lot in with the Antichrist, incurring the wrath of God and assuming a final resting place in the lake of fire.

We must take our stand. We must not look back. We must lift our eyes beyond this life—for it will only get worse—and look ahead to the glory that awaits us. Then, we will have no regrets. So, let us be ever so conscious of any mark whose acceptance means acceptance of a man as God, and let us refuse it!

The Church with Christ
(Rev. 14:1-5)
ΑΩ

The vision of 144,000 people standing on Mt. Zion looks ahead and anticipates the final outcome of the tribulation. This vision pictures for us the hope of all Christians: We will see Christ with our eyes, and we will be made like him (1 John 3:2). We will see the glory that Christ had before the foundation of the world, and we will share in that glory (John 17:22, 24). We will see Christ the Victor stand on Mount Zion, and we will stand with him (Rev. 14:1). We who are scattered because of persecution will be gathered under one shepherd. The church that appears weak and destitute will be made strong and whole.

These people, in contrast to those who had received the mark of the Antichrist, had received the seal of God on their foreheads. Before God poured out his wrath on the earth, he had sealed his own people so as to distinguish them from unbelievers and to protect them from his wrath (Rev. 7:2-3). This was not a physical mark, which could be felt or seen; rather, it was the divine election of those who belong to God. Now, these 144,000 people have come through the tribulation, they have kept their faith in Jesus Christ, and they stand with Christ on the Victor's stand.

Who are these people? We have previously identified these people as the believing remnant of Israel, a subset of the church (see chapter entitled "The Two Visions of the Church" in Part Two).

The present passage further describes this assembly. Revelation 14:3 says that they were singing a new song that no one else could learn. This new song is the song of redemption. No other class of creatures, except humans, is able to sing this song, for Jesus Christ did not die for any other class of creatures. He came once to make redemption possible and has appeared again to bring salvation to those who eagerly long for his appearing. These have been "redeemed from the earth" (Rev. 14:3) and "redeemed from mankind as firstfruits for God and the Lamb" (Rev. 14:4).

Christ's work on the cross is the reason why we are persecuted in this life, and Christ's work on the cross is the basis for our deliverance at his appearing. We are persecuted now because of our faith in Christ's death, burial, and resurrection. Soon we will be delivered from this persecution because of this same faith.

The church is unwavering in its faith in Jesus Christ, and its devotion is manifest by how these Christians had lived during the tribulation. That these individuals had "not defiled themselves with women" expresses their single-hearted devotion to Christ and their refusal to share this devotion with anyone, particularly with the Antichrist and his followers (Rev. 14:4). They were, in this respect, virgins.

The 144,000 servants of God were undefiled by the pollution that surrounded them. Instead, they had followed the Lamb. Their lives were characterized by the ideals set forth in the teachings of Jesus. They were poor in spirit, thirsty for righteousness, and pure in heart. Although they were accused of wrongdoing and suffered for it, they were not guilty of any of it. No evil could be found in them (Rev. 14:4-5).

Now, they stand victoriously with Christ.

The Message of the Three Angels (Rev. 14:6-13)
ΑΩ

John looks up into the sky and sees three angels flying overhead. As each angel passes by, it heralds a message for all to hear. The end is coming. Now is the time to choose sides. The angels encourage people to choose the winning side.

The First Angel

The first angel calls people to "Fear God and give him glory" (Rev. 14:7). Most of us generally care about what other people think about us. We want to be loved. We want to belong. We don't want to be laughed at or scorned. And we certainly do not want to be hurt or abused. But, during the tribulation, we must resist such natural tendencies. We must choose God over man. While people can harm the body, God can send both body and soul to hell. For this reason, we should fear God more than man. This may necessitate being hated by people and suffering the expression of people's hatred.

The Second Angel

The second angel announces, "Fallen, fallen is Babylon the great, she who made all nations drink the wine of the passion of her sexual immorality" (Rev. 14:8). This announcement warns people not to partake in the deception of the Antichrist. Babylon is the capital city of the Antichrist's empire, and her sexual immorality is his rebellion against God. We should have nothing to do with the wickedness of the Antichrist, for his kingdom will end in complete destruction.

The Third Angel
The third angel declares the judgment that will come upon anyone who receives the mark of the Antichrist (Rev. 14:9). He will drink the wine of God's wrath (Rev. 14:10a). He will be tormented with fire and sulfur (Rev. 14:10b). And he will have no rest from his torment, day or night, forever (Rev. 14:11). This announcement warns people not to accept the mark of the Antichrist, lest they share in his judgment.

The Exhortations
Christians need to heed the messages of these angels. We need to fear God and give him glory. We need to have no part in the wickedness and blasphemy of the Antichrist. And we need to refuse the mark of the Antichrist.

Christians need to follow the commands of God rather than buckle under the pressure of the Antichrist. We need to love God more than life. We need to hold to our confession of faith. We need to endure until the end, even if it means death. Such endurance will be worth it all. A voice from heaven declares, "Blessed are the dead who die in the Lord from now on" (Rev. 14:13a), and the Spirit concurs, "Blessed indeed...that they may rest from their labors, for their deeds follow them!" (Rev. 14:13b).

Those who refuse the mark of the Antichrist will not receive any rest in this life. They will be the target of the Antichrist's fury. Yet, God will remember their stand of faith and will reward them accordingly. They will be granted rest from their labors; they will never suffer again. These people stand in sharp contrast to those who receive the mark of the Antichrist. Those who receive the mark of the Antichrist may find immediate relief from his threats, but they will not find eternal rest. They will be tormented day and night forever.

The Harvest of the Earth (Rev. 14:14-20)
ΑΩ

God's Purpose in Wrath

God's wrath is never intended for his people. While God's people and his enemies have lived side-by-side throughout the course of history, God will make a clear distinction between these two groups at the end of time. God will gather his people together in order to reward them, and he will gather his enemies together in order to judge them. Pictured as ripe grapes plump with sin, God's enemies are harvested in season and thrown into the winepress of God's wrath. There they will be trampled until their juices fill the valley outside the city of Jerusalem.

This passage brings to mind Christ's parable of the weeds:

> The kingdom of heaven may be compared to a man who sowed good seed in his field, but while his men were sleeping, his enemy came and sowed weeds among the wheat and went away. So when the plants came up and bore grain, then the weeds appeared also.
>
> And the servants of the master of the house came and said to him, "Master, did you not sow good seed in your field? How then does it have weeds?"
>
> He said to them, "An enemy has done this."
>
> So the servants said to him, "Then do you want us to go and gather them?"
>
> But he said, "No, lest in gathering the weeds you root up the wheat along with them. Let both grow together until the harvest, and at harvest time I will tell the reapers,

Gather the weeds first and bind them in bundles to be burned, but gather the wheat into my barn."

Matt. 13:24-30 (paragraphs mine)

Like the passage in Revelation, the parable of the weeds affirms that God's people and his enemies will live side-by-side throughout the course of history. As wheat can be more easily distinguished from weeds at maturity, so the distinction between the righteous and unrighteous will be most pronounced during the tribulation. At the end of this time, God will separate these two groups of people. God will gather his people to himself, like a farmer gathers wheat into his barn; and God will gather his enemies to judge them, like a farmer gathers weeds into bundles to burn.

Both of these passages assure us that God's intentions for us are only good. Though we live among unbelievers, we will not be judged with unbelievers. God will deliver us from his wrath.

The Angels with the Last Plagues (Rev. 15)
ΑΩ

John sees a great and marvelous sign in heaven: seven angels who are about to pour out the fullness of God's wrath.

An Assembly of Martyrs

Before the first angel pours out his bowl, heaven pauses and contemplates what is about to take place. John specifically takes notice of those who have conquered the Antichrist, his image, and his mark. From an earthly perspective, these people did not win. They had been assaulted and killed by the Antichrist. But, from a heavenly perspective, these people did win. They had held fast to their profession of faith, and now they stand with God in glory.

The goal of the Antichrist is to make Christians renounce their faith and swear allegiance to himself. These Christians, though, did not budge. They remained true. They did not give in to the relentless pressure of the Antichrist, even when family members and friends urged them to give up and submit to his authority. They did not bow their knee to his image. They did not accept his mark. They, in fact, won.

These Christians now stand victoriously in heaven. They stand in God's presence. They are alive and well. They are strong in number. They are given authority and power. And they sing of God's great and marvelous works. Who better to sing of God's holiness in wrath than those who were unjustly persecuted and martyred in this life!

The Justice of God's Wrath

Earlier in the book of Revelation, John noted the souls under the altar and their cry, "How long before you will judge and avenge our blood on those who dwell on the earth?" (Rev. 6:10). Now the time of God's judgment is here. The innocent blood of the righteous will be avenged. The divine scales of justice will be balanced. Those who destroyed will be destroyed. Those who persevered will be rewarded.

God's righteous acts will be clearly manifested in his wrath. The martyred saints now sing, "Great and amazing are your deeds, O Lord God the Almighty! Just and true are your ways, O King of the nations!" (Rev. 15:3). God is both just and true in the outpouring of his wrath. God is just in that he is punishing the wicked and clearing the innocent. And God is true in that he had warned the wicked of their destruction and promised deliverance to the righteous.

The Unity of God's People

Interestingly, this group sings both the song of Moses and the song of the Lamb. While the book of Revelation primarily seeks to encourage the last generation of Christians, it also addresses the injustices lodged against the people of God throughout the course of history. The last generation of Christians represents believers throughout time and in both dispensations. This group of believers represents the predominately Jewish believers of the Old Testament and the predominately Gentile believers of the New Testament.

Revelation records the culmination and outcome of the history-long struggle between God's people and his enemies. While we may not experience God's justice in our lifetime; nonetheless, it is coming. While we may not realize God's promises in our lifetime, they will be fulfilled. While we may not know God's vindication in our lifetime, still our name will be cleared. While we may not experience God's deliverance in our lifetime, most certainly he will save. This vision assures us of God's ultimate plans.

This group of people standing by the sea of glass represents us. Their vindication is our vindication. Their hope is our hope. Their song is our song. Their satisfaction is our satisfaction. And their victory is our victory. May we find solace in this heavenly scene!

The Seven Bowls (Rev. 16)
ΑΩ

Christ's Victory

Without further delay, the angels one by one pour out their bowls until the kingdom of the Antichrist collapses under the weight of God's wrath. An epidemic of painful boils breaks out upon humanity, the sea turns to blood and all its creatures die, the rivers and springs also turn to blood, the sun becomes unbearably hot and scorches people with its flames, the world is suddenly plunged into darkness, the kings of the earth are once again deceived and gather their armies for one final battle, and then it is done. The capital city of the Antichrist's empire collapses. The Antichrist and all who have followed him have been defeated. His rule is over. Christ has won.

The Exclusion of the Church

God's wrath is expressly directed at the Antichrist and his followers. The boil epidemic spreads among "the people who bore the mark of the beast and worshiped its image" (Rev. 16:2). The waters turn to blood because "they have shed the blood of saints and prophets" (Rev. 16:6). The sun scorches people who curse God and refuse to repent (Rev. 16:9). God pours out his wrath because "God remembered [the sin of] Babylon the great" (Rev. 16:19). And finally, one hundred pound hailstones crush people who continue to curse God (Rev. 16:21).

God's wrath is nowhere directed at God's people in the book of Revelation. God's wrath is always directed at the Antichrist and his followers. This is consistent with the whole of Scripture. The church, because of her faith in Jesus Christ, will be saved from the coming wrath. God's people will not face his wrath.

What is unclear in the book of Revelation is whether the church is present on earth during the outpouring of God's wrath. A case could be made either way from the present passage. On the one hand, someone may argue that to specify one group of people (that is, those who received the mark of the Antichrist) implies the presence of another group of people (that is, those who refused the mark of the Antichrist). On the other hand, someone may argue that the author is simply highlighting the justice of God's wrath by describing the remaining human population with such specification. Nowhere does the passage explicitly state that the saints are present or absent.

The Absence of the Church

We are sorely disappointed by this passage because we want to establish a timeline of end-time events. The book of Revelation does not concern itself with chronology as much as with principles. This chapter is a case in point. We want to know whether the church is present or absent during the outpouring of God's wrath. This passage, however, does not mention the church. Instead, this passage emphasizes the point that God will judge the Antichrist and all who side with him, and that this judgment will be severe.

Although the book of Revelation does not provide a clear-cut timeline of end-time events, I will attempt to answer our question from other principles we glean from the book of Revelation. While I believe the church will be present during the tribulation, I believe that the church will be absent during the outpouring of the seven bowls of God's wrath. I offer the following three reasons.

First, God will not unleash his wrath until all Christians who are to be martyred are martyred. In Revelation 6:11, the souls under the altar are told that their blood would not be avenged until the number of their fellow servants who were to be killed should be complete. Since the Antichrist will be "allowed to make war on the saints and to conquer them" during the tribulation, we must conclude that there are few, if any, Christians left on earth when God's unleashes his wrath (Rev. 13:7).

Second, John recorded several visions of Christians safely in glory (the 144,000 on Mt. Zion, the harvest of the earth, and those who had conquered the Beast standing by a sea of glass) before he recorded this vision of the seven bowls of wrath.

Third, John does not explicitly mention the presence of any Christians on earth in the present passage. Being an argument from silence, this admittedly is a weak argument; however, as collaborative evidence, it supports the previous two arguments.

The Justice of God's Wrath

The present passage teaches us that, while God's wrath is severe, it is also just. God is justified in his wrath because these people had attacked his people. God is avenging the blood of his servants. God is pouring out his wrath on those who had assaulted and killed his people.

The angel in charge of the waters declared:

> Just are you, O Holy One, who is and who was,
>   for you brought these judgments.
> For they have shed the blood of saints and prophets,
>   and you have given them blood to drink.
> It is what they deserve! Rev. 16:5-6

And the altar under which the souls stood and at which the prayers of the saints were offered concurred:

> Yes, Lord God the Almighty,
>   true and just are your judgments! Rev. 16:7

God is further justified in that these people still do not repent even when they are being punished for their sins (Rev. 16:9, 11). Although God is applying his hand of discipline, they still do not acknowledge their wrongdoing. They think that they are in the right and God is in the wrong. They are obstinate in their rebellion, and they are justified in their own eyes. Instead of confessing their sins, they curse God.

The text points out three times that these people continue to curse God. Revelation 16:9 says, "They were scorched by the fierce heat, and they *cursed the name of God* who had power over these plagues" (italics mine). Revelation 16:10-11 says, "People gnawed their tongues in anguish and *cursed the God of heaven* for their pain and sores" (italics mine). And, finally, Revelation 16:21 says, "Great hailstones, about one hundred pounds each, fell from heaven on people; and they *cursed God* for the plague of the hail, because the plague was so severe" (italics mine).

These verses highlight the depravity of man and the hardness of their hearts. It is not that God is unwilling to forgive, but they are unwilling to repent. While God wants everyone to be saved, the will of these people cannot be broken. They are set in their antagonism toward God. Therefore, they are deserving of this punishment from God. God is indeed true and just in his judgments.

Christ's Word of Encouragement

Almost out of nowhere, we hear Christ speak. He interrupts this scene of devastation and offers a word of encouragement: "Behold, I am coming like a thief! Blessed is the one who stays awake, keeping his garments on, that he may not go about naked and be seen exposed!" (Rev. 16:15).

In this statement, Christ reminds us that this horrific scene is the fate of the unbelieving world and that we do not need to be among these people. Instead, we need to stay away and keep our garments on. If we have not done so already, we need to repent of our wickedness. We need to acknowledge the righteousness of God. We need to refuse the mark of the Antichrist. We need to abhor the worship of his image. And we need to cling to our faith in Jesus Christ.

As life's circumstances grow worse and worse, Christ's appearance and his deliverance draw closer and closer. May we find encouragement in Christ's soon return!

The Prostitute and the Beast (Rev. 17)
ΑΩ

Revelation 17 describes for us the city of Babylon, the capital city of the Antichrist's empire. Revelation 18 laments the fall of Babylon.

The Description of the Prostitute

One of the seven angels who had the seven bowls invites John to see the great prostitute with whom all the nations of the earth committed spiritual apostasy (Rev. 17:1-2). John sees a woman, promiscuously dressed in red and lavishly adorned with fine jewelry, riding on a blasphemous Beast with seven heads and ten horns (Rev. 17:3).

The woman is Babylon, and the Beast is the Antichrist. In ancient history, Babylon was the capital city of the Assyrian empire. In the book of Revelation, Babylon represents the capital city of the Antichrist's empire. Babylon is the city from which the Antichrist will exert his influence, display his power, enact his agenda, and enforce his policies. As such, it will become the center of the world's commerce, politics, wickedness, and persecution against Christians.

The Display of the World's Wealth

Babylon will be the display of the world's wealth. Babylon is described as "arrayed in purple and scarlet, and adorned with gold and jewels and pearls" (Rev. 17:4). She pampers herself as she lives in luxury (Rev. 18:7, 9). She does not know, nor has she ever seen, poverty (Rev. 18:7). She is wealthy (Rev. 18:17), full of the world's splendors and delicacies (Rev. 18:14).

The merchants of the earth will grow rich from her marketplace (Rev. 18:3). There they will buy and sell "gold, silver, jewels, pearls, fine linen, purple cloth, silk, scarlet cloth, all kinds of scented wood, all kinds of articles of ivory, all kinds of articles of costly wood, bronze, iron and marble, cinnamon, spice, incense, myrrh, frankincense, wine, oil, fine flour, wheat, cattle and sheep, horses and chariots, and slaves" (Rev. 18:12-13). All of the world's wealth will pass through her (Rev. 18:17-19).

Babylon will be the happening place. There, people will find much to see and to do. There, people can go and hear "the sound of harpists and musicians, of flute players and trumpeters" (Rev. 18:22a). There, people can go and buy the product of any craft and eat the richest cuisine (Rev. 18:22b). There, people can go and enjoy all the night life (Rev. 18:23a). There, people can go and celebrate all the momentous occasions in their lives (Rev. 18:23b).

The Capital of the World's Government

Babylon will be the capital of the world's government. Revelation 17:1 pictures Babylon, the great prostitute, as sitting on many waters. Revelation 17:15 explains the vision: "the waters that you saw, where the prostitute is seated, are peoples and multitudes and nations and languages." In other words, Babylon will sit over all the nations of the world. She will subdue the kings of the earth and rule over a worldwide empire.

Babylon will view herself as a queen and the nations of the earth as her subjects (Rev. 18:7). She will deceive the nations of the earth with her sorcery (Rev. 18:23). The kings of the earth will commit sexual immorality with her, and the inhabitants of the earth will all become drunk with the wine of her sexual immorality (Rev. 17:2; 18:3). After all, Babylon is "the great city that has dominion over the kings of the earth" (Rev. 17:18).

The Haunt of the World's Depravity

Babylon will be the haunt of the world's depravity. She is pictured as "sitting on a scarlet beast that was full of blasphemous names" (Rev. 17:3), and she is "holding in her hand a golden cup full of abominations and the impurities of her sexual immorality" (Rev. 17:4). She is furthermore described as the "mother of prostitutes and of earth's abominations" (Rev. 17:5). On three occasions, the text notes that the kings of the earth commit sexual immorality with her:

> [With her] the kings of the earth *have committed sexual immorality*, and with the wine of whose sexual immorality the dwellers on earth have become drunk. Rev. 17:2 (italics mine)

> For all nations *have drunk the wine of the passion of her sexual immorality*, and the kings of the earth have committed immorality with her, and the merchants of the earth have grown rich from the power of her luxurious living. Rev. 18:3 (italics mine)

> And the kings of the earth, who *committed sexual immorality* and lived in luxury *with her*, will weep and wail over her when they see the smoke of her burning. Rev. 18:9 (italics mine)

Sexual immorality pictures her spiritual apostasy, and drunkenness depicts the extent of her apostasy. Her sins and iniquities will be "heaped high as heaven" (Rev. 18:4-5). She will seek her own welfare, and she will take advantage of others (Rev. 18:6-7). In her gates, the souls of men will be bought and sold. Slave trade will once again be legalized, and people's freedom will be exploited for a profit (Rev. 18:13).

The Seat of the World's Antagonism

Babylon will be the seat of the world's antagonism against Christianity. While promiscuity and lawlessness are worthy of judgment, the sin above all sins is Babylon's affront to God and his Christ. Babylon will demonstrate her hatred of God by her overt persecution of Christians. Babylon will forbid the free exercise of religion. Anyone who breaks this law will be arrested, tried, and executed. God will judge Babylon severely for her antagonism toward Christianity.

Consider the following verses.

> And I saw the woman, *drunk with the blood of the saints, the blood of the martyrs of Jesus.* When I saw her, I marveled greatly. Rev. 17:6 (italics mine)

> Pay her back *as she herself has paid back others,* and repay her double for her deeds; mix a double portion for her *in the cup she mixed.* Rev. 18:6 (italics mine)
>
> Rejoice over her, O heaven, and you saints and apostles and prophets, for *God has given judgment for you against her!* Rev. 18:20 (italics mine)
>
> And *in her was found the blood of prophets and of saints,* and of all who have been slain on earth. Rev. 18:24 (italics mine)

No one touches God's people without God himself noticing. Though people in authority may "get away" with persecuting Christians now, God will not forget the pain they have inflicted. The day of his reckoning is coming. When Christ comes, the unbelieving world will be judged, and all believers past, present, and future will be vindicated. Until then, let us rest content in this future judgment and heed the words of the apostle Paul:

> Repay no one evil for evil, but give thought to do what is honorable in the sight of all. If possible, so far as it depends on you, live peaceably with all. Beloved, never avenge yourselves, but leave it to the wrath of God, for it is written, "Vengeance is mine, I will repay, says the Lord." To the contrary, "if your enemy is hungry, feed him; if he is thirsty, give him something to drink; for by so doing you will heap burning coals on his head." Do not be overcome by evil, but overcome evil with good.
> Rom. 12:17-21

The Description of the Beast

The description of the Beast in this passage reinforces the vision we have already seen about the Antichrist. He masquerades as Christ who had lived, died, and was raised again (Rev. 17:8). He will cause all who dwell on the earth to marvel, and he will deceive everyone whose name is not found in the Book of Life (Rev. 17:8). Christians will be able to see through the deception and know the true identity of the woman and the Beast (Rev. 17:9).

The Prostitute and the Beast (Rev. 17)

The Antichrist will reign ruthlessly for a set time, yet his doom is soon and sure (Rev. 17:10-11). The kings of the earth will yield their authority and pledge their allegiance to the Antichrist (Rev. 17:12-13, 17). The Antichrist will unite them in their antagonism toward Christians and in their effort to overthrow the rule of Jesus Christ (Rev. 17:14). Jesus, though, will conquer them, for Jesus is indeed "Lord of lords" and "King of kings" (Rev. 17:14). Christians will share in this victory—both now in their struggle with the Antichrist and in the end (Rev. 17:14).

The Fall of Babylon
(Rev. 18-19:10)
ΑΩ

The Troubled Soul

The psalmist declared the Lord's goodness to Israel in the introductory verse of Psalm 73. The psalmist, though, did not stop there; he went on to confess his doubt in the Lord's goodness in his own life. He explained, "For I was envious of the arrogant when I saw the prosperity of the wicked" (Ps. 73:3). The wicked are full of pride, violence, envy, and insolence; and yet, "they are not in trouble as others are; they are not stricken like the rest of mankind" (Ps. 43:5).

Nothing undermines one's motivation for godly living as much as the prevalence of social injustice in this world. "Why make the effort if it's all in vain?" a believer is tempted to think. This is what the psalmist thought: "All in vain have I kept my heart clean and washed my hands in innocence" (Ps. 73:13). Thus the twin questions "Why do the wicked prosper?" and "Why do good people suffer?" have plagued believers throughout the course of history.

The quandary of social injustice will be most pronounced during the tribulation, for the contrast between the righteous and the wicked will be the greatest during this period of time. Christians will face their greatest suffering, and the ungodly will enjoy their greatest freedom. Evil will rule the day, and righteousness will be bound. People will do whatever they want, and Christians will be persecuted for righteousness' sake.

The End of the Wicked

The soul of the psalmist was quieted when he went into the sanctuary of God. There he saw the end of the wicked. There he prayed, "Truly you set them in slippery places; you make them fall to

The Fall of Babylon (Rev. 18-19:10)

ruin. How they are destroyed in a moment, swept away utterly by terrors!" (Ps. 73:18-19).

Like Psalm 73, Revelation 18 reminds us that the wicked do not always prosper, and the righteous do not always suffer. Despite all appearances to the contrary, Revelation 18 encourages Christians to maintain their stand. As the city of Babylon is prosperous and wicked, so shall her judgment be swift and complete.

> Alas! Alas! You great city,
>   you mighty city, Babylon!
> For in a single hour your judgment has come.
>   Rev. 18:10 (cf. Rev. 18:8, 17, 19)

Babylon is coming down. God is going to judge her. God will do to her as she has done to others, particularly to the people of God. God will pay her back double for her wicked deeds (Rev. 18:6). God will bring upon her plagues of death, mourning, and famine (Rev. 18:8). All of her glory and splendor will be laid waste (Rev. 18:17). She will be razed to the ground with fire (Rev. 18:8). She will become a desolate wasteland for wandering animals and dejected demons (Rev. 18:2). She will be wiped off the map (Rev. 18:21).

The Exhortation to Christians

The present passage contains a single exhortation to Christians: "Come out of her, my people, lest you take part in her sins, lest you share in her plagues" (Rev. 18:4). God's wrath is never intended for Christians. We are supposed to judge ourselves, so that we will not be judged with the world (1 Cor. 11:31-32).

When the Antichrist begins to exert his authority, we should have no part in his agenda or in his programs. As persuasive and popular as they may be, they are designed to bring all society under his control and to execute all kinds of atrocities—crimes against humanity and attacks against Christians. Don't be a part of it! Stand opposed to it! Speak out against it! To go along with the flow is to choose the side of man and to share in his ultimate judgment.

The Praise of Heaven

At the fall of Babylon, heaven erupts in praise. The great crowd of Christians praises the Lord because he has dispensed true justice

(Rev. 19:1). The wicked have been punished, for God has destroyed Babylon on account of her wickedness; and the righteous have been vindicated, for God has avenged the blood of his servants (Rev. 19:2). The twenty-four elders and the four living creatures affirm the assessment of God's judgment and echo the praise of his people (Rev. 19:4).

A voice from the throne exhorts the people of God:

> Praise our God,
> all you his servants,
> you who fear him,
> small and great. Rev. 19:5

The fall of Babylon marks a decisive blow against the Antichrist and his kingdom. This is a cause of great rejoicing. The history-long battle between God's people and his enemies is nearly done. The patient endurance of the saints in the face of antagonism, persecution, and suffering is almost over. The long-awaited union between Christ and his people is nearly here.

All of God's people have reason to celebrate. This moment is not simply for Christians who have endured the tribulation; this moment is for everyone who has believed in Jesus Christ. Since Christ's ascension in the first century, Christians have looked forward to the day when evil would be destroyed and righteousness would prevail. More than that, Christians have longed for the moment when Christ would appear and they would see him face-to-face. God incarnate will live among us. He will be our God, and we will be his people.

The Marriage Supper

The marriage supper of the Lamb has come. Those who are invited will be blessed in that they will not be judged with the Antichrist and his followers. Moreover, they are blessed because they will be in the presence of the Lamb and enjoy the favor of God forever.

The White Robes of the Saints

The saints will be clothed in white robes. These white robes represent their holiness, that is, their confession of faith in Jesus Christ and their commitment to follow him at all costs. These white robes distinguish these people from the rest of humanity. These people were characterized by holiness. They are the ones who, while living on earth, had a hunger and thirst for righteousness. They are now pictured in heaven, with Christ, dressed in their holiness.

These white robes were both given to and acquired by the saints. Our holiness is a divine-human cooperative. By this, I mean, our holiness is something that we actively pursue ("his Bride has made herself ready" and "the fine linen is the righteous deeds of the saints"), and it is something that is given to us ("it was granted her to clothe herself with fine linen, bright and pure").

We should not wait until our wedding day to be dressed in white. We should be preparing ourselves now to meet our future husband, for this is why Christ died for us.

> Christ loved the church and gave himself up for her, that he might sanctify her, having cleansed her by the washing of water with the word, so that he might present the church to himself in splendor, without spot or wrinkle or any such thing, that she might be holy and without blemish. Eph. 5:25-27

Figuratively speaking, we are even now sewing our garments for the wedding ceremony. No, we are not perfect, nor will we be. However, we should pursue that for which Christ apprehended us.

Like the apostle Paul, we should "press on toward the goal for the prize of the upward call of God in Christ Jesus" (Phil. 3:14). Our goal is to be found blameless and pure when Christ appears for his bride. Thus, Peter wrote: "Since you are waiting for [the coming of the Lord], be diligent to be found by him without spot or blemish, and at peace" (2 Peter 3:14).

The Rider on the White Horse
(Rev. 19:11-21)
ΑΩ

The Identity of the Rider

Jesus Christ rides on the white horse. His name reflects his character. He is faithful to his servants and true to his word. He executes justice and wages war in perfect righteousness. He condemns the guilty and acquits the innocent. He calls good, "good" and evil, "evil." His focus is intense; and his authority, manifold. The basis of his authority is his death, burial, and resurrection.

The Impotence of Man

Jesus and his armies have come to engage the Antichrist and his armies in one final battle. The contest can hardly be called a battle as Christ does not even raise an arm to strike. We do not see the clashing of swords and shields as the opposing armies collide. Christ does not stand in the midst of a whirl of activity as he commands his troops to victory. Christ does not spoil or tear his garments from combat. Christ simply speaks. His word alone goes out like a sharp sword and attacks the nations. By his word, Christ secures the victory and treads the winepress of the wrath of God. Christ demonstrates that he is, in fact, the King of kings and Lord of lords (Rev. 19:16).

Man is no match for Jesus Christ. Christ's power differs from man's power in quality, not simply in quantity. Christ's power is uncreated, independent of everyone. Man's power is created, dependent upon his Maker. It is sheer absurdity for man to think that he can somehow oust Christ. Those who have received the mark of the Beast and who worship his image have clearly been deceived (Rev. 19:20).

The Rider on the White Horse (Rev. 19:11-21)

The Anointed of the Lord

This battle scene reflects the teaching of Psalm 2. The Lord has installed his king on Mt. Zion. While the nations object to the Lord's selection and take up arms against him, the Lord knows the futility of their frenzied activity, and he laughs from heaven.

> Why do the nations rage
>   and the peoples plot in vain?
> The kings of the earth set themselves,
>   and the rulers take counsel together,
>   against the Lord and against his anointed, saying,
> "Let us burst their bonds apart
>   and cast away their cords from us."
>
> He who sits in the heavens laughs;
>   the Lord holds them in derision.
> Then he will speak to them in his wrath,
>   and terrify them in his fury, saying,
> "As for me, I have set my King
>   on Zion, my holy hill."
>
> I will tell of the decree:
> The Lord said to me, "You are my Son;
>   today I have begotten you.
> Ask of me, and I will make the nations your heritage,
>   and the ends of the earth your possession.
> You shall break them with a rod of iron
>   and dash them in pieces like a potter's vessel."
>
> Now therefore, O kings, be wise;
>   be warned, O rulers of the earth.
> Serve the Lord with fear,
>   and rejoice with trembling.
> Kiss the Son,
>   lest he be angry, and you perish in the way,
>   for his wrath is quickly kindled.
> Blessed are all who take refuge in him.
>
> Psalm 2:1-12

Encouragement for Us

This vision of Christ on a white horse was not written for unbelievers but for us. It was not intended to enlighten the deceived but to encourage the saints. While struggling in the here and now, we often lose sight of the omnipotence of Christ. In the present, we see the prevalence of evil all around us. We feel as though evil is on par with Christ. The truth of this passage is clear. There is no contest. Christ just has to say the word, and it's done.

The Thousand Years (Rev. 20)
ΑΩ

Christ casts the Antichrist and the False Prophet into the lake of fire, he binds Satan in the Abyss, he raises those who belong to him from the dead, and he establishes his millennial rule over the earth. Christ appoints Christians to fill the various offices in his newly formed theocracy. They will serve as kings, judges, and priests. Christians will, as the apostle Paul reminded his readers, judge the world (1 Cor. 6:2). Christians will, as Jesus had taught the crowds, inherit the earth (Matt. 5:5). These promises will find their fulfillment, at least in part, during these thousand years.

Millennial Kingdom for All Believers

We should not think that these promises are limited only to the last generation of believers. Admittedly, special emphasis is given to those who—on account of their faith and witness—refused to worship the Antichrist or to accept his mark (Rev. 20:4). And perhaps these martyrs will receive the more prominent positions in Christ's kingdom. This emphasis is right and proper, for these Christians endured the brunt of the history-long antagonism that has existed against the people of God. Furthermore, the book was written to prepare these believers *for* the coming tribulation and to encourage these believers *during* the tribulation.

Yet, Christ's millennial kingdom is for all believers. The book of Revelation teaches that there are two resurrections: one prior to the thousand years and another subsequent to the thousand years. Those who participate in the first resurrection will live and reign with Christ for a thousand years. They will not be cast into the lake of fire, for the second death does not have authority over them (Rev. 20:6). In contrast, those who participate in the second resurrection will stand before God and be judged according to their works (Rev. 20:12). Anyone whose name is not found in the Book of Life will be cast into the lake of fire (Rev. 20:15).

We are not among those who are raised only to be condemned; we are among those who trust in Jesus Christ and are consequently saved. We are those who have been delivered from the condemnation of sin and who walk according to the Spirit (Rom. 8:1-4). We are those who have passed from death to life (John 3:16-21, 36; 1 John 3:14). We are those who have been sanctified in Christ Jesus. We therefore must be among those who participate in the first resurrection and enter Christ's millennial reign.

This teaching agrees with the prophet Daniel who spoke of two resurrections: one to everlasting life and another to everlasting condemnation (Dan. 12:2). It also agrees with Jesus Christ who declared that, "an hour is coming when all who are in the tombs will hear his voice and come out, those who have done good to the resurrection of life, and those who have done evil to the resurrection of judgment" (John 5:28-29).

We, therefore, must conclude that Revelation 20:4-6 speaks of the resurrection of all believers, though it focuses its attention on a subgroup of believers, the tribulational saints. This conclusion reaffirms the truth that Revelation records the culmination of history. As such, the message is not simply for those who will live through the tribulation, but it is also for us who precede this tumultuous period of time. We can be assured that we will participate in the first resurrection.

One Final Revolt

At the conclusion of the thousand years, Satan will lead one final revolt to overthrow the reign of Christ. This battle is even feebler than the first. Satan rallies a mass of troops and surrounds the capital city of Christ's kingdom. Christ does not mount his horse. Christ does not call out the troops. Christ does not even enter the picture. Fire bursts down out of heaven and engulfs the threat, and it's over.

The End of the Devil

The Devil who stood behind the Antichrist and the False Prophet now joins his puppets in the lake of fire. Satan does not hold any authority in the lake of fire, as we so often think. He does not hold a pitchfork as his scepter, he does not wear a cynical grin, and he does not torment fallen humanity. Rather, the one who devoted his existence to opposing God and deceiving humanity will himself be tormented day and night forever (Rev. 20:10). Christ has crushed the head of the serpent, fulfilling the hopeful promise made by the Lord to humanity back in the garden of Eden (Gen. 3:15).

The Justice of God's Judgment

The dead are judged according to their works. Although the courtrooms on earth witness a lot of injustice, none will take place on the Day of Judgment. The heavenly records are accurate and complete. People will give account for every word they have spoken, every deed they have done, and every thought that has passed through their minds. Christ not only knows the outward acts of a person, but he also knows the inward thoughts of the heart. Consequently, Christ will make no mistakes. Christ will judge with perfect knowledge and equity. He will reward those who fear his name and destroy those who destroyed the earth (Rev. 11:18).

The Book of Life reminds us that our salvation does not find its basis in our works. If a person's name is not found in the Book of Life, he will be cast into the lake of fire (Rev. 20:15). If it were not for the Book of Life, we all would be cast into the lake of fire. For there is no one who is righteous; no one who understands God's ways; and no one who seeks after God. Instead, we all are silenced before God (Rom. 3:10-11, 19-20). Yet, through our unwavering faith in Christ's work on the cross, we may be assured of eternal life.

All Things New (Rev. 21-22:5)
ΑΩ

A New Heaven and Earth

Heaven and earth with all its physical upheaval, moral corruption, and tyrannical governance will flee from the face of him who sits on the throne. Created in perfect beauty but corrupted by sin, the present heaven and earth will serve no more purpose in the future. Their usefulness is gone. They will be discarded. There will be no place for them in the new order (Rev. 20:11).

Whereas some Scripture emphasizes the continuity between this earth and the next (Isa. 11:1-9; 35:1-9; Mal. 3:1-4; 4:1-3; Acts 3:19-21; Rom. 8:19-21), the present passage emphasizes the discontinuity. Such an emphasis is appropriate for Christians who are suffering persecution. For them, there are few, if any, redeeming qualities in this world. Instead, a new heaven and a new earth will serve as the eternal habitation for humanity.

All things will be made new (Rev. 21:5). The chaos that existed on the old earth will not exist on the new earth. Everything that caused pain, hardship, and tears will be gone. There will be no more aging. There will be no more corruption. There will be no more persecution. The curse imposed in the garden of Eden will be reversed. Redeemed humanity will once again live in an ideal world.

The Human Heart Satisfied

The deepest desire of the human heart is to know God. Augustine captured this thought in the opening paragraph of his *Confessions*:

> Man is one of your creatures, Lord, and his instinct is to praise you. He bears about him the mark of death, the sign of his own sin, to remind him that you thwart the proud.

But still, since he is a part of your creation, he wishes to praise you. The thought of you stirs him so deeply that he cannot be content unless he praises you, because you made us for yourself and our hearts find no peace until they rest in you.[5]

In the garden of Eden, people enjoyed a perfect relationship with God. God would come, walk, and converse with Adam and Eve in the cool of the day. This relationship was marred forever the moment Adam ate of the forbidden fruit. Adam's eyes were opened, and the presence of God terrified him. Because of his sin, humanity was banished from the garden of Eden and, more significantly, from the Tree of Life. Humanity no longer had access to the source of life; instead, we were plunged into a life filled with sin and despair.

Although the deepest desire of the human heart is to know God, our sinfulness has prevented us from pursuing this relationship. But, what was impossible for us was possible for God. God took the initiative and provided a way through Christ by which we can pass from death to life. Through faith in Jesus Christ, we can once again know God forever. The desire of the human heart can be satisfied: God will once again live among us. All this was accomplished, not by anything that we did, but by Christ's death, burial, and resurrection. All this was accomplished to the praise, honor, and glory of God.

> And I heard a loud voice from the throne saying, "Behold, the dwelling place of God is with man. He will dwell with them, and they will be his people, and God himself will be with them as their God. Rev. 21:3

> No longer will there be anything accursed, but the throne of God and of the Lamb will be in it, and his servants will worship him. They will see his face, and his name will be on their foreheads. Rev. 22:3-4

While the new earth has its benefits—no more heartache, no more suffering, no more crying, no more dying, etc.—these pale in comparison to being in the presence of God and enjoying his favor forever. His presence satisfies our deepest longings and fills us with immeasurable joy. All these other benefits flow spontaneously from a benevolent God who loves his people and showers his blessings upon them.

The Certainty of the End

God is the Alpha and the Omega, the Beginning and the End. As I write, the story is incomplete. The wicked prevail, and the righteous suffer. God, though, will bring the story to a perfect conclusion. God and his creatures will be reconciled. God will once again dwell among people. The wicked will be punished, and the righteous will be vindicated.

The Thirsty Are Satisfied

He who thirsts for the consummation of history will drink fully of its reality (Rev. 21:6). His thirst will be quenched. He who takes a stand for Christ and refuses to worship the Beast will enjoy the restoration of all creation. He will receive the new earth as his inheritance (Rev. 21:7a); and he will have a special relationship with God: God will be his God, and he will be God's son (Rev. 21:7b).

This passage challenges us to foster a thirst for the new heaven and the new earth. If we want to dwell on the new earth, then we have to be faithful now. If we want to stand with God then, we have to side with God now. We may be called to suffer, but the eternal weight of glory far surpasses any temporal hardship we may experience, even if it means death or the constant threat of it.

The Exclusion of the Wicked

Many people—the vile, the murderers, the sexually immoral, the sorcerers, the idolaters, and all liars—will be excluded from the new earth (Rev. 21:8). The sins that identify these people characterize the moral climate in which the last generation of Christians will live. It will be marked by lawlessness. Moreover, these sins identify people who have aligned themselves with the Antichrist and who have persecuted the people of God.

While these people caused a great deal of sorrow for Christians on the old earth, they will not be able to cause sorrow for anyone on the new earth. They will not be able to do so, because they will not be there. They will be banned from the new heaven and the new earth.

Instead, they will be assigned a place in the lake of fire (Rev. 21:8). With the wicked out of the picture, we will find rest on the new earth.

Though the wicked may torment us in this life, we can be assured that our present experience will not be our eternal experience. Let us take comfort in this truth.

The Exclusion of the Cowardly and Faithless

The cowardly and the faithless are also excluded from the new earth. These two categories of people may surprise us. After all, no one is perfect, and we all get scared at times. "Are these not normal human emotions?" we may think. Yet, these two sins are listed first (Rev. 21:8). While being fearful and faithless may not seem like a big deal to us, these two sins are a big deal to God. They will keep people from the new heaven and the new earth.

The cowardly are people who know the right course of action but are too afraid to follow it. They choose comfort in this life rather than comfort in the life to come. They choose immediate, temporal relief rather than eventual, eternal relief. The faithless are people who know the right course of action and even follow it for a time, but when opposition and persecution come, they waver in their faith and give up. They succumb to the thinking that nothing can stop the relentless onslaught of evil, so why try? They succumb to the thinking that they can bear no more, so they cave in.

A Warning to Us

My friends, this is a warning to us all. The promises contained in the book of Revelation are only offered to those who conquer. They are not offered to those who have good intentions. Good intentions will only get us a place in the lake of fire. We must take a stand. We must not retreat from this position. This is a war for our soul, and we must not lose. We must fight until the end.

The book of Revelation defines Christians as those who conquer. They cling to their confession of faith and never let it go. As the author of Hebrews wrote, "We are not of those who shrink back and are destroyed, but of those who have faith and preserve their souls" (Heb. 10:39). If we do our part, we can be assured that God will do his part, for "it is God who works in you, both to will and to work for his good pleasure" (Phil. 2:13). After all, God "is able to keep you from stumbling and to present you blameless before the presence of his glory with great joy" (Jude 24).

The Bride of the Lamb

One of the angels who had poured out one of the bowls of God's wrath invited the apostle John, "Come, I will show you the Bride, the wife of the Lamb" (Rev. 21:9). The angel then took John to the top of a high mountain and showed him the Holy City of Jerusalem which had descended from heaven. Interestingly, the angel did not show John a woman, or an assembly of people, but a city. The implication is clear: The city of Jerusalem is the Bride, the wife of the Lamb.

The New Jerusalem therefore must be a figurative representation of the people of God. This visual description of the people of God agrees with John's earlier description of the New Jerusalem in Revelation 21:2. There the apostle John wrote, "I saw the holy city, new Jerusalem, coming down out of heaven from God, prepared as a bride adorned for her husband." This description also aligns with other Scripture that associates the people of God with a heavenly city.

For instance, the apostle Paul wrote in Galatians:

> Abraham had two sons, one by a slave woman and one by a free woman....Now Hagar is Mount Sinai in Arabia; she corresponds to the present Jerusalem, for she is in slavery with her children. But the Jerusalem above is free, and she is our mother. Gal. 4:22, 25-26

And, the author of Hebrews wrote:

> You have come to Mount Zion and to the city of the living God, the heavenly Jerusalem, and to innumerable angels in festal gathering, and to the assembly of the firstborn who are enrolled in heaven, and to God, the judge of all, and to the spirits of the righteous made perfect, and to Jesus, the mediator of a new covenant, and to the sprinkled blood that speaks a better word than the blood of Abel. Heb. 12:22-24

The Splendor of the Church

Since the city of Jerusalem is the wife of the Lamb, the description of the city does not describe our new residence; rather, it describes us. It describes the people of God in their heavenly splendor.

On earth, the church appears small, weak, and destitute because of the activity of the Antichrist. The church is small because the Antichrist has deceived many professing Christians and lured them away with a false gospel. He has also driven away the cowardly and the faithless from the true gospel. The church is weak because the Antichrist has waged an all-out war against the church and killed many of her members. And the church is destitute because the Antichrist has forbidden her members from working, buying, selling, or engaging in any type of business.

The heavenly perspective of the church is radically different than the earthly perspective of the church. In heaven, the church appears glorious, powerful, and full of splendor. Ultimately, it is God's perspective that prevails.

The Unity of God's People

God's people includes believers of both dispensations: those who lived under the old covenant, and those who lived under the new covenant. The twelve gates of the city are inscribed with the names of the twelve tribes of Israel. Salvation is of the Jews, and God's people include the Jews. The twelve foundations of the city are inscribed with the names of the twelve apostles. The church is built upon the teaching of the apostles, and the apostles took the gospel and proclaimed it among the Gentiles. God's people include the Gentiles.

The Purity of God's People

God has purified his people. They are no longer a mixture of sheep and wolves, genuine believers and false imitators, or precious metal filled with impurities. The city of God is made of "pure gold, like clear glass" (Rev. 21:18, 21). God has expelled everything unclean and everyone who commits abominable acts and speaks lies. The enemies of God who had infiltrated the church on the old earth will not take up residence in the New Jerusalem.

Only those whose names are written in the Lamb's Book of Life will be granted entrance into this city (Rev. 21:27). These people have washed their robes, that is, they have stood the test and kept themselves from the wiles of the Antichrist (Rev. 22:14). They will not only be granted entrance into the city, but they will also be allowed to eat from the Tree of Life (Rev. 22:14). They alone will be able to enjoy the blessing of walking in right relationship with God forever. Everyone else—the dogs, the sorcerers, the sexual immoral, the murderers, the idolaters, the deceivers, and the deceived—will be denied entrance into the city. They will be forbidden access to the blessings found in it (Rev. 22:15).

The Presence of God

No temple will stand in the New Jerusalem, for "its temple is the Lord God the Almighty and the Lamb" (Rev. 21:22). This again illustrates for us that the deepest desire of the human heart will be fulfilled. God will once again live among his people: we will be his people, and he will be our God. In the Old Testament, the temple represented the presence of the Lord among his people. The temple could in no way contain the Creator of heaven and earth; yet it was through the temple that the Lord uniquely displayed his presence among his people (1 Kings 8:27-30). No such temple will be needed in the New Jerusalem, for Jesus Christ—God in flesh—will live among his people.

The fulfillment of this desire is also illustrated in the next verse: No sun or moon will shine over the city, for "the glory of God gives it light, and its lamp is the Lamb" (Rev. 21:23). Throughout the Bible, light is used to image God, his attributes, and/or his Word. For example, 1 John 1:5 reads, "God is light, and in him is no darkness at all." And Psalm 119:105 declares, "Your word is a lamp to my feet and a light to my path." In the New Jerusalem, believers will bask in the light of the Lord forever.

The Personal Knowledge of God

The context of this passage emphasizes the far-reaching, deep-penetrating knowledge of God. In the New Jerusalem, people will not need the sun or any other celestial luminaries. No longer will we need pastors, teachers, and fellow believers to encourage us in our walk with the Lord. Instead, God himself will live among us and "enlighten" us. He himself will guide us into all truth and lead us in the way everlasting. All these other sources of truth, while they reflected the Truth and served the purpose for which they were given, will no longer be necessary. The Truth will be among us.

Then, the prophecy of Jeremiah will be fulfilled in its fullness:

> "This is the covenant I will make with the people of Israel after that time," declares the Lord. "I will put my law in their minds and write it on their hearts. I will be their God, and they will be my people. No longer will they teach their neighbor, or say to one another, 'Know the Lord,' because they will all know me, from the least of them to the greatest," declares the Lord. Jer. 31:33-34

And the anticipatory statement of 1 Corinthians 13 will be reality:

> For we know in part and we prophesy in part, but when the perfect comes, the partial will pass away. When I was a child, I spoke like a child, I thought like a child, I reasoned like a child. When I became a man, I gave up childish ways. For now we see in a mirror dimly, but then face to face. Now I know in part; then I shall know fully, even as I have been fully known. 1 Cor. 13:9-12

The River of Life

In the New Jerusalem, a river will flow from the throne of God and along the main street of the city. When a river flows through a parched land, it brings life. Vegetation springs up and wild animals find habitation. Like a river, God is the source of life. Everything we enjoy on earth comes from the hand of God. He is the giver of all good gifts, and he gives us these gifts for our enjoyment.

The food we eat, the clothes we wear, the house in which we reside, the family and friends whom we love, the air that we breathe—all come from God. While we may be denied the basic necessities in this life, we will never be lacking in the life to come. We will continually enjoy the abundance that God supplies, and we will continually find our greatest satisfaction in him.

The Tree of Life

The Tree of Life will stand in the middle of the city, and the inhabitants of the city will have access to its fruit (Rev. 22:2, 14). The reference to the Tree of Life in the final chapter of Revelation brings resolution to the overarching story of the Bible. When God created the father and mother of the human race, he gave Adam and Eve permission to eat fruit from any tree but one in the garden of Eden (Gen. 2:16). Although man was prohibited from eating the fruit of the tree of the knowledge of good and evil, he could eat from the Tree of Life (Gen. 2:9).

When Adam transgressed against God's command, the judgment of death came upon all people. God had warned Adam, "In the day that you eat of it you shall surely die" (Gen. 2:17). As a result of Adam's sin, the human race was expelled from the garden of Eden (Gen. 3:24a). More significantly, we were barred from the Tree of Life (Gen. 3:24b). God had reasoned, "lest [man] reach out his hand and take also of the tree of life and eat, and live forever" (Gen. 3:22). Without access to the Tree of Life, death would characterize human history.

The account of Adam's descendants tells the story. When Adam had lived 130 years, he fathered Seth. Adam then lived another 800 years, *and he died*. When Seth had lived 105 years, he fathered Enosh. Seth then lived another 807 years, *and he died*. When Enosh had lived 90 years, he fathered Kenan. Enosh then lived another 815 years, *and he died*. When Kenan had lived 70 years, he fathered Mahalalel. Kenan then lived another 840 years, *and he died*. When Mahalalel had lived 65 years, he fathered Jared. Mahalalel lived another 830 years, *and he died*. When Jared had lived 162 years, he fathered Enoch. Jared lived another 800 years, *and he died*. When Enoch had lived 65 years, he fathered Methuselah. Enoch lived another 300 years, *and he*—in contrast to the other ancients—*did not die*, but he walked with God. When Methuselah had lived 187 years, he fathered Lamech. Methuselah lived another 782 years, *and he died*. When Lamech had lived 122 years, he fathered Noah. Lamech lived another 595 years, *and he died*.

This abridged account of Genesis 5 shows how death reigned from Adam to Noah. Death has so characterized human history that we think it is a normal part of the life cycle: We are born, we live, and we die. Death, though, is not natural. Death was not part of the original creation. Death was foreign to God's creative acts in the garden of Eden. Death was introduced by our own sin and rebellion.

In the New Jerusalem, the curse of death will no longer plague the people of God (Rev. 22:3). The Tree of Life will sprout leaves for the healing of the nations and produce fruit for the nourishing of people. We will not deteriorate with age. We will not die. Our lives will no longer be a chasing after the wind. We will build houses and live in them. We will plant vineyards and enjoy their fruit. We will love people, and they will love us back. The wounds that we have received will be healed. The pains that we have endured will be alleviated. The fears that have troubled us will be calmed.

The mention of the Tree of Life reminds us that, while the book of Revelation was written to encourage the last generation of Christians, it also brings encouragement to those believers who have lived throughout the course of history. The book of Revelation offers hope to everyone who fears God—from Adam who lived in the garden of Eden, to the last martyr who dies for the cause of Christ. The hope pictured in the Tree of Life is our hope. May we cling to it whenever we feel the shadow of death coming over us!

The Epilogue (Rev. 22:6-21)
ΑΩ

Two Bookends

The prologue and epilogue serve as bookends to the book of Revelation. As such, they tie all of its contents together. Both the introduction and the conclusion state that God sent his angel to show his servants the events that are about to happen (Rev. 1:1; 22:6). Both pronounce a blessing upon the person who heeds the warnings and exhortations found in the pages of the book (Rev. 1:3; 22:7). Both reveal that the time is near (Rev. 1:3; 22:10). Both declare that Jesus is the Alpha and Omega (Rev. 1:8; 22:13). Both identify Jesus as the originator of the revelation and the sender of the angel (Rev. 1:1; 22:16). Both identify the seven churches as the recipients of the prophecy (Rev. 1:4; 22:16).

These bookends make it abundantly clear that this prophecy is a single piece of literature. It's no wonder that God warns against tampering with this book:

> I warn everyone who hears the words of the prophecy of this book: if anyone adds to them, God will add to him the plagues described in this book, and if anyone takes away from the words of the book of this prophecy, God will take away his share in the tree of life and in the holy city, which are described in this book. Rev. 22:18-19

The Imminence of Christ's Return

The book concludes by emphasizing the imminence of the events written in it. Revelation 22:6 identifies the content of the revelation as "what must soon take place." The blessing recorded in Revelation 22:7 presumes that the reader of the prophecy will live to see the events recorded in the prophecy. The angel forbids the apostle John from sealing up the words of his prophecy in Revelation 22:10. This prohibition stands in contrast to the instruction given to the prophet Daniel in the Old Testament. Daniel is told to "shut up the words and seal the book, until the time of the end" (Dan. 12:4). For Daniel, the end was far away; but, for John, the end was near. Thus, the two prophets are given two different instructions. What is implied is then expressly stated in the same verse, "for the time is near."

Revelation 22:11 calls people, both the righteous and the wicked, to complete their role in the story. Jesus speaks, in Revelation 22:12, and says, "Behold, I am coming soon." The certainty of these events may be found in his self-identification, "I am the Alpha and the Omega, the first and the last, the beginning and the end" (Rev. 22:13).

Revelation 22:14, like verse 7, presumes that the reader will live to see the events recorded in the prophecy. The Spirit of God and the people of God both call for the soon return of Christ in Revelation 22:17. Jesus again announces, "Surely, I am coming soon" (Rev. 22:20a). And the apostle John concludes his prophecy with a benediction and a prayer for Jesus to come soon (Rev. 22:20b).

Our Response

Since Christ is coming soon, we need to be all the more diligent in our responsibilities. Our responsibilities are threefold.

First, we need to accept the testimony of Revelation (Rev. 22:18-19). Lest we end up on the wrong side of the battle lines and come under the judgment of God, we should not alter the text, meaning, or application of Revelation. Instead, we should keep the words of this prophetic book, so that we may receive its blessing (Rev. 1:3; 22:7).

Second, we need to wash our garments in the blood of the Lamb (Rev. 22:14-15). While we must prepare for Christ's return, our salvation does not find its basis in our works. Our salvation finds its basis in the finished work of Christ on the cross, and it finds its fulfillment in the coming of Christ as described in this prophecy. In light of this, we must place our faith in Jesus Christ, for our "salvation is nearer to us now than when we first believed" (Rom. 13:11).

And, third, we need to keep our garments clean (Rev. 19:7-8). Although we live in a morally corrupt world, we should pursue what is right and holy (Rev. 22:11). Since we anticipate being made like Christ when he comes, we should seek to be like him while we wait (1 John 3:2-3). Moreover, Christ is coming to reward his servants, "to repay each one for what he has done" (Rev. 22:12; cf. Rev. 11:18). In light of this, we should live so as to hear the words, "Well done, good and faithful servant" (Matt. 25:21).

Part Three

Confessions

Introduction
ΑΩ

There are two ways to read the book of Revelation.

The first way to read the book of Revelation is from a *theological* approach. A theological approach starts with a pre-manufactured framework of end-time events and then fits the details of Revelation into this humanly constructed theology. According to our theology, the next major event on God's timeline of future events is the rapture of the church. Once the church is safely in heaven, God will turn his attention back to the nation of Israel. The Antichrist will rise to power and make a pact with Israel for seven years, but half-way through this time he will break this agreement and seek to assimilate the Jews. For this reason, this period of time is called "a time of distress for Jacob" (Jer. 30:7). At the end of this time, Christ will step into history, deliver the people of Israel, destroy the kingdom of the Antichrist, and set up his own kingdom on earth for a thousand years.

The second way to read the book of Revelation is from an *exegetical* approach. An exegetical approach starts with the text of Revelation and allows the text to speak for itself. We do not impose a pre-manufactured framework onto the text. Following an exegetical approach, we recognize that the book of Revelation identifies itself as a book of prophecy addressed to the church, written for the benefit of the church, describing future events that will affect the church. It was written not only to tell the church how to live in the present (Rev. 1-3) but also how to prepare for the future (Rev. 4-22). The book of Revelation reveals that the church will be persecuted (Rev. 4-13); her persecutors will be punished (Rev. 14-18); and the church will be delivered (Rev. 19-22). In light of these future events, the church is called to endure to the end (Rev. 13:10; 14:12).

Introduction

These two approaches lead to opposite conclusions. A theological approach presumes the church will *not* be present on earth during the tribulation. The reason? Our theology has already established this point even before we open the book of Revelation. An exegetical approach presumes that the church *will* be present on earth during the tribulation. The reason? The book of Revelation was written to prepare the church for things to come. Jesus wanted to warn the church about the rise of the Antichrist and to provide the church with the needed encouragement for the coming tribulation. These two conclusions cannot both be true.

We in the evangelical community have fully embraced the theological approach. This approach is espoused by many of our churches, taught in many of our Bible colleges and seminaries, and disseminated in a lot of our literature. This approach was popularized through the publication of the *Scofield Reference Bible* in 1909, Hal Lindsey's *The Late, Great Planet Earth* in 1970, and Tim LaHaye and Jerry B. Jenkins' *Left Behind* series between 1995-2007.

Although we have fully embraced a theological approach, there are serious problems with this approach. To begin with, it fails to see how the book of Revelation is relevant to the church. It has effectively taken the book of Revelation away from the church. The assumption of this approach has blinded us to the obvious and prevented us from hearing the message of Revelation. It is high time that we acknowledge the weaknesses of our theological approach, even as we consider another approach that better aligns with Scripture.

Exegetical Weakness
ΑΩ

Exegesis vs. Eisegesis

Exegesis is the interpretative process whereby we draw meaning *out of* the text. It involves the study of vocabulary and grammar, the consideration of the literary genre and surrounding context, and the examination of the historical and cultural background. This careful, painstaking work seeks to uncover what the original author intended to communicate to his audience.

Eisegesis stands in contrast to exegesis. Whereas exegesis seeks to draw meaning *out of* the text, eisegesis reads meaning *into* the text. It begins with a preconceived idea and tries to find the idea in the text. The idea itself does not come from the text, but rather the interpreter brings the idea to the text. This creative, subjective work allows the interpreter to make the text say whatever he or she wants.

Figure 3: Exegesis vs. Eisegesis

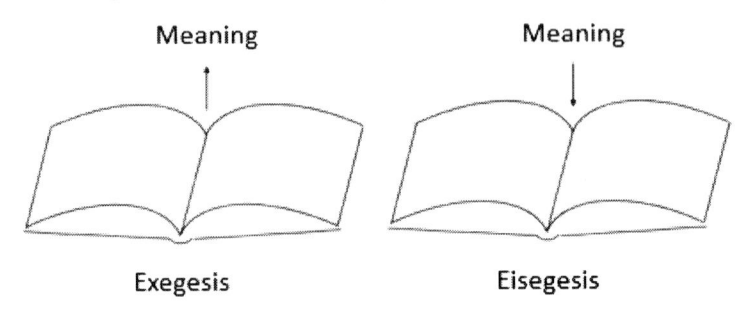

Meaning	Meaning
Exegesis	Eisegesis

Our theological approach to the book of Revelation is guilty of eisegesis. Coming to the text with a pre-manufactured framework of end-time events, we bring all kinds of preconceived ideas to the text. Two such ideas include the seven-year tribulation and the rapture of

Exegetical Weakness

the church. Both of these ideas find their biblical basis elsewhere in Scripture. They are then packed with additional meaning and imposed upon our reading of Revelation.

The Seven-Year Tribulation

Our theology teaches that there is a seven-year period of time reserved for God's dealings with the nation of Israel and God's wrath against the unsaved world. This period of time is commonly referred to as the tribulation. The nature of the tribulation, as it has been traditionally taught, necessitates the removal of the church prior to its commencement. According to our theology, the tribulation is a period of time reserved for God's dealings with the nation of Israel, not the church. In addition, the tribulation is a period of time reserved for God's wrath against the unsaved world. The church is exempt from God's wrath. For both of these reasons, the church must necessarily be removed before the tribulation.

The primary biblical basis for a seven-year tribulation is Daniel 9:24-27. In this passage, seventy weeks of years are decreed for the nation of Israel. This period of time may be divided into three smaller periods of time: seven weeks, sixty-two weeks, and one week. The first seven weeks focus on the rebuilding of the city of Jerusalem. The next sixty-two weeks end with the cutting off of the Anointed One. And the last week supposedly lays in the future. It will begin with a covenant between the Antichrist and the nation of Israel. This covenant will be broken halfway through the week. This last week of seven years, according to our theology, is the tribulation.

Interestingly, the book of Revelation nowhere mentions a seven-year period of time. It does occasionally refer to a three-and-a-half-year period of time (Rev. 11:1-3; 12:5-6, 14; 13:5); however, it is left up to the interpreter whether this period of time corresponds to the first half of Daniel's seventieth week, the second half of Daniel's seventieth week, or whether it refers to Daniel's seventieth week at all. In any case, the idea of a seven-year tribulation is brought to the text of Revelation.

What's more, the book of Revelation describes this three-and-a-half-year period of time differently than our theology has defined the seven-year tribulation. Our theology describes the tribulation as a period of time when God is dealing with the nation of Israel; however, the book of Revelation describes it as a period of time when God is also working among the Gentiles. In Revelation 12, the apostle John sees a vision of a woman clothed with the sun, with the moon under her feet, and a crown of twelve stars on her head. During the tribulation, the woman (commonly understood to be the nation of Israel) will be pursued by the dragon; however, God will prepare for her a place in the wilderness where she will be protected from the dragon and nourished for 1,260 days (Rev. 12:5-6). Unable to touch the woman, the dragon will turn his fury "on the rest of her offspring, on those who keep the commandments of God and hold to the testimony of Jesus" (Rev. 12:17). That is, the dragon will pursue those who believe in Jesus who are outside the nation of Israel.

Whereas our theology describes the tribulation as a period of time when God pours out his wrath on the unsaved world, the book of Revelation describes it as a period of time when the Antichrist exercises great authority in this world. In Revelation 11:1-2, the nations will trample the Holy City for 42 months. In Revelation 11:3, God's two witnesses will prophesy against the atrocities of the Antichrist for 1,260 days. In Revelation 12:5-6 and 12:14, the woman will be protected from the onslaught of the Antichrist for 1,260 days. And, in Revelation 13:5, the Beast of the sea is allowed to exercise authority and speak blasphemous words for 42 months. Nowhere in the book of Revelation is God's wrath associated with this three-and-a-half-year period of time.

The Rapture of the Church

Our theology teaches that there is an event that will occur prior to the tribulation when Christ will descend from heaven, snatch up and meet the church in the air, and usher them into heaven to be with him forever. We commonly refer to this event as the rapture, or the rapture of the church.

The primary biblical basis for the rapture is 1 Thessalonians 4:13-18. In this passage, the apostle Paul comforted the Thessalonians who were needlessly saddened over the deaths of their fellow believers. They were afraid that these loved ones, because they had died prior to the return of Christ, were somehow lost forever. In response, the

Exegetical Weakness

apostle Paul assured them that, when Christ appears, he will gather to himself both the living and the dead. Paul wrote: "The dead in Christ will rise first. Then we who are alive, who are left, will be caught up together with them in the clouds to meet the Lord in the air, and so we will always be with the Lord" (1 Thess. 4:16-17).

Interestingly, the book of Revelation nowhere mentions the removal of the church prior to the tribulation. This is read into the text.

Many have found the rapture of the church in Revelation 3:10, where Jesus promised to keep the church of Philadelphia from the hour of trial that is coming on the whole world. However, there are many problems with this interpretation. First, the phrase "to keep from" does not necessarily mean "removal from." It may also mean "preservation in" (cf. James 1:27). Second, the phrase "the hour of trial" may refer to the outpouring of God's wrath, not the persecution brought on by the Antichrist. The tribulation and the outpouring of God's wrath are not the same thing. Third, this promise, if it refers to a pre-tribulational rapture of the church, runs counter to the prophecy in Revelation 2:10, where Jesus predicted that the church will have tribulation for ten days.

Others have found the rapture of the church in Revelation 4:1 where a voice commands the apostle John to "Come up here, and I will show you what must take place after this." This interpretation, though creative, has no biblical basis. The object of the call is the apostle John, not the church. Furthermore, the purpose of the call is to show John what is to come, not to remove him from persecution. This verse simply introduces the next vision. It orients the reader to a new setting—heaven versus earth—and marks a change in subject— things to come versus things that are. Anything beyond this is supplied by the reader; it is not in the text itself.

Grappling to find the rapture of the church in the book of Revelation, John F. Walvoord suggested that "the morning star" in Revelation 2:28 might refer to the rapture of the church. In his commentary, he wrote, "The Scriptures do not explain this expression, but it may refer to participation in the rapture of the church before the dark hours preceding the dawn of the millennial kingdom."[6] While there is an interesting comparison between the rapture of the church and the morning star, there is no biblical basis for this interpretation. Walvoord himself acknowledged this shortcoming when he wrote, "The Scriptures do not explain this expression."

The most logical identification of the rapture is found in Revelation 14:14-20 where the text describes the harvest of the earth. The Son of Man seated on the cloud first gathers the good grapes to himself (Rev. 14:14-16). He then gathers the sour grapes and throws them into the wine press of God's wrath (Rev. 14:17-20). This passage immediately follows the persecution of the church in Revelation 13 and immediately precedes the outpouring of God's wrath in Revelation 15-16. We, though, do not want to accept this placement of the rapture, because it does not fit with our theology. Instead, we try to find it elsewhere in the text, preferably before the tribulation.

The silence of Revelation about the rapture of the church is deafening. In a book that was written to the church and that purports to tell us about things to come, we would expect to hear something about the rapture. After all, the rapture of the church is undoubtedly the most significant future event for the church. Yet, if we say that the harvest of the earth does not relate to the church, then the book of Revelation has failed to talk about the greatest hope of the believer.

In his book entitled *The Church and the Tribulation*, Robert H. Gundry expressed his dismay with this perspective of Revelation:

> It is incongruous that the major book of prophecy in the NT, written to churches for the express purpose of instructing them regarding final events, should not contain a full description of the hope of the Church and yet in its major portion painstakingly chronicle events which according to pretribulationism have no direct bearing upon the Church.[7]

We must therefore conclude that either the book of Revelation has missed the mark, which is not likely, or our theological approach is wrong.

Theology and Exegesis

One voice stands behind all of Scripture. To hear this voice, we need to bring together everything that Scripture says about a particular topic into a cohesive, consistent statement of thought. This is the purpose of theology.

Theology is a human enterprise whereby we seek to synthesize everything that Scripture says about a particular topic. When our theology leads to a conclusion that contradicts the clear testimony of Scripture, then our theology, which is a man-made structure, must yield to the testimony of Scripture, which is the infallible Word of God.

In other words, our exegesis should inform our theology, and not the other way around.

Hermeneutical Weakness
ΑΩ

Interpreting the Bible

Interpreting the Bible is like assembling a puzzle. When assembling a puzzle, we start with the easy parts of the puzzle, usually the border with its easily recognizable, straight-edged pieces. Once the easy parts of the puzzle are complete, we move on to the more difficult parts, the interior with its indistinguishable, homogenous pieces. We continue this process until all of the gaps are filled in and the picture is complete. When interpreting the Bible, we should similarly start with the clearer passages of Scripture. Once we have a firm understanding of these passages, we can use these passages to help us understand the harder passages of Scripture.

Figure 4: Assembling a Puzzle

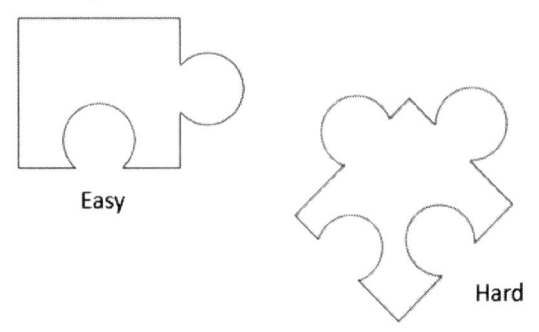

This practice of using the clearer parts of Scripture to interpret the harder parts of Scripture is a fundamental principle in hermeneutics. The reformers called this principle the "Analogy of Faith" and explained its application in the *Westminster Confession* of faith. The *Confession* states: "The infallible rule of interpretation of Scripture is the Scripture itself; and therefore, when there is a question about the true and full sense of any Scripture (which is not manifold, but one), it must be searched and known by other places that speak more clearly."[8]

Scripture itself acknowledges that not all Scripture is the same. Speaking of Paul's writings, Peter wrote that "there are some things in them that are hard to understand, which the ignorant and unstable twist to their own destruction, as they do the other Scriptures." (2 Peter 3:16). For this reason, new believers should start with the basic principles of the Word of God before they move on to the hard sayings of the Bible. The author of Hebrews compared new believers to newborn babies who first need to drink milk before they eat solid food (Heb. 5:12-14). As new believers mature, they will be better equipped to digest the harder passages of Scripture.

Although starting with the clearer parts of Scripture is a fundamental principle in hermeneutics, our theological approach to the book of Revelation does not follow this principle.

A Hard Passage: Daniel 9:24-27

Our theological approach uses Daniel 9:24-27 as the interpretative key for unlocking the book of Revelation. In this passage, seventy weeks of years are decreed for the nation of Israel. According to our theology, sixty-nine of these weeks lie in the past, and the last week of seven years lies in the future. This final seven years is commonly referred to as the tribulation. Our theology teaches us that the book of Revelation, specifically chapters 4-19, refers to this period of time. Since this period of time has been set apart for the nation of Israel, our theology reasons that the church is not present on earth during this time.

The problem with this approach is that Daniel 9:24-27 is one of the most difficult passages in the whole Bible. In four short verses, this passage raises one question after another. Consider some of the questions with which scholars have to wrestle:

- What is a "week"? Does a "week" refer to seven days, seven weeks, or seven years?
- Does the "seventy weeks" refer to one, uninterrupted period of time? Or, does it refer to three separate periods

of time (seven weeks, sixty-two weeks, and one week) with indefinite breaks of time between them?
- Are these literal weeks? Or, are these figurative or symbolic weeks?
- What do each of the following phrases mean: "to finish the transgression", "to put an end to sin", "to atone for iniquity", "to bring in everlasting righteousness", "to seal both vision and prophet", and "to anoint a most holy place"?
- What human decree fulfilled the "going out of the word"?
- Who is the "anointed one"? Has this individual already come, or is he yet to come?
- Does the subordinate clause "after the sixty-two weeks" mean during the final week? Or, does it mean outside the seventy weeks altogether?
- What does the statement mean that the "anointed one shall be cut off and have nothing"?
- Who is the coming "prince"? Is he the same person as the "anointed one"?
- How will the city and the sanctuary be destroyed? And, how extensive will be the destruction?
- Who, or what, will end with a flood?
- Who will make a strong covenant?
- With whom will he make it?
- What will be the terms of this covenant?
- What is the beginning and ending point of the seven weeks, the sixty-nine weeks, and the final week?
- How does Daniel's prophecy of seventy weeks relate to Jeremiah's prophecy of seventy years (Jer. 25:8-14)?
- How does this passage harmonize with the rest of Scripture and with theology?

When a reader of the Bible encounters a question in the text, the surrounding context normally leads the reader toward an answer. In this passage, every verse raises multiple questions, and every verse is surrounded by other verses that raise multiple questions. There's nowhere to get a solid foothold to begin chipping away at the rest. It is no wonder why Edward J. Young wrote in his commentary, "This passage...is one of the most difficult in all the OT, and the interpretations which have been offered are almost legion."[9]

Although Daniel 9:24-27 is one of the hardest passages in the Bible, our theological approach has reached a "definitive" interpretation of this passage, and it uses this interpretation as the chronological framework for understanding the book of Revelation. By way of example, John F. Walvoord wrote in his commentary, "The Book of Daniel describes in detail the period from Daniel's time to Christ's first coming and speaks briefly of the Tribulation and Christ's rule on earth. But the Book of Revelation amplifies the great end-time events with many additional details, culminating in the new heaven and the new earth."[10]

An Easy Passage: Revelation 1:4

I do not intend to unpack Daniel 9:24-27, nor do I intend to offer my own interpretation of this passage. I only point out that we use one of the most difficult passages of Scripture as the interpretative lens through which to read the book of Revelation. Rather than using Daniel 9:24-27 as the foundation for understanding the book of Revelation, let us start with something that is more clear and move on from there.

Revelation 1:4 declares that the book of Revelation was written to, for, and about the church. There is no ambiguity there. Let us first read the book of Revelation from this perspective. Once we get this part of the puzzle put together, then let us figure out how Daniel 9:24-27 fits into the picture. No doubt it does, for the Bible tells one story and all the pieces relate to this story. But let's start with an easier part of the puzzle.

Structural Weakness
AΩ

Complicating the Simple

In our study of the Bible, we tend to make topics more complicated than they need to be. This is especially true of end-time events. We have complicated the study of eschatology by drawing distinctions where there are none and creating categories that are foreign to the text. All of these intricacies obscure the clarity of Scripture and prevent us from hearing the message of Revelation. The key to simplicity is to say enough to capture the point but no more than what is necessary. In the words of Albert Einstein, "Everything should be made as simple as possible, but no simpler."

Figure 5: Simple Foundation and Complex Structure

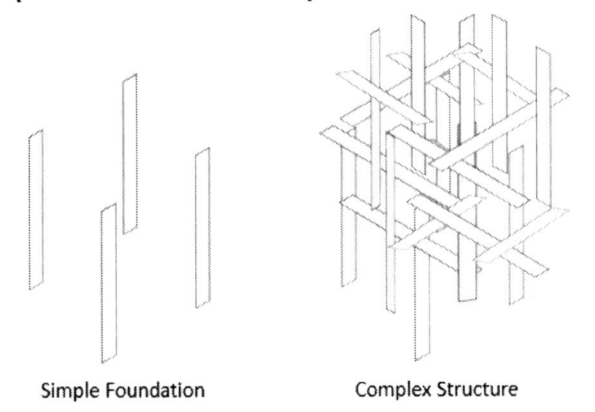

Simple Foundation　　　Complex Structure

The book of Revelation lays a simple, but solid foundation on which to build a theology of end-time events: The church will be persecuted (Rev. 4-13); her persecutors will be punished (Rev. 14-18); and the church will be delivered (Rev. 19-22). On this simple foundation, we have built an overbearing structure. We have so complicated

Structural Weakness

eschatology that we have to construct elaborate, and sometimes enormous, charts to explain what we believe and how all the pieces fit together. The complexity of the structure is so crisscrossed that, if one piece was pulled out, the whole structure would collapse.

Let us consider how we have complicated the study of end-time events and offer a simpler alternative.

Two Comings of Christ

The Bible teaches that there are two comings of Christ. Christ came the first time to suffer, and Christ will come a second time to enter into his glory. After his resurrection, Jesus scolded his disciples, saying, "O foolish ones, and slow of heart to believe all that the prophets have spoken! Was it not necessary that the Christ should suffer these things and enter into his glory?" (Luke 24:25-26). Christ came the first time to deal with sin, and Christ is coming again to save those who long for his appearing. Thus, the author of Hebrews wrote, "Christ, having been offered once to bear the sins of many, will appear a second time, not to deal with sin but to save those who are eagerly waiting for him" (Heb. 9:28).

Although the Bible teaches that there are two comings of Christ, we have introduced a third coming of Christ. Accordingly to our theology, the second coming of Christ includes two different events: the rapture of the church and the revelation of Jesus Christ. The rapture of the church is when Christ descends from heaven, raises the dead in Christ, translates the living believers, and meets the church in the air (1 Thess. 4:13-18). The revelation of Jesus Christ is when Christ comes to purge the nation of Israel from her wickedness and to destroy her enemies (Rev. 14:1-5; 19:11-16). By splitting the second coming of Christ into two different events, we have effectively created a third coming of Christ.

Certainly, Jesus Christ is coming to meet the church in the air and to visit the nation of Israel. But, who says that these are two distinct events? Are they not two aspects of the same event? Are we not complicating the simple? Does not the Bible clearly declare that Christ will come once as a suffering servant, and he will come again as a reigning king? When he comes again, he will not only snatch up those who believe in him, but he will also come to the rescue of Israel.

Two Resurrections

The Bible teaches that there are two resurrections: There is a resurrection of the righteous to life and a resurrection of the unrighteous to damnation. This is what Daniel had prophesied. Daniel 12:2 reads, "And many of those who sleep in the dust of the earth shall awake, some to everlasting life, and some to shame and everlasting contempt." This is what Jesus affirmed. John 5:28-29 reads, "An hour is coming when all who are in the tombs will hear his voice and come out, those who have done good to the resurrection of life, and those who have done evil to the resurrection of judgment." And this is what was revealed to the apostle John. Revelation 20:6 reads, "Blessed and holy is the one who shares in the first resurrection!" and "The rest of the dead did not come to life until the thousand years were ended."

Although the Bible teaches that there are two resurrections, we have added many more resurrections. John F. Walvoord identified these resurrections in his commentary on Revelation:

> Christ was "the Firstfruits" (1 Cor. 15:23), which was preceded by the token resurrection of a number of saints (Matt. 27:52-53). Then will occur the Rapture of the church, which will include the resurrection of dead church saints and the translation of living church saints (1 Thes. 4:13-18). The resurrection of the two witnesses will occur in the Great Tribulation (Rev. 11:3, 11). Then the resurrection of the martyred dead of the Great Tribulation will occur soon after Christ returns to earth (20:4-5). To these may be added the resurrection of Old Testament saints which apparently will also occur at this time, though it is not mentioned in this text (cf. Isa. 26:19-21; Ezek. 37:12-14; Dan. 12:2-3).[11]

Certainly, everyone—Old Testament saints, New Testament saints, martyred saints, and the rest of the dead—will be resurrected. But, who says that these people will rise from the dead at different times? Are we not complicating the simple? Does not the Bible repeatedly declare that there are but two resurrections: one for the righteous, and another for the wicked? Will not God simply raise all of the righteous at the time of Christ's appearing, and all of the unrighteous at the time of judgment?

One Judgment

The Bible teaches that there is one, final judgment. Everyone will stand before God and be judged for what they have done, whether good or bad. During his ministry on earth, Jesus had said, "I tell you, on the day of judgment people will give account for every careless word they speak, for by your words you will be justified, and by your words you will be condemned" (Matt. 12:36-37). To which the apostle Paul elaborated, "[God] will render to each one according to his works: to those who by patience in well-doing seek for glory and honor and immortality, he will give eternal life; but for those who are self-seeking and do not obey the truth, but obey unrighteousness, there will be wrath and fury" (Rom. 2:6-8).

Although the Bible teaches that there is one, final judgment, we have envisioned multiple judgments. According to our theology, there is the judgment of the church-age saints, whose works will pass through a fire so as to determine their reward (1 Cor. 3:10-15). There is the judgment of the Old Testament and martyred saints, who will be given positions of authority in the millennial kingdom (Ezek. 20:33–38; Rev. 20:4). There is the judgment of the nations, so as to evaluate how Gentile people treated Jewish people (Matt. 25:31-46). And there is the judgment of the dead, who will be judged according to their works and thrown into the lake of fire (Rev. 20:11-15).

Certainly, everyone—believers and unbelievers, Jews and Gentiles, nations and individuals—will be judged. But, who says that these judgments will take place at different times? Are we not complicating the simple? Does not the Bible clearly declare that "we will all stand before the judgment seat of God" (Rom. 14:10-11)? Thankfully, another book, that is, the Book of Life, will be opened. Those whose names are found in that book will find mercy (Rev. 20:11-15).

One People

The Bible teaches that there is one people of God. God is forming for himself one people from every tribe and language and people and nation. For this reason, the four living creatures and the twenty-four elders sang a new song about the Lamb, "Worthy are you to take the scroll and to open its seals, for you were slain, and by your blood you ransomed people for God from every tribe and language and people and nation, and you have made them a kingdom and priests to our God, and they shall reign on the earth" (Rev. 5:9-10). This one people of God is illustrated by many analogies throughout Scripture: one flock (John 10:16), one tree (Rom. 11:17), one man (Eph. 2:14-15), and one building (Eph. 2:20-21).

Although the Bible teaches that there is one people of God, we have insisted that there are multiple people of God. John F. Walvoord emphasized this point in his commentary:

> One of the false interpretations that has plagued the church is the concept that God treats all saints exactly alike…Instead of treating all alike, God indeed has a program for Israel as a nation and also for those in Israel who are saved. He also has a program for Gentiles in the Old Testament who come to faith in God. And in the New Testament He has a program for the church as still a different group of saints. Again in the Book of Revelation the Tribulation saints are distinguished from other previous groups. It is not so much a question of difference in blessings as it is that God has a program designed for each group of saints which corresponds to their particular relationship to His overall program.[12]

Certainly, there are differences between Israel and the church. Israel refers to an ethnic category, and the church refers to a spiritual category. But, who says that there are multiple people of God? Are we not complicating the simple? Is not God bringing all people under one head, even Christ (Eph. 1:16-23)? Does not the Bible clearly declare that we "are all one in Christ Jesus" (Gal. 3:28)? Does not the multi-nationality of God's people magnify both the depth of his wisdom (Rom. 11:33-36) and the wonder of his redemption (Rev. 5:9-10)?

The Original Meaning

While we should strive to keep our interpretation of Revelation simple, recovering the intent of the original author is more important than insisting on simplicity. After all, meaning resides not in our interpretation of the text but in the message that the author intended to communicate to his audience. Did Jesus Christ have all of these complexities in mind when he gave the apostle John this revelation? Did the apostle John have all of these intricacies in mind when he penned this revelation? Did the seven churches in Asia recognize all of these distinctions when they heard this revelation?

The testimony of Revelation answers "no" to all of these questions. Jesus Christ did not mention the rapture of church apart from his revelation when he gave the apostle John this revelation. The apostle John only spoke about two resurrections and one final judgement when he penned this revelation. And the seven churches in Asia did not think that God was working with the nation of Israel as a separate people of God when they heard this revelation. From this perspective, the book of Revelation is quite simple. We have made it complicated!

Historical Weakness
ΑΩ

The Early Church

From a historical perspective, our theological approach to the book of Revelation is a modern phenomenon. The proposition of an appearance of Christ separate from and prior to his revelation saw its beginnings about two hundred years ago.[13] This was not the perspective of the early church. Those who lived closest to the apostle John and the seven churches in Asia followed an exegetical approach to the book of Revelation.

The *Didache*, also called the *Teaching of the Twelve Disciples*, is one of the oldest surviving documents from the early church. This document served as a handbook for new Christians, teaching them about a variety of topics: ethics, baptism, fasting and prayer, the Lord's Supper, hospitality, church leadership, and—yes—future events. Written a mere 20-30 years after the book of Revelation, the *Didache* allows us to hear the perspective of the early church.

The following excerpt, translated and edited by Tony Jones, has been re-paragraphed here:

> Watch over your life, that your lamps are never quenched, and that your loins are never unloosed. Be ready, for you do not know on what day your Lord is coming. Come together often, seeking the things that are good for your souls. A life of faith will not profit you if you are not made perfect at the end of time.
>
> For in the last days false prophets and corrupters will be plenty, and the sheep will be turned into wolves, and love will be turned into hate. When lawlessness increases,

they will hate and persecute and betray one another, and then the world-deceiver will appear claiming to be the Son of God, and he will do signs and wonders, and the earth will be delivered into his hands, and he will do iniquitous things that have not been seen since the beginning of the world.

Then humankind will enter into the fire of trial, and many will be made to stumble and many will perish; but those who endure in their faith will be saved from under the curse itself. And then the signs of the truth will appear: the first sign, an opening of the heavens; the second sign, the sounding of the trumpet; and the third sign, the resurrection of the dead—not of every one, but as it is said: "Then the Lord my God will come, and all the holy ones with him."

Finally, "Then the sign of the Son of Man will appear in heaven, and then all the tribes of the earth will mourn, and they will see the Son of Man coming on the clouds of heaven' with power and great glory."[14]

The *Didache* does not suggest that Christ will remove the church prior to the tribulation. Quite the opposite is true. It teaches that false prophets are coming, people's faith will be tested, signs will appear in the heavens, and then Christ will break into history. Interestingly, the *Didache* holds in perfect tension the imminence of Christ's return ("Be ready, for you do not know on what day your Lord is coming") and the certainty of preceding signs ("And then the signs of the truth will appear"). In short, it supports an exegetical approach to the book of Revelation.

The New Hampshire Confession

While the church has taken various millennial positions throughout the centuries, the church has consistently believed the book of Revelation relates to the church. As recently as the nineteenth century, the church continued to follow an exegetical approach to the book of Revelation. Written by the Board of the Baptist Convention in 1833 and revised by the editorial secretary of the American Baptist

Publication Society in 1853, the *New Hampshire Confession* provides a succinct statement concerning the world to come.

> [We believe] That the end of this world is approaching: that at the last day, Christ will descend from heaven, and raise the dead from the grave to final retribution; that a solemn separation will then take place; that the wicked will be adjudged to endless punishment, and the righteous to endless joy; and that this judgment will fix forever the final state of men in heaven or hell, on principles of righteousness.[15]

The *New Hampshire Confession* does not distinguish between the rapture of the church and the revelation of Jesus Christ. Nor does it mention multiple resurrections of believers, multiple judgments of mankind, or multiple peoples of God. Rather, the *New Hampshire Confession* reflects the simplicity found in the book of Revelation. Christ will break into history, separate the righteous from the unrighteous, throw the unrighteous into the lake of fire, and usher the righteous to their eternal home.

Lest we think that we are smarter than eighteen hundred years of church history, let us accept the testimony of the church.

Theological Weakness
ΑΩ

Our theological approach has given rise to some unintended theologies to make the system work. These resulting theologies are not simply necessary conjectures; they contradict the clear teaching of the Bible. Specifically, they include a theology of second chances, a theology of purgatory, a theology of escapism, and a theology of abandoned Christians. Like cracks in a foundation, these unbiblical theologies show the failure of our theological position.

In the subsequent chapters, I will talk about each of these derived theologies and show how they contradict the clear teaching of Scripture. For sake of illustration, I have used Tim LaHaye and Jerry B. Jenkins' novel entitled *Left Behind* to show how each theology has permeated our thinking. This section is not a critique of their novel but of our theology that is represented in their novel. From a literary perspective, they have done a commendable job imagining what the end of the world may be like from the perspective of our theology.

In addition, I will address the two strongest arguments for a pretribulational rapture of the church. The first argument relates to the relationship of Israel and the church, and the second argument relates to the relationship of God's wrath and the church. The first argument says that, since God has a separate plan for Israel and the church, and since the tribulation is for Israel and not the church, then the church must be raptured before the tribulation. The second argument says that, since God has promised to deliver the church from the coming wrath, and since the tribulation is the period of God's wrath, then the church must be raptured before the tribulation.

In these chapters, I will seek to clarify what the Bible does and does not teach. In so doing, I hope to provide some direction toward a biblical response.

Second Chances
ΑΩ

The Sealing of Our Fate

The Bible teaches that death seals our fate. The only unpardonable sin is a rejection of the Son of God (John 3:16-18, 36). As long as we have life, we have an opportunity to repent and believe in Jesus Christ. Thus, Hebrews 3:15 says, "Today, if you hear his voice, do not harden your hearts as in the rebellion." Once we die, our judgment has been sealed. There is no longer an opportunity for us to change our mind (Ps. 88:10-12; 115:17-18; Luke 16:19-26). In light of this, it is imperative that we respond now, for we do not know how long we have to live (Luke 12:16-21).

Not only does death seal our fate, Christ's second coming also seals our fate. The author of Hebrews made this point in Hebrews 9:27-28. There he compared the finality of death to Christ's second coming. He wrote, "And just as it is appointed for man to die once, and after that comes judgment, so Christ…will appear a second time, not to deal with sin but to save those who are eagerly waiting for him."

Christ's second coming seals our fate because it will be accompanied by the judgment of the dead. With the sounding of the seventh trumpet, the voices of heaven declare the coming of Christ, "The kingdom of the world has become the kingdom of our Lord and of his Christ, and he shall reign forever and ever" (Rev. 11:15). To which, the twenty-four elders respond with the declaration of God's final judgment, "the time [has come] for the dead to be judged, and for rewarding your servants, the prophets and saints, and those who fear your name, both small and great, and for destroying the destroyers of the earth" (Rev. 11:18).

Although we understand that the second coming of Christ seals our fate, our theology has formulated a theology of second chances. By separating the rapture of the church from the revelation of Jesus Christ, we have interjected a period of time in which people can reconsider their relationship with God and place their faith in Jesus Christ.

Left Behind Illustration

In the novel *Left Behind*, Rayford Steele was a nominal Christian. Although he did not attend church regularly or make any profession of faith, he led a morally upright life and supported his wife, Irene, who was a genuine Christian. Irene, on the other hand, was a vibrant Christ-follower who was getting more and more eccentric about her faith. Then, it happened. The rapture. His wife was gone. While the world scratched their heads wondering the whereabouts of millions of people, Rayford knew exactly what had happened. His wife had talked to him about the rapture on a number of occasions, and more so recently.

Although Rayford knew what had happened, he had his own struggles. Rayford did not struggle with the mystery of the disappearances. He knew exactly what had happened: Jesus had come and taken his followers out of the world. Rayford did not struggle with concern for his wife. He knew exactly where she was. She was safe with Jesus Christ in heaven, apart from the havoc taking place on earth. Rayford's biggest struggle was the uncertainty of his own fate. "If Jesus has come for his followers, and I now realize my mistake, is it too late?" Rayford despaired, fearing the worst.

Listen in as Rayford thinks through what has happened:

> If the disappearances were of God, if they had been his doing, was this the end of it? The Christians, the real believers, get taken away, and the rest are left to grieve and mourn and realize their error? Maybe so. Maybe that was the price. But then what happens when we die? he thought. If heaven is real, if the Rapture was a fact, what does that say about hell and judgment? Is that our fate? We go through this hell of regret and remorse, and then we literally go to hell, too?

Second Chances

> Irene had always talked of a loving God, but even God's love and mercy had to have limits. Had everyone who denied the truth pushed God to his limit? *Was there no more mercy, no second chance?* Maybe there wasn't, and if that was so, that was so.[16]

In desperation, Rayford contacted the church where his wife had attended. On the pre-recorded message, he learned about the availability of a video tape that the senior pastor had made for such an occasion. Rayford went to the church, picked up the tape, and returned home. Later that evening, he watched the video. Pastor Vernon Billings appeared on the screen, introduced himself, and explained the mass disappearance of people.

> You may wonder why this has happened. Some believe this is the judgment of God on an ungodly world. Actually, that is to come later. Strange as this may sound to you, this is God's final effort to get the attention of every person who has ignored or rejected him. He is allowing now a vast period of trial and tribulation to come to you who remain. He has removed his church from a corrupt world that seeks its own way, its own pleasures, its own ends.
>
> *I believe God's purpose in this is to allow those who remain to take stock of themselves and leave their frantic search for pleasure and self-fulfillment, and turn to the Bible for truth and to Christ for salvation.*[17]

Pastor Vernon exhorted those who were watching:

> It doesn't make any difference, at this point, why you're still on earth. You may have been too selfish or prideful or busy, or perhaps you simply didn't take the time to examine the claims of Christ for yourself. *The point now is, you have another chance. Don't miss it.*
>
> The disappearance of the saints and children, the chaos left behind, and the despairing of the heartbroken are evidence that what I'm saying is true. *Pray that God will help you. Receive his salvation gift right now.* And resist

the lies and efforts of the Antichrist, who is sure to rise up soon. Remember, he will deceive many. Don't be counted among them.[18]

In response to the video, Rayford slid to his knees, prayed to God for forgiveness, and placed his faith in Jesus Christ. His struggle with the uncertainty of his fate was over. He had found salvation in Jesus Christ, and he found fellowship in a new community of believers at New Hope Village Church. Having been given a second chance, Rayford's mind was flooded with new thoughts.

Rayford knew he had been forgiven for mocking his wife, for never really listening, for having ignored God for so many years. *He was grateful he had been given a second chance* and that he now had new friends and a place to learn the Bible.[19]

Problems with Second Chances

There are three problems with a doctrine of second chances.

First, the second coming of Christ marks the end of God's patience. The apostle Peter taught us that the Lord is delaying his coming because of his patience. In his second letter, Peter wrote, "The Lord is not slow to fulfill his promise as some count slowness, but is patient toward you, not wishing that any should perish, but that all should reach repentance" (2 Peter 3:9). Once the time of the Lord's patience is over, then the Lord will come. There will be no second chances; rather, "the day of the Lord will come like a thief, and then the heavens will pass away with a roar, and the heavenly bodies will be burned up and dissolved, and the earth and the works that are done on it will be exposed" (2 Peter 3:10).

Second, the hardness of hearts will prevent people from accepting Christ. It's not that God is unwilling to forgive people, but that people are unwilling to repent. On several occasions, the book of Revelation notes the refusal of people to repent. As God is meting out punishment for sin—an act that should call people to repentance—people still refuse to acknowledge that he is right and they are wrong. They are obstinate in their unbelief. Far from repenting, they curse God for the misery they are experiencing.

> And in those days people *will seek death* [instead of repentance] and will not find it. They *will long to die*, but death will flee from them. Rev. 9:6 (italics mine)
>
> The rest of mankind, who were not killed by these plagues, *did not repent* of the works of their hands nor give up worshiping demons and idols of gold and silver and bronze and stone and wood, which cannot see or hear or walk, *nor did they repent* of their murders or their sorceries or their sexual immorality or their thefts. Rev. 9:20-21 (italics mine)
>
> They were scorched by the fierce heat [of the sun], and they *cursed the name of God* who had power over these plagues. They *did not repent* and give him glory. Rev. 16:9 (italics mine)
>
> People gnawed their tongues in anguish and *cursed the God of heaven* for their pain and sores. They *did not repent* of their deeds. Rev. 16:10-11 (italics mine)
>
> And great hailstones, about one hundred pounds each, fell from heaven on people; and they *cursed God* for the plague of the hail, because the plague was so severe. Rev. 16:21 (italics mine)

These verses demonstrate that the wrath of God is completely holy and just. These people are hardened in their unbelief and sinfulness. As it relates to the possibility of second chances, the inhabitants of the earth will not be inclined to seek after God. Blinded by the deceitfulness of sin, they will be convinced of their own righteousness and of God's injustice. They will believe that God who has the authority over the plagues, which he does, is the cause of their misery, which he is not. Unwilling to acknowledge their sinfulness, they will not seek God's forgiveness.

Third, the conditions of society will not be favorable toward accepting Christ. In his book entitled *The Bible & Future Events*, Leon Wood raised the question, "How can one account for the large number of people who will be saved during the tribulation period, when wickedness will reign as never before?" To which question, Wood provided the following answer:

> Two principle matters may be noted in answer. First, the rapture will have occurred, which certainly will have brought great psychological shock to millions of people. They will have experienced the sudden departure from the world of their finest friends and relatives. This will force them to think seriously of religious matters, in a way they have never before desired or thought necessary. Second, there will be a marked increase of sinful activity in the world, over anything known before (2 Thess. 2:6-8), and this will likely be repugnant, especially at first, to a significant number of people. Reacting against it, many will be led to a source of refuge from it, as found in Jesus Christ.[20]

Such an answer ignores the condition of the human heart. Those who are outside of Christ do not seek God. Romans 3:10-11 makes this clear: "None is righteous, no, not one; no one understands; no one seeks for God." Moreover, those who are outside of Christ cannot seek God. They are spiritually impotent. They are enslaved to sin (Rom. 6:15-23), and their affections are hostile toward God (Rom. 8:5-8; Gal. 5:17). A sudden change of events is not going to change the heart. Thus, Revelation 22:11 declares, "Let the evildoer still do evil, and the filthy still be filthy, and the righteous still do right, and the holy still be holy."

Even if the rapture of the church causes people "to think seriously of religious matters," the upsurge of evil will have the opposite effect. Without the restraining influence of the Holy Spirit (2 Thess. 2:6-8) and the seasoning presence of the church (Matt. 5:13), people will be free to pursue their base desires. Those who had some semblance of morality will abandon it. Jesus prophesied, "And because lawlessness will be increased, the love of many will grow cold" (Matt. 24:12). Far from causing a revival, the increase in lawlessness will loosen people's inhibitions and embolden people to greater acts of wickedness. For this reason, God will send "a strong delusion, so that they may believe what is false, in order that all may be condemned" (2 Thess. 2:11-12).

Today is the Day

In short, there are no second chances. Today is the day of salvation.

If the Lord is convicting you of sin, now is the time to repent and believe in Jesus. Don't ignore his prompting in your life. No mercy will be shown to those who neglect such a great salvation (Heb. 2:1-4). Only a fearful expectation of judgment and a fury of fire awaits the adversaries of God (Heb. 10:26-27).

When Christ appears in the clouds, "all the tribes of the earth will mourn" (Matt. 24:30; Rev. 1:7). Why? People will know that the time of God's patience is over, and the time of God's wrath has come (Rev. 6:12-17). Their fate is sealed. It's too late.

Purgatory
ΑΩ

The Sufficiency of Christ's Death

The Bible teaches us that Christ's death on the cross is sufficient for all of our sins. Unlike the Levitical priests who had to offer animal sacrifices year after year because these sacrifices could not remove sin, Christ offered himself once as the perfect sacrifice. The author of Hebrews wrote, "But when Christ had offered for all time a single sacrifice for sins, he sat down at the right hand of God, waiting from that time until his enemies should be made a footstool for his feet. For by a single offering he has perfected for all time those who are being sanctified" (Heb. 10:12-14).

Because of Christ's sacrifice, we no longer have to fear any punishment for our sin. The apostle Paul wrote, "There is therefore now no condemnation for those who are in Christ Jesus" (Rom. 8:1). "Therefore, since we have been justified by faith, we have peace with God through our Lord Jesus Christ" (Rom. 5:1). Peace with God means salvation from the coming wrath. Paul continued, "Since, therefore, we have now been justified by his blood, much more shall we be saved by him from the wrath of God. For if while we were enemies we were reconciled to God by the death of his Son, much more, now that we are reconciled, shall we be saved by his life" (Rom. 5:9-10).

Although we recognize that the Bible teaches us that Christ's death on the cross is sufficient for all our sins, our theology has introduced a Protestant version of purgatory. According to Catholic theology, purgatory refers to a place that people go after they die where they undergo temporal suffering so as to purge any remaining sin from them and to prepare them for heaven. Similarly, our theology speaks of a kind of purgatory for those who place their faith in Christ *after* the rapture of the church. This purgatory is called the tribulation.

People who place their faith in Jesus Christ *before* the rapture will escape the tribulation and go immediately to be with Christ; however, people who place their faith in Jesus *after* the rapture will live through the tribulation. This latter group of people will experience the wrath of God, and their faith will be tested by the Antichrist.

There are many similarities between the Catholic theology of purgatory and our view of the tribulation. Like purgatory, the tribulation is a temporary period of time, seven years to be exact. Like purgatory, only some Christians—namely, those who did not believe before the rapture—will go there. Like purgatory, Christians who go there will experience suffering; they will be pursued by the Antichrist and martyred for their faith. Like purgatory, the tribulation will awaken these individuals out of spiritual slumber and prepare them to live in the presence of God.

Apparently Christ's sacrifice is not sufficient for these believers, for they must pay the penalty for their initial unbelief.

Left Behind Illustration

In the novel *Left Behind*, Bruce Barnes had been left behind. The rapture of the church revealed the insincerity of his faith and drove him to trust in Christ. Bruce wished he had come to Christ years ago rather than now, for his former pastor warned about the hardships that lay ahead for those left behind. In a prerecorded video, Pastor Billings prepared those left behind for things to come:

> The Bible teaches that the Rapture of the church ushers in a seven-year period of trial and tribulation, during which terrible things will happen. If you have not received Christ as your Savior, *your soul is in jeopardy.* And because of the cataclysmic events that will take place during this period, *your very life is in danger.* If you turn to Christ, *you may still have to die as a martyr.*[21]

> You'll find that government and religion will change, *war and inflation* will erupt, there will be *widespread death and destruction, martyrdom of saints,* and even *a devastating earthquake.* Be prepared.[22]

Pastor Billings had believed in Jesus *before* the rapture of the church. Consequently, he was safe in heaven, removed from the coming wrath. Bruce, on the other hand, believed in Jesus *after* the rapture of the church. Consequently, he was left behind, facing the greatest period of distress the world has ever known. His initial sin of unbelief would cost him seven years of tribulation. Apparently, Christ's death was not sufficient for all of his sins. Some purification would be necessary.

While this makes for a great novel, such thinking is horrible theology. In Romans 5:9, the apostle Paul wrote: "Since, therefore, we have now been justified by his blood, much more shall we be saved by him from the wrath of God." This promise of salvation did not come with any qualifications; it was not limited only to those who believe *before* the rapture of the church. It applies to everyone who has been justified by Christ's blood. Christ's death is sufficient for all of our sins.

Escapism
AΩ

A Life of Persecution

In the Sermon on the Mount, Jesus pronounced a blessing on those who are persecuted. He said, "Blessed are you when others revile you and persecute you and utter all kinds of evil against you falsely on my account. Rejoice and be glad, for your reward is great in heaven, for so they persecuted the prophets who were before you" (Matt. 5:11-12). Those who are persecuted are blessed because they stand in good company.

In the upper room, Jesus explained why his disciples would experience persecution. Jesus said, "If you were of the world, the world would love you as its own; but because you are not of the world, but I chose you out of the world, therefore the world hates you" (John 15:19). Jesus continued, "Remember the word that I said to you: 'A servant is not greater than his master.' If they persecuted me, they will also persecute you" (John 15:20). Believers are persecuted because of their association with Jesus.

Since we all associate ourselves with Jesus Christ, we all should expect to be persecuted. For this reason, the apostle Paul wrote, "all who desire to live a godly life in Christ Jesus will be persecuted" (2 Tim. 3:12). The absence of persecution in our lives should give us pause for reflection. Have we grown so accustomed to this world that we cannot be differentiated from it? Have we drifted so far away from Christ that we cannot be identified with him?

Although Jesus taught that persecution is a way of life for the believer, our theology has cultivated a theology of escapism. We view the rapture of the church as a "benefit" of accepting Christ as our Savior. We consider it a benefit because we will evade the worst period of distress the world has ever seen. We cannot fathom the proposal that God would call Christians to endure such persecution. We apparently do not see the value of persecution in the life of the believer.

Left Behind Illustration

In the novel *Left Behind*, Bruce Barnes, a church staff member who was left behind, presented the gospel to Rayford's daughter Chloe. Wanting some time to think it over, Chloe responded, "Surely this [Christianity] isn't something you rush into." Bruce, though, emphasized the urgency of the matter from his own personal experience. If only he had accepted Christ sooner, Bruce muses, he would not be in the present troublesome situation.

> "Well, let me tell you," Bruce said. "It's something I wish I had rushed into. I believe God has forgiven me and that I have a job to do here. But I don't know what's going to happen now, with the true Christians all gone. I'd sure rather have come to this point years ago than now, when it was nearly too late. You can imagine that I would much rather be in heaven with my family right now."[23]

Although Bruce did not know what was going to happen, he knew it was not going to be good. With the true Christians all gone, wickedness would prevail. Thus, he comments, "I'd sure rather have come to this point years ago than now." He knew that only hardships lie in the future for those who were left behind, but those who had accepted Christ prior to the rapture were in a safe and secure place. Chloe is urged to believe in Jesus, not so that she might be preserved in suffering, but so that she might escape future suffering. This is the theology of escapism.

The Perspective of Jesus

Jesus had a different perspective about suffering. In his high priestly prayer, he prayed for his disciples: "I do not ask that you take them out of the world, but that you keep them from the evil one. They are not of the world, just as I am not of the world. Sanctify them in the truth; your word is truth." (John 17:15-17). Jesus did not pray that the

Father would remove the disciples from the earth, but that he would sanctify them through the word on the earth.

The book of Revelation shares this same perspective. Speaking about the souls under the altar, Robert H. Mounce wrote:

> The martyrs had given up their lives because of the word of God and the testimony they had borne...Note that John knows nothing of a "rapture" of the church by which Christians are spared the tribulation that normally accompanies a godly life (cf. 2 Tim 3:12). They "ascend to heaven through suffering and death, as Jesus did: they are not taken to heaven to escape the sufferings of earth."[24]

As Jesus had prayed, God did not take these believers out of the world; rather, they ascended to heaven through a violent death. Nonetheless, God did keep them from the evil one: they held fast to their confession of faith in the face of strong opposition. Apparently God saw the necessity and value of their suffering. This is a perspective that we have trouble seeing. For this reason, let us consider some of the purposes for persecution.

The Purposes of Persecution

Persecution serves at least three purposes.

First, persecution provides evidence that we belong to Christ. As we have already explained, every disciple is like his master. If the world persecuted Christ, they will also persecute us. If we did not belong to Christ, the world would love us as its own; but, because we belong to Christ, the world hates us. While no one likes to be persecuted, belonging to Christ is more valuable than being accepted by the world. In Christ, we have been reconciled to God, and we will be saved from the coming wrath (Rom 5:9).

Second, persecution provides evidence that we are communicating the gospel effectively. The apostle Paul explained the foolishness of the gospel to the Corinthians:

> The word of the cross is folly to those who are perishing, but to us who are being saved it is the power of God...For Jews demand signs and Greeks seek wisdom, but we preach Christ crucified, a stumbling block to Jews and

folly to Gentiles, but to those who are called, both Jews and Greeks, Christ the power of God and the wisdom of God. 1 Cor. 1:18, 22-24

Certainly, we can be obnoxious when we present the gospel; however, even when we present the gospel with graciousness and tact, people will still not understand. The Jews could not understand how the Messiah could be crucified; the Messiah was supposed to reign over the house of David forever. The Gentiles could not understand how any convicted and executed felon could be an influential spiritual leader. Yet, for us, we recognize the significance of Christ's cross. He who knew no sin became sin for us, so that we might become the righteousness of God in him (2 Cor. 5:21).

Third, persecution provides evidence that we will share in Christ's glory. Since Christ is our master and we are his disciples, the pattern of our lives will follow the pattern of Christ's life. As Christ came first to suffer and then to enter his glory, we also will first suffer and then enter into his glory (Luke 24:25-27). Thus, the apostle Peter encouraged the exiled believers with these words:

> Beloved, do not be surprised at the fiery trial when it comes upon you to test you, as though something strange were happening to you. But rejoice insofar as you share Christ's sufferings, that you may also rejoice and be glad when his glory is revealed. 1 Peter 4:12-13

> Yet, if anyone suffers as a Christian, let him not be ashamed, but let him glorify God in that name. For it is time for judgment to begin at the household of God; and if it begins with us, what will be the outcome for those who do not obey the gospel of God? 1 Peter 4:16-17

> And after you have suffered a little while, the God of all grace, who has called you to his eternal glory in Christ, will himself restore, confirm, strengthen, and establish you. 1 Peter 5:10

In his suffering, Christ left us an example, so that we might follow in his steps (1 Peter 2:21). The example is this: Christ suffered and then ascended to the right hand of the throne of God. Following his example, we also will suffer and then ascend to the heavenly throne room of God. When we suffer persecution for the sake of Christ, this persecution gives us confidence that our momentary affliction is preparing for us an eternal weight of glory that will outweigh it all (2 Cor. 4:17).

Impersonal Gospel Agents
AΩ

God's Chosen Instrument

God has chosen to use people to proclaim the gospel.

After his resurrection, Jesus directed his disciples to a mountain in Galilee. There he commissioned his disciples, saying, "Go into all the world and proclaim the gospel to the whole creation" (Mark 16:15; cf. Matt. 28:18-20; Luke 24:46-49). Once they were endowed with the Holy Spirit, they were faithful to this mission. Peter, standing with the eleven, proclaimed the gospel: at Pentecost (Acts 2:14-41), at the temple (Acts 3:11-26), and before the council (Acts 4:1-22; 5:27-32). As the gospel spread, others joined them. Stephen proclaimed Christ before the high priest in Jerusalem (Acts 7:1-53), and Philip proclaimed Christ to the crowds in the city of Samaria (Acts 8:4-8).

God used Philip to bring the Ethiopian eunuch to faith in Christ. Although the Ethiopian eunuch had the very Word of God in his hands and was reading the Messianic prophecies of Isaiah, God still chose to use a person to effect faith. God directed Philip to a deserted road where his path would intersect with that of the eunuch. Philip asked, "Do you understand what you are reading?" (Acts 8:30). And the eunuch answered, "How can I, unless someone guides me?" (Acts 8:31). As God supernaturally brought Philip, so God supernaturally took Philip from the scene. Once the eunuch came to faith and was baptized, "the Spirit of the Lord carried Philip away, and the eunuch saw him no more, and went on his way rejoicing" (Acts 8:39).

God used Ananias, a disciple at Damascus, to bring Saul, a persecutor of the church, to faith in Christ. Although Jesus himself appeared to Saul while on the way to persecute disciples in Damascus, God still chose to use another person to effect faith. The Lord spoke to

Ananias in a vision, "Rise and go to the street called Straight, and at the house of Judas look for a man of Tarsus named Saul" (Acts 9:11). After initially objecting, Ananias went to the house, found Saul, and laid his hands on him. Saul regained his sight, was filled with the Holy Spirit, and was baptized by Ananias.

God called Saul, who was also called Paul, to proclaim the gospel throughout the world. When the Lord commanded Ananias to go and find Paul, the Lord explained to Ananias why he was being sent to a persecutor of the church. Speaking about Paul, the Lord said to Ananias, "Go, for he is a chosen instrument of mine to carry my name before the Gentiles and kings and the children of Israel" (Acts 9:15). And, indeed, Paul was that instrument.

The book of Acts recounts Paul's travels. Paul went on three missionary trips, proclaiming the gospel as he traveled. On his first trip, he took the gospel to Salamis, Perga, Antioch in Pisidia, Iconium, Lystra, and Derbe. On his second trip, he took the gospel to Troas, Neapolis, Philippi, Amphipolis, Thessalonica, Berea, Athens, Corinth, and Cenchreae. On his third trip, he took the gospel to Assos, Mitylene, Miletus, Rhodes, and Patara. Returning to Jerusalem, Paul was arrested. Appealing to Caesar, Paul was escorted to Rome, the capital of the known world. There he "welcomed all who came to him, proclaiming the kingdom of God and teaching about the Lord Jesus Christ with all boldness and without hindrance" (Acts 28:30-31).

While general revelation is sufficient to condemn people, it is not sufficient to save people. People must hear about Jesus in order to be saved. For the Scripture says, "everyone who calls on the name of the Lord will be saved" (Rom. 10:13; cf. Joel 2:32). In light of this, Paul raised the question, "How are they to call on him in whom they have not believed? And how are they to believe in him of whom they have never heard? And how are they to hear without someone preaching? And how are they to preach unless they are sent?" (Rom. 10:14-15a). Consequently, Paul concluded with Scripture, "How beautiful are the feet of those who preach the good news!" (Rom. 10:15b; cf. Isa. 52:7).

Other Gospel Agents

Although we recognize that God has chosen to use people to proclaim the gospel, we have adopted a theology in which God uses impersonal agents to spread the gospel. If the church is raptured at the beginning of the tribulation, and if there are saints who live during the tribulation, the question must be raised, "Where did these believers come from?" With the church gone, how did they find out about Jesus Christ? Who proclaimed the gospel to them?

In his book *The Bible & Future Events,* Leon J. Wood suggested "The principal source...will probably be Bibles, religious books, and tracts, which will still be here in the world. From reading these, people will be able to learn of the gospel and be prompted to place their trust in Christ."[25] In other words, God will use impersonal agents to proclaim the gospel during the tribulation.

Left Behind Illustration

Tim LaHaye and Jerry B. Jenkins used impersonal agents to spread the gospel in their novel *Left Behind.* When Rayford Steele was left behind, he desperately wanted to know what was happening. The rapture of the church had awakened him out of spiritual apathy, and he wanted to know more. The only problem was his wife was gone. Hoping to find answers, he looked for his wife's Bible.

> [Rayford] wanted to investigate, to learn, to know, to act. He started by searching for a Bible, not the family Bible that had collected dust on his shelf for years, but Irene's. Hers would have notes in it, maybe something that would point him in the right direction.[26]

Rayford then decided to call the church where his wife had been attending. When he called, he heard an offer to receive a videotape that had been recorded for such an occasion.

> You have reached New Hope Village Church. We are planning a weekly Bible study, but for the time being we will meet just once each Sunday at 10 a.m. While our entire staff, except me, and most of our congregation are gone, the few of us left are maintaining the building and distributing a videotape our senior pastor prepared for a time such as this. You may come by the church office anytime to pick up a free copy, and we look forward to seeing you Sunday morning.[27]

Rayford stopped by the church, picked up the video, returned home, and popped the video into his VCR. Through the prerecorded message of Pastor Vernon Billings, Rayford became a believer. Rayford acknowledged his sins to God and placed his trust in Jesus Christ.

God's Perspective

While the use of impersonal gospel agents sounds like a reasonable explanation from a human perspective, this is not a reasonable explanation from a divine perspective. Certainly, God can use impersonal agents to bring people to faith in his Son. This, however, is not the means that he has chosen.

God has chosen to use people to proclaim his message. More specifically, God has ordained the church to proclaim the gospel. This is what we were commissioned to do. This is the example that the apostles set for us. This is why the feet of those who proclaim the gospel are called "beautiful." When the church is removed from the earth, so is God's witness.

Abandoned Christians
ΑΩ

The Unity of the Church

The Bible teaches that those who believe in Jesus Christ belong to his body, the church.

In Acts 2, Luke recounted the birth of the church. On the day of Pentecost, God poured out his spirit on the followers of Jesus, and they all began proclaiming the mighty works of God in other languages. As people tried to make sense of what was happening, Peter stood up, explained the phenomenon as the fulfillment of prophecy, and accused the crowd of crucifying the Messiah. Convicted, they cried out, "Brothers, what shall we do?" Peter answered, "Repent and be baptized every one of you in the name of Jesus for the forgiveness of your sins." Three thousand people responded, and the church was born.

As we witness the life of the early church, we realize that it was a tight-knit community. They "devoted themselves to the apostles' teaching and the fellowship, to the breaking of bread and the prayers" (Acts 2:42). Moreover, "all who believed were together and had all things in common" (Acts 2:44). They were "selling their possessions and belongings and distributing the proceeds to all, as any had need" (Acts 2:45). Everyday they worshiped together in the temple, they ate meals together in their homes, and they praised God and earned the respect of outsiders (Acts 2:46-47). No believer was left out, rather "the Lord added to their number day by day those who were being saved" (Acts 2:47).

This unity of the church continued to be emphasized throughout the first century. To the divided church at Corinth, Paul asked rhetorically, "Is Christ divided?" (1 Cor. 1:13) and explained by way of analogy, "For just as the body is one and has many members, and all the members of the body, though many, are one body, so it is with Christ" (1 Cor. 12:12). More than an analogy, Paul explained that this was our experience: "For in one Spirit we were all baptized into one body—Jews or Greeks, slaves or free—and all were made to drink of one Spirit" (1 Cor. 12:13). Because of this reality, Paul urged the Ephesians "to maintain the unity of the Spirit in the bond of peace (Eph. 4:3). To Titus, Paul indicated that God did not simply want to save individuals but "to purify for himself a [singular] people for his own possession who are zealous for good works" (Titus 2:14).

Peter also emphasized the corporate unity of the church. He wrote, "You yourselves like living stones are being built up as a spiritual house, to be a holy priesthood, to offer spiritual sacrifices acceptable to God through Jesus Christ" (1 Peter 2:5). And, "You are a chosen race, a royal priesthood, a holy nation, a people for his own possession, that you may proclaim the excellencies of him who called you out of darkness into his marvelous light" (1 Peter 2:9).

When someone comes to faith in Jesus Christ, they are simultaneously incorporated into the body of Christ. There is no such thing as a Lone Ranger Christian. In Paul's words, "none of us lives to himself, and none of us dies to himself" (Rom. 14:7). We all belong to one another.

Although the Bible teaches that those who believe in Jesus Christ belong to the church, our theology imagines Christians who are not part of the church. Our theology teaches that there will be people who come to faith in Jesus Christ after the rapture of the church. The faith of these people will be so strong that they will be willing to die for their faith. Yet, these believers will not be part of the church, for the church, having been raptured, is in heaven and they are on earth. These believers are all by themselves. They have been left behind, abandoned.

Left Behind Illustration

In the novel *Left Behind*, Rayford Steele, shaken up by the rapture of the church, asks Bruce Barnes, "How do we become true Christians?"

Bruce responds:

> First, we have to see ourselves as God sees us. The Bible says all have sinned, that there is none righteous, no not one. It also says we can't save ourselves. Lots of people thought they could earn their way to God or to heaven by doing good things, but that's probably the biggest misconception ever.[28]

He continues:

> Jesus took our sins and paid the penalty for them so we wouldn't have to. The payment is death, and he died in our place because he loved us. When we tell Christ that we acknowledge ourselves as sinners and lost, and receive his gift of salvation, he saves us.[29]

Bruce then invites Rayford to accept this gift.

> I have to ask you...something I never wanted to ask people before. I want to know if you're ready to receive Christ right now. I would be happy to pray with you and lead you in how to talk to God about this.[29]

Although Rayford did not immediately respond to this invitation, Rayford later prayed in the confines of his home.

> Dear God, I admit that I'm a sinner. I am sorry for my sins. Please forgive me and save me. I ask this in the name of Jesus, who died for me. I trust in him right now. I believe that the sinless blood of Jesus is sufficient to pay the price for my salvation. Thank you for hearing me and receiving me. Thank you for saving my soul.[30]

Food for Thought

How can people come to faith in Jesus Christ and not be part of the church? To whom do they belong? They cannot belong to the church, for the church is in heaven and they are on earth. If they are members of the church, then they have been separated from the church. They have been severed from the body of Christ. They have been orphaned from their spiritual family. The church has been taken away, while they are left alone.

Left Behind Illustration (continued)

The novel *Left Behind* resolves this problem with the formation of a new church. Bruce Barnes organizes a meeting for all those who are trying to make sense of the recent events. He recounts his journey of faith, he invites those in attendance to a Bible study, and he shows a video created by his former pastor. Moved by the video, more than a hundred people pray with the pastor at the end of his message; and dozens, including Rayford, come down the aisle to declare their newfound faith. Bruce sings a brief song from Scripture and closes the meeting in prayer.

The narrative describes what follows.

> People seemed reluctant to leave, even after Bruce closed in prayer. Many stayed to get acquainted, and it became obvious a new congregation had begun. The name of the church was more appropriate than ever. New Hope. Bruce shook hands with people as they left, and no one ducked him or hurried past.[31]

More Food for Thought

This solution only exasperates the problem.

How can there be a church apart from the church? How does the church on earth relate to the church in heaven? Why does the church on earth have to suffer persecution while the church in heaven rests from its labor? Why does the church on earth have to live through the wrath of God while the church in heaven escapes it completely? How can the church be raptured before the tribulation, yet the church remains on earth during the tribulation?

These questions demonstrate that something is seriously wrong with our theology. Christ's body has not been mutilated; rather, we all are one body.

Israel and the Church
ΑΩ

The First Argument

The strongest argument for a pretribulational rapture of the church relates to the relationship of Israel and the church. It reasons that since God has a separate plan for Israel and the church, and since the tribulation is for Israel and not the church, then the church must be raptured before the tribulation.

In his book entitled *The Late Great Planet Earth*, Hale Lindsey gave five reasons he believed in a pretribulational view of the rapture. Recognizing the strength of this argument, Lindsey listed the relationship of Israel and the church as his number one reason. He wrote:

> First, there is a great distinction between God's purpose for the nation of Israel and His purpose for the church, which is His main program today. The church is composed of both Gentiles and Jews. We are now living during the church age and the responsibility for evangelizing the world rests upon the church...During the Tribulation the spotlight is on the Jew—in the Book of Revelation the Jew is responsible for evangelizing the world again.[32]

In this chapter, I want to explain what our theology teaches about the relationship of Israel and the church and then explain what the Bible teaches about the same.

The Teaching of Our Theology

Our theology teaches us that Israel and the church are distinct categories. According to our theology, Israel refers to the descendants of Abraham, to whom God has made certain irrevocable promises of land, blessing, and children. The church refers to people who have placed their faith in the death, burial, and resurrection of Jesus Christ for the forgiveness of sins and hope of eternal life.

Figure 6: Israel and the Church as Distinct Categories

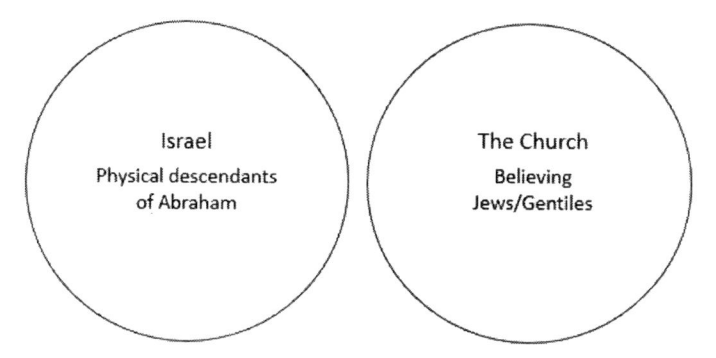

Israel
Physical descendants of Abraham

The Church
Believing Jews/Gentiles

Israel and the church are mutually distinct categories of people.

Furthermore, these categories do not overlap with one another. God has one plan for Israel and another for the church. During the Old Testament era, God was actively working to fulfill the promises that he had made to Israel; but when the Messiah arrived on the scene, Israel rejected him. So, God turned his attention away from the nation of Israel and to the saving of the nations. God is now building his church through the proclamation of the gospel. When God is done working among the Gentiles, he will turn his attention back to the nation of Israel.

Israel is destined for a millennial kingdom, and the church is destined for heaven. The promises that God made to Israel relate to this earth: He promised Israel a land in the Middle East; he promised them descendants beyond number; he promised them a kingdom of worldwide influence; he promised them material prosperity and national security. The promises that God made to the church relate to heaven: God promised us forgiveness of sins through faith in his Son; God promised us justification in his sight and adoption into his family;

God promised us an inheritance that never will fade away; God promised us the guarantee of the Holy Spirit.

The church represents a parenthesis in God's plan for Israel. According to Daniel's prophecy, God has decreed seventy weeks for the nation of Israel. Sixty-nine of these weeks have been fulfilled, and one week still lies in the future. At the moment, we live in an interim period of time of unknown length, commonly called the church-age. During this period of time, God is working among the Gentiles, calling them to repentance and faith in his Son. Once the church is removed, God will once again turn his attention to the nation of Israel.

The introduction of the church was a mystery in the plan of God. God had clearly revealed his plan for the nation of Israel in the Old Testament; however, God did not so clearly speak of Israel's rejection of her Messiah and God's turning to the Gentiles. For this reason, the apostle Paul called the church-age a "mystery" in the plan of God. To the Romans Paul wrote, "I do not want you to be unaware of this mystery, brothers: a partial hardening has come upon Israel, until the fullness of the Gentiles has come in" (Rom. 11:25; cf. Eph. 1:9; 3:1-6; 6:19; Col. 1:24-27; 4:3-4).

The second coming of Christ is a two-stage event. First, Christ comes *for* the saints at the *beginning* of the tribulation. This is commonly known as the rapture of the church. Then, Christ comes *with* the saints at the *end* of the tribulation. This is commonly known as the revelation of Jesus Christ. The first stage of Christ's coming is for the benefit of the church. Christ will meet the church in the air and remove her from the earth, so that she will not have to endure the tribulation. The second stage of Christ's coming is for the benefit of Israel. Christ will come in flaming fire to take vengeance on those who do not know God and to stand with the redeemed on Mount Zion.

The Teaching of the Bible

Having looked at what our theology teaches, I would now like to explain what the Bible teaches.

While Israel and the church are distinct categories, these categories are not mutually exclusive; rather, they overlap with one another. The word "Israel" denotes a racial distinction (whether an individual is a physical descendant of Abraham), and the word

Israel and the Church

"church" denotes a spiritual distinction (whether an individual has placed his faith in Jesus Christ). These categories represent two different ways of classifying people: one based on race, and another based on faith. It is, therefore, possible for someone to belong to both categories. For instance, the apostle Paul was both a citizen of Israel and a member of the church. Similarly, the apostle John, who penned the book of Revelation, belonged to Israel and the church.

This may be visually depicted by two overlapping circles.

Figure 7: Israel and the Church as Overlapping Categories

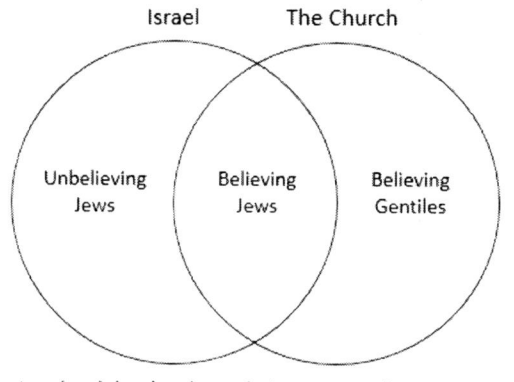

```
         Israel        The Church

    ┌─────────┐   ┌─────────┐
    │         │   │         │
    │Unbelieving│ Believing │Believing│
    │  Jews    │   Jews    │ Gentiles│
    │         │   │         │
    └─────────┘   └─────────┘
```

Israel and the church are distinct, yet overlapping categories of people.

God has one plan for all mankind. God plans to bring all people, Jews and Gentiles, under one head, Christ. The apostle Paul laid out this plan in Ephesians 1:9-10 where he wrote "[God made] known to us the mystery of his will, according to his purpose, which he set forth in Christ as a plan for the fullness of time, to unite all things in him, things in heaven and things on earth." This plan is illustrated by many analogies: one flock, one tree, one man, one building, etc. Jesus said, "And I have other sheep that are not of this fold. I must bring them also, and they will listen to my voice. So there will be *one flock*, one shepherd" (John 10:16, italics mine). The apostle Paul wrote, "some of the branches were broken off, and you, although a wild olive shoot, were grafted in among the others and now share in the nourishing root of *the olive tree*" (Rom. 11:17, italics mine). Paul wrote, "For he himself is our peace, who has made us both one and has broken down in his flesh the dividing wall of hostility...that he might create in himself *one new man* in place of the two, so making peace" (Eph. 2:14-15, italics mine). Paul wrote, "[You are] built on the foundation of the apostles and prophets, Christ Jesus himself being the cornerstone, in whom the whole structure, being joined together, grows into *a holy temple* in the Lord" (Eph. 2:20-21, italics mine).

The remnant of Israel and the saved of the Gentiles share a common destiny. God has made certain irrevocable promises to the nation of Israel. These promises he will indeed fulfill through the remnant of Israel, that is, the physical descendants of Abraham who place their faith in Jesus Christ. The Gentiles may also participate in these promises by exhibiting the same kind of faith as Abraham (Gal. 3:7-9). This does not mean that the Gentiles become Jews. Faith in Jesus does not change our racial identity. It only changes our spiritual standing before God. Through the death of Christ on the cross, the blessing of Abraham was extended to the Gentiles (Gal. 3:13-14). For this reason, Paul was able to declare, "There is neither Jew nor Greek, there is neither slave nor free, there is no male and female, for you are all one in Christ Jesus. And if you are Christ's, then you are Abraham's offspring, heirs according to promise" (Gal. 3:28-29).

The book of Revelation recognizes the shared destiny of Jews and Gentiles. In chapter 21, the apostle John described the New Jerusalem coming down out of heaven from God. It had twelve gates on which were inscribed "the twelve tribes of the sons of Israel," and it had twelve foundations on which were inscribed "the twelve names of the twelve apostles of the Lamb" (Rev. 21:12, 14). The twelve tribes of the sons of Israel represent the descendants of Abraham, and the twelve names of the twelve apostles of the Lamb represent the church. The remnant of Israel and the saved of the Gentiles will spend all of eternity together.

The church represents a continuation in the plan of God. This may be demonstrated from the consistency in the message that was preached from John the Baptist through the time of the church. It may also be demonstrated by the biblical support for the message that was preached by the apostles in the early church. And it may be demonstrated from the teaching of the apostle Paul, who, because he was a Jew, had a vested interest in the matter. Let us look at each of these proofs in turn.

The kingdom of God was preached from John the Baptist through the time of the church. John the Baptist preached the kingdom of God (Matt. 3:2). Jesus preached the kingdom of God (Matt. 4:17, 23; 9:35). The apostles preached the kingdom of God (Matt. 10:7; 24:14). This message of the kingdom, often thought only to refer to the nation of Israel, continued to be proclaimed well after Jesus' death, burial, and resurrection (Acts 1:3; 8:12; 19:8; 20:25; 28:23, 31).

The Old Testament was used to demonstrate that Jesus was the Christ. Jesus explained how Moses and the Prophets spoke about Christ's passion and the proclamation of repentance and forgiveness of sins throughout the whole world (Luke 24:25-27, 44-47). Peter argued that the outpouring of the Spirit and the resurrection of Christ were in fulfillment of the Scriptures (Acts 2:15-21, 24-28). Stephen demonstrated through the Scriptures that the Jewish leaders always resisted the Holy Spirit, which culminated in their rejection of Christ (Acts 7:51-53). Philip the evangelist explained to the Ethiopian eunuch how the prophet Isaiah spoke about the passion of Christ (Acts 8:32-35). Wherever the apostle Paul traveled, he would enter the local synagogue, argue from the Scriptures that Jesus is Christ, and try to persuade his fellow Israelites to believe in Jesus (Acts 13:13-16; 14:1; 17:1-3, 10, 17; 18:4, 5, 19; 19:8; 20:18-21; 26:22-23; 28:30-31).

The apostle Paul taught that the church represented a continuation in the plan of God. In Romans 11:1, Paul confronted the question head-on. "Has God rejected his people?" he wrote. Paul responded adamantly, "By no means!" He then provided three proofs of the continuation of God's plan: 1) Paul himself was a descendant of Abraham through whom God was fulfilling his purposes for Israel (Rom. 11:1-2); 2) At the present time, there was a remnant of believing Israelites through whom God was fulfilling his promises for Israel (Rom. 11:2b-6); and 3) The partial hardening of Israel was also fulfilling God's purposes for Israel (Rom. 11:7-10).

The "mystery" of which the apostle Paul spoke is not the introduction of the church but the extension of the gospel to the Gentiles. Paul gave this meaning of the mystery in Ephesians 3:6, where he wrote, "This mystery is that the Gentiles are fellow heirs, members of the same body, and partakers of the promise in Christ Jesus through the gospel." Paul went on to explain how his whole ministry was devoted to this mystery. "To me, though I am the very least of all the saints, this grace was given, to preach to the Gentiles the unsearchable riches of Christ, and to bring to light for everyone what is the plan of the mystery hidden for ages in God who created all things" (Eph. 3:8-9). This mystery took the early church by surprise (Acts 10:45; 11:1, 18; 13:46-48; 14:27), raised a lot of questions in the Jewish community (Acts 10:9-29; 11:1-18), and required a thoughtful response by the Jerusalem council (Acts 15:1-21).

The second coming of Christ is a single, unified event. One of the primary themes of 1 & 2 Thessalonians is the second coming of Christ. In these two short letters, the apostle Paul expressly mentions the coming of Christ five times (1 Thess. 2:19; 3:13; 4:15; 5:23; 2 Thess. 2:1). These letters also contain the primary instruction on the rapture (1 Thess. 4:13-18), and they speak about the eternal destruction that will accompany the revelation of Jesus Christ (2 Thess. 1:5-10). Interestingly, nowhere does the apostle Paul break apart the coming of Christ into two stages. Rather, he moves imperceptibly back and forth between these concepts as though it is a single, unified event.

For instance, Paul pronounces a blessing upon the so-called "church-age" saints that their hearts will be blameless at the coming of our Lord Jesus Christ *with* all his saints (1 Thess. 3:11-13). Similarly, he promises deliverance to the "church-age" saints at the revelation of Christ, when Christ inflicts punishment on those who persecute Christians (2 Thess. 1:5-7). After he explains the rapture of the church (1 Thess. 4:13-18), he immediately describes the sudden destruction that will come upon those who think they live in security (1 Thess. 5:1-3). Then, he comments that that day (that is, the revelation of Jesus) will not surprise the Thessalonians (that is, "church-age" saints) as a thief in the night (1 Thess. 5:4). Clearly, the apostle Paul does not differentiate between two separate stages.

God's Wrath and the Church
ΑΩ

The Second Argument

The second strongest argument for a pretribulational rapture of the church relates to the relationship of God's wrath and the church. It reasons that, since God has promised to deliver the church from the coming wrath, and since the tribulation is the period of God's wrath, then the church must be raptured before the tribulation.

In this chapter, I want to explore what the Bible teaches us about God's wrath and the church, and what the Bible does *not* teach us about God's wrath and the church.

What the Bible Teaches

The Bible teaches that the church is exempt from the coming wrath.

In his letter to the Romans, the apostle Paul wrote "God shows his love for us in that while we were still sinners, Christ died for us. Since, therefore, we have now been justified by his blood, much more shall we be saved by him from the wrath of God" (Rom. 5:8-9). To the Thessalonians, Paul described how they had turned from idols to serve the true and living God, and how they are now waiting for his Son from heaven, "Jesus who delivers us from the wrath to come" (1 Thess. 1:10). In the same letter, Paul later wrote, "For God has not destined us for wrath, but to obtain salvation through our Lord Jesus Christ" (1 Thess. 5:9).

Consistent with the rest of the New Testament, the book of Revelation affirms the truth that the church is exempt from the coming wrath. In Revelation 3:10, Jesus makes a promise to the believers at Philadelphia, saying, "I will keep you from the hour of trial that is coming on the whole world, to try those who dwell on the earth." This promise is fulfilled as you read through the rest of Revelation. God's judgments are specifically targeted against unbelievers. Believers are not mentioned in these contexts. This is true of the seven seals (Rev. 6:1-17, esp. v. 10, 15-16), the seven trumpets (Rev. 8:6-9:21, esp. vv. 8:13; 9:4-6, 20-21), and of the seven bowls (Rev. 16:1-21, esp. vv. 2, 5-6, 8-9, 10-11, 21).

What the Bible Does Not Teach

While the book of Revelation teaches that the church is exempt from the coming wrath, the book of Revelation does not specify how God will keep his people from the coming wrath.

One Option

God could remove the church prior to the tribulation, as our theology insists. However, there are many problems with this position. This position assumes that the tribulation is a seven-year period of time (a length of time that is nowhere mentioned in the book of Revelation) and that this entire period is characterized by the outpouring of God's wrath (Revelation speaks of a period of 42 months or 1,260 days; but this period of time is associated with the reign of the Antichrist, not the wrath of God). It also assumes a sharp distinction between Israel and the church (a topic discussed in the previous chapter), and a clear differentiation between the rapture of the church and the revelation of Jesus Christ (a distinction that does not arise from Scripture but from our theology). And it runs against the foundational premise that the book of Revelation was written to, for, and about the church.

Moreover, a pretribulational rapture of the church does not solve the problem of God's wrath. Although the church would not be on earth during the tribulation, the pretribulational view acknowledges the presence of other believers on earth during the tribulation. We call these believers "tribulational saints." Having been justified by the blood of Christ, they also would be promised salvation from the wrath of God (Rom. 5:9). If the rapture of the church is the means by which God keeps his people from the hour of trial that is coming on the whole world, then God has not kept his promise to these believers.

A Second Option

God could remove the church prior to the seven bowls of God's wrath, as the text of Revelation suggests. We have wrongly assumed that the tribulation is the same period of time as the outpouring of God's wrath. The tribulation is associated with the reign of the Antichrist and the persecution of the saints, but it is not associated with God's wrath. The period of God's wrath follows, or is at the tail end of, the tribulation.

The seven bowls are specifically identified as "the seven bowls of the wrath of God" (Rev. 16:1). With the outpouring of the seven bowls "the wrath of God is finished" (Rev. 15:1). Prior to the introduction of the seven bowls, God's wrath is spoken of as imminent but not yet started (Rev. 6:16-17; 11:18). Once the angels begin to pour out the bowls of God's wrath, no more mention is made of believers; rather, the bowl judgments come upon "the people who bore the mark of the beast and worshiped its image" (Rev. 16:2).

Since the tribulation and the outpouring of God's wrath are not the same period of time, it is possible for the church to go through the tribulation and escape the period of God's wrath. The closest description of the rapture of the church in the book of Revelation is the harvest of the earth (Rev. 14:14-16). This event immediately follows the tribulation (Rev. 13:1-18) and precedes the trampling of the grape harvest in the wine press of God's wrath (Rev. 14:17-20). The church may, therefore, be removed at this point in time and escape the period of God's wrath.

A Third Option

God could preserve his people through the outpouring of his wrath, as God is able to do.

Some have argued that, given the universal nature of the coming wrath and the severity of this wrath, it will be impossible for anyone on earth to escape its effects. While this may seem like a plausible argument from a human perspective, it carries no weight from a divine perspective. In his second letter, the apostle Peter wrote, "the Lord knows how to rescue the godly from trials, and to keep the unrighteous under punishment until the day of judgment" (2 Peter 2:9).

To illustrate his point, Peter provided two examples: Noah and Lot. Of Noah, Peter wrote, "[God] preserved Noah, a herald of righteousness, with seven others, when he brought a flood upon the world of the ungodly" (2 Peter 2:5). Though the floodwaters covered the whole earth, God saved Noah. Of Lot, Peter wrote, "[God] rescued righteous Lot, greatly distressed by the sensual conduct of the wicked" (2 Peter 2:7). Though the cities of Sodom and Gomorrah were razed to the ground, God saved Lot.

The Old Testament provides other examples of how the Lord protected his own people, even while he unleashed judgment on the unrighteous. For instance, the Lord protected the nation of Israel when he sent plagues against the land of Egypt. Though the plagues devastated the whole land of Egypt, God made a sharp distinction between the Israelites and the Egyptians.

With the fourth plague of flies, Moses said to Pharaoh, "But on that day I will set apart the land of Goshen, where my people dwell, so that no swarms of flies shall be there, that you may know that I am the Lord in the midst of the earth. Thus I will put a division between my people and your people" (Ex. 8:22-23).

With the fifth plague on the livestock, Moses said to Pharaoh, "But the Lord will make a distinction between the livestock of Israel and the livestock of Egypt, so that nothing of all that belongs to the people of Israel shall die" (Ex. 9:4). Moses then recounted, "And the next day the Lord did this thing. All the livestock of the Egyptians died, but not one of the livestock of the people of Israel died. And Pharaoh sent, and behold, not one of the livestock of Israel was dead" (Ex. 9:6-7).

With the seventh plague of hail, Moses commented, "Only in the land of Goshen, where the people of Israel were, was there no hail" (Ex. 9:26).

With the eighth plague of darkness, Moses again commented, "They did not see one another, nor did anyone rise from his place for three days, but all the people of Israel had light where they lived" (Ex. 10:23).

Finally, with the death blow to the firstborn, the Lord says through Moses, "There shall be a great cry throughout all the land of Egypt, such as there has never been, nor ever will be again. But not a dog shall growl against any of the people of Israel, either man or beast, that you may know that the Lord makes a distinction between Egypt and Israel" (Exodus 11:6-7).

The book of Revelation also shows how the Lord protects his own people, even while he unleashes judgment on the unrighteous.

God protected his 144,000 servants by putting his seal on their forehead. Before the sounding of the seven trumpets, an angel declared to the four destroying angels, "Do not harm the earth or the sea or the trees, until we have sealed the servants of our God on their foreheads" (Rev. 7:3). This seal would identify God's people, so that they would not be harmed by God's judgments. When the fifth angel blew his trumpet, the scorpions were told "not to harm the grass of the earth or any green plant or any tree, but only those people who do not have the seal of God on their foreheads" (Rev. 9:4).

God protected his two witnesses by enabling them to breathe out fire on anyone who would harm them (Rev. 11:5-6). He gave them this special protection so that they might prophesy against the Antichrist for 1,260 days (Rev. 11:3-4).

God protected the woman who gave birth to the male child by preparing a place in the wilderness to which she could flee (Rev. 12:5-6). There, she would be safe, not only from the dragon, but also from God's wrath (Rev. 12:13-17).

God's Faithfulness

God has promised to save his people from the coming wrath, and God will keep his promise; however, how he brings about this salvation is up to him.

God could remove the church prior to the tribulation, as our theology contends, or he could remove the church prior to the outpouring of his wrath, as the text of Revelation suggests. However, he does not have to take either of these courses of action. As he has done before, so he could do again. God could protect his people through the outpouring of his wrath.

No matter how God chooses to deliver us from the coming wrath, let us be clear in this: God *will* keep his promise.

Logical Weakness
ΑΩ

The word "church" appears twenty times in the book of Revelation. It appears nineteen times in the first three chapters of the book (Rev. 1:4, 11, 20; 2:1, 7, 8, 11, 12, 17, 18, 23, 29; 3:1, 6, 7, 13, 14, 22), and it appears once more in the last chapter of Revelation (Rev. 22:16). It does not appear in Revelation 4-19 where the tribulation is described. This observation is often used to show that the church has been raptured prior to the tribulation. However, it must be noted that this is an argument from silence.

An argument from silence is a weak logical argument. Rather than drawing a conclusion based on the presence of evidence, it draws a conclusion based on the absence of evidence. At best, an argument from silence raises suspicion. It causes the reader to ask, "Why does the word "church," which appears so frequently in the first three chapters of Revelation, seemingly disappear from the text?" According to our theology, the answer is obvious. The church has been raptured; it is in heaven, not on earth, during the tribulation. This, though, is a false conclusion based on a weak argument.

If this same logic was applied to the rest of the New Testament, then much of the New Testament would not apply to the church. For instance, only the gospel of Matthew would have any bearing on the church, for it is the only gospel to explicitly mention the church. Romans 1-15, which provides the fullest explanation of the gospel, would have nothing to do with the church, for the word "church" does not appear until the final chapter of the book. Although Paul addressed Galatians "to the churches of Galatia" (Gal. 1:2) and employed the word "church" twice more in the first chapter (Gal. 1:13; 1:22), the rest of the letter would not pertain to the church. Similarly, only the first chapter of 2 Thessalonians would relate to the church. And 2 Timothy, Titus, 1 & 2 Peter, and 1 & 2 John should probably be removed from the Christian canon altogether, for the word "church" does not appear in any of these letters.

There may be other reasons why the author chose not to use the word "church" in Revelation 4-19.

The apostle John reserved the Greek word "church" (ἐκκλησία) to refer to a local assembly of believers (in addition to the references above; see also 3 John 1:6, 9-10). One reason why the apostle John may have refrained from using the word "church" in Revelation 4-19 is because, during the tribulation, believers will not be gathered, but scattered, because of the persecution. Another reason may be that, during the tribulation, the only visible church will be the apostate church. As he demands the worship of himself, the Antichrist will prohibit the worship of the one true God. There will be no true church, only the "church" of the Antichrist.

Whether these suggestions are right or wrong does not matter. Absence of evidence is just that, absence of evidence. It does not establish a fact but only raises a possibility. For the sake of veracity, we need actual evidence. Rather than arguing from the *absence* of evidence, let us argue from the *presence* of evidence.

The church *is* mentioned in Revelation 4-19, though other words are used to describe its presence. One of these words is the word "saints." The word "saints" appears thirteen times in the book of Revelation (Rev. 5:8; 8:3-4; 11:18; 13:7, 10; 14:12; 16:6; 17:6; 18:20, 24; 19:8; 20:9). Twelve of these occurrences appear in Revelation 4-19, where the church is supposedly absent. The book of Revelation uses the word "saints" to distinguish God's people from those who dwell on the earth. More broadly, the New Testament most commonly uses the word "saints" to speak of Christians, that is, members of the church (Acts 9:13, 32, 41; 26:10; Rom. 1:7; 1 Cor. 1:2; 14:33; 2 Cor. 1:1; Eph. 1:1, 15, 18; 2:19; Phil. 1:1; Col. 1:2, 12; Heb. 13:24; Jude 3).

Our theology ignores this evidence by creating different categories of "saints" and selecting the appropriate category of "saints" depending on the context. The "saints" mentioned in Revelation 5:8 and 8:3-4 are church-age saints because they are seen in heaven and are engaged in intercessory prayer. The "saints" mentioned in

Revelation 13:7 are tribulational saints because the Antichrist fights against them and conquers them. The "saints" mentioned in Revelation 13:10 and 14:12 are tribulational saints because they are called to endure the atrocities of the Antichrist. The "saints" mentioned in Revelation 16:6; 17:6; and 18:20, 24 are tribulational saints because their blood was shed by the Antichrist. The "saints" mentioned in Revelation 19:8 are church-age saints because they are seen in heaven, identified as the bride of Christ, and clothed with the righteousness of Christ. Finally, the "saints" mentioned in Revelation 20:9 are Jewish saints as they stand on earth in Jerusalem, surrounded by nations that are intent on wiping them out, and with God fighting for them as prophesied in the Old Testament.

The book of Revelation does not differentiate between different categories of saints. Without any qualifications, the book of Revelation uses the word "saints" (ἅγιοι) for God's people throughout its pages. These different categories of saints come from our theology. We have added these categories of saints to the text.

The book of Revelation views the "saints" as a singular category. This is evidenced by the pairing of the word "saints" with Old Testament "prophets" in Revelation 11:18. With the blowing of the seventh trumpet, loud voices in heaven proclaim, "[The time has come] for rewarding your servants, *the prophets and saints*, and those who fear your name, both small and great, and for destroying the destroyers of the earth" (Rev. 11:18, italics mine; cf. Rev. 18:24). This is also evidenced by the pairing of the word "saints" with New Testament "apostles" in Revelation 18:20. At the fall of Babylon, all the shipmasters and seafaring men cried out, "Rejoice over her, O heaven, and *you saints and apostles and prophets*, for God has given judgment for you against her!" (Rev. 18:20, italics mine).

Certainly, saints have lived in different periods of time throughout the course of history: some lived shortly after the world was created, and others have seen a man step on the moon. Certainly, saints have had different experiences: some have enjoyed a rich and abundant life, and others have lived in abject poverty. Certainly, saints have lived under different dispensations: some have offered sacrifices in the temple in obedience to the law, and others have celebrated Christ's sacrifice through their participation in communion. Despite all of these differences, we all belong to one community. We all are saved by grace through faith.

As we read the book of Revelation, we must recognize that we who believe in Jesus now and those who will believe in Jesus later belong to the same community of faith. We share a common identity in Christ. We belong to them, and they belong to us. Their struggles are our struggles, and their victory is our victory. As the saints of God, we stand together against those who destroy the earth; and, one day, we will stand together with Christ on the new heaven and the new earth.

Even John F. Walvoord, who elsewhere distinguishes between different categories of saints, speaks of "saints" as a singular category at the end of his commentary.

> Probably no other book of Scripture more sharply contrasts the blessed lot of the saints with the fearful future of those who are lost. No other book of the Bible is more explicit in its description of judgment on the one hand and the saints' eternal bliss on the other. What a tragedy that so many pass by this book and fail to fathom its wonderful truths, thereby impoverishing their knowledge and hope in Christ Jesus. God's people who understand and appreciate these wonderful promises can join with John in his prayer, "Come, Lord Jesus."[33]

If the saints are present on earth during the tribulation, and the saints belong to a single community of faith called the church, how can we argue from silence and say the church is *not* present on earth during the tribulation? The evidence is in. A verdict may be reached. The church *is* present on earth during the tribulation.

Literary Weakness
AΩ

The book of Revelation is a literary work. As such, it exhibits the four elements of literature. The four elements of literature are: (1) characters; (2) plot; (3) theme, or statement; and (4) style. "A good writer tries to balance these elements to create a unified work of art."[34] The book of Revelation is no exception. God, working through man, has created the most marvelous piece of literature bar none.

Characters

Characters are the central interest of a literary work. "Writers must know their characters thoroughly and have a clear picture of each one's looks, speech, and thoughts."[34]

In the book of Revelation, we encounter multiple characters. They include God (Rev. 1:1), the apostle John (Rev. 1:1-2), the seven churches that are in Asia (Rev. 1:4, 10-11), Jesus Christ (Rev. 1:12-16), the One seated on the throne (Rev. 4:2-6), the four living creatures (Rev. 4:6b-8), the twenty-four elders (Rev. 4:9-11), the Lamb that had been slain (Rev. 5:6-10), the souls under the altar (Rev. 6:9-11), the 144,000 servants of Israel (Rev. 7:2-8), the innumerable multitude (Rev. 7:9-10), the two witnesses (Rev. 11:3-6), the woman clothed with the sun (Rev. 12:1-2), the dragon and his hordes (Rev. 12:7-9), the beast rising from the sea (Rev. 13:1-3), the beast rising from the earth (Rev. 13:11-14), and the great prostitute (Rev. 17:1-5).

But, the main character on the stage of earth is the church. To this point, reread the chapter entitled "About the Church" in Part One.

Our theology suffers from character crisis. While the book of Revelation presents the church as the main character of the story, our theology cannot figure out who the main character of Revelation is.

Our theology insists that part of the book focuses on the church and part of the book focuses on the nation of Israel. Unable to decide between Israel and the church, our theology settles on both characters.

Plot

"Plot tells what happens to the characters in a story. A plot is built around a series of events that take place within a definite period....A unified plot has a beginning, a middle, and an end. That is, an author leads us from somewhere (a character with a problem), through somewhere (the character facing the problem), to somewhere (the character overcoming or being overcome by the problem)." [34]

"In literary terms, we speak of a story having an exposition, a rising action, a climax, and a denouement, or outcome. The exposition gives the background and situation of the story. The rising action builds upon the given material. It creates suspense, or a reader's desire to find out what happens next. The climax is the highest point of interest. The denouement ends the story." [34]

In the book of Revelation, the plot centers on the main character, the church. The church is introduced in Revelation 1-3. This is the exposition of the story. The church is persecuted in Revelation 4-13. This is the rising action of the story. The church is avenged in Revelation 14-18. This is the climax of the story. And the church is delivered in Revelation 19-22. This is the denouement of the story.

Our theology makes a mess of the plot. According to our theology, the church is introduced (Rev. 1-3) but then exits (Rev. 4-6). Israel enters (Rev. 7), is persecuted (Rev. 8-13), and is delivered (Rev. 14-19). Israel then reigns with Christ for a thousand years (Rev. 20). Israel exits, and the church enters. The church lives happily ever after (Rev. 21-22). Our theology treats the nation of Israel like a stunt man for the church. When life gets tough, the church leaves the set and Israel takes her place. When the danger is over, the church is allowed to return.

While this may work for our theology, it makes for a bad story.

Theme

"Theme, or statement, is the basic idea expressed by a work of literature. It develops from the interplay of character and plot. A theme may warn the reader to lead a better life or a different kind of life." [34] In the book of Revelation, the primary theme of the story is endurance. The book of Revelation pictures the climatic struggle between God and Satan for the hearts of mankind. In this heated contest, the church needs encouragement. The book of Revelation serves as "a call for the endurance and faith of the saints" (Rev. 13:10; cf. 14:12). This theme is explored at length in the chapter entitled "Endure to the End" in Part Four.

Although the book of Revelation is a single piece of literature, our theology fails to appreciate the literary unity of the book. Instead, we treat the book of Revelation as a theological textbook with separate units of study. These units of study include the church age (Rev. 1-3), the tribulation (Rev. 4-19), the millennial reign of Christ (Rev. 20:1-10), and the eternal state (Rev. 21-22).

Each unit of study represents a different dispensation in God's economy, and each dispensation is separated by a major event: the rapture of the church (Rev. 4:1), the return of Christ (Rev. 19:11-21), and the great white throne judgment (Rev. 20:11-15). Since God works differently in each period of time, our theology insists that each unit should be studied separately, and the units of thought should not overlap with one another.

Style

"Style is the way a writer uses words to create literature. It is one word following another, and one paragraph leading to the next....The way writers write is part of what they have to say." [34] From a stylistic perspective, the book of Revelation may be classified as apocalyptic literature. "Apocalyptic writings are marked by distinctive literary features, particularly prediction of future events and accounts of visionary experiences or journeys to heaven, often involving vivid symbolism."[35]

Revelation, as apocalyptic literature, tells of "things that must soon take place" (Rev. 1:1). Revelation is comprised of a series of visions. The apostle John saw a vision of the throne in heaven (Rev. 4), the scroll and the Lamb (Rev. 5), the seven seals (Rev. 6), the 144,000 servants of God (Rev. 7:1-8), a great multitude (Rev. 6:9-17), and more. And Revelation is riddled with symbolism. Such symbols include stars, lampstands, trees, manna, stones, garments, trumpets, bowls, beasts, water, and fire, to name a few.

Thankfully, our theology has left the style of Revelation alone.

Moral Weakness
ΑΩ

Adding to this Prophecy

The book of Revelation warns against adding to its message. Revelation 22:18-19 states, "If anyone adds to [the words of the prophecy of this book], God will add to him the plagues described in this book." Although the prophecy of Revelation warns against adding to the text, our theology has added many ideas to the message of Revelation.

Throughout Part Three of this book, we have shown how our theology has added to the book of Revelation. Our theology has superimposed Daniel's seventieth week on the text. We have introduced the rapture of the church to the text. We have separated the rapture of the church from the revelation of Jesus Christ. We have created multiple categories of believers, multiple resurrections, and multiple judgments. We have introduced unbiblical teachings as it relates to second chances, purgatory, escapism, impersonal gospel agents, and detached Christians.

All of these additions alter the message of Revelation and prevent us from hearing what the Spirit says to the churches. We need to prepare ourselves for things to come. We need to wash ourselves in the blood of the Lamb. We need to clothe ourselves with the righteous deeds of the saints. We need to stand firm in our faith. And we need to endure to the end.

Taking from this Prophecy

The book of Revelation warns against taking away from its message. Revelation 22:19 states, "If anyone takes away from the words of the book of this prophecy, God will take away his share in the tree of life and in the holy city, which are described in this book." Although the prophecy of Revelation warns against taking away from the text, our theology has taken away the message of Revelation from the church.

The book of Revelation was written to prepare the church for things to come, particularly the tribulation. However, when we develop a theology that says the church will not be here, there is no longer a message for us. We have effectively taken away the book of Revelation from the church. This will leave the church ill-prepared for things to come and vulnerable to the deception of the Antichrist.

For the person who advocates a theology that detracts from the message of Revelation, God minces no words. God will take away his share in the Tree of Life and in the Holy City. In other words, he will not be saved but fall under the fiery indignation of God. He will receive a portion in the lake that burns with fire and sulfur, which is the second death.

Taking Heed to this Warning

These warnings should cause us to stop and think twice about our theological approach to the book of Revelation. Does our theological approach represent the clear teaching of Scripture? If so, then there is nothing to worry about. If not, then we may be guilty of tampering with the Word of God. Let us be humble enough to admit when we are wrong, and let us be receptive enough to be corrected. Then we will have God's blessing rather than his judgment.

Pastoral Weakness
ΑΩ

The book of Revelation offers a blessing to those who read, hear, and obey its message (Rev. 1:3; 22:7). Yet, we have adopted a view of Revelation that makes its message irrelevant.

To be sure, we hear many sermons about the seven churches as described in the opening chapters (Rev. 2-3). And we hear many sermons about the eternal state as described in the concluding chapters (Rev. 21-22). However, we do not hear much about the tribulation as described in the body of the book (Rev. 4-19).

The reason for this negligence is clear. According to our theology, the tribulation relates to the nation of Israel, not to the church. Therefore, there is no immediate application for the church. Any relevancy is indirect at best.

What's more, many of us do not care what the book of Revelation has to say about things to come. We know what we believe and how it all fits together, or we think the book of Revelation is too difficult to understand, or we think the book of Revelation only stirs up division. In any case, we do not see any value in studying the book of Revelation. Instead, we flippantly say, "I am not a-mil or pre-mil but pan-mil. I believe it will all pan out in the end!"

Such apathy will be costly. In the Olivet Discourse, Jesus warned his disciples about false christs and false prophets so that they would not be led away (Matt. 24:24-26). The book of Revelation serves this same purpose. It was written to prepare the church for things to come. If we ignore its message, we will be ill-prepared for the future. We will be either surprised because we were not raptured as we thought or deceived because we were not looking out for antichrists.

While our theological approach sees little value in the book of Revelation, an exegetical approach sees the book of Revelation as immensely valuable for the church. The book of Revelation serves two purposes for the church.

First, the book of Revelation prepares the church *for* the tribulation. Jesus, knowing that his disciples would experience a time of testing before his return, did not want his disciples to be ill-prepared. So, he gave them the inside scoop. He told them what would take place before it happened. Unlike servants who do not know what their master is doing, the disciples of Jesus are his friends, to whom he has made known what is to come (John 15:15). The church is therefore "in the know" as it relates to future events.

Second, the book of Revelation will encourage the church *during* the tribulation. When the time of testing comes, Christians will be able to look beyond their immediate circumstances and see the final outcome of all things. They will understand that their "light momentary affliction" is preparing for them "an eternal weight of glory" that will surpass it all (2 Cor. 4:17). Though the Antichrist and his followers will appear to have the upper hand, Christians will know the final Victor. The kingdom of the Antichrist will fall, and Christ will triumph. Christians may take comfort in this fact.

While we may not be the generation of Christians who will live through the tribulation, the book of Revelation still offers us hope. When life is good, the coming of Christ means little to us. When the world turns against us, the coming of Christ means everything to us. We long for his appearance. We long for the day when the wicked are punished and the righteous are vindicated. We long for the restoration of all creation. The book of Revelation assures us that, despite what we may go through, Christ is coming soon, and his reward is with him (Rev. 22:12).

For these reasons, a blessing accompanies those who read, hear, and obey the message of Revelation.

Part Four

Application

Introduction
ΑΩ

The book of Revelation offers a blessing to those who read, hear, and obey its message. Revelation 1:3 says, "Blessed is the one who reads aloud the words of this prophecy, and blessed are those who hear, and who keep what is written in it, for the time is near."

This blessing is offered not once, but twice, in the pages of Revelation. Revelation 22:7 repeats this blessing when it says, "Blessed is the one who keeps the words of the prophecy of this book."

In both instances, this blessing is placed in a prominent place in the text.

In the first instance, the blessing stands at the head of the prologue. As such, it tells the reader how to read the book. The book should not be read to create elaborate timelines or to satisfy speculative curiosity; rather, the book should be read with an intent toward obedience. The mind should ask, "What does the text say I am to do?" The heart should say, "Yes, Lord, I am listening." And the hands should be prepared to do what is asked.

In the second instance, the blessing stands at the head of the epilogue. As such, it bridges the gap between the eschatological vision and practical life. Having just heard about the things that are to come, the reader is called to consider how he ought to live in the here and now. With the restatement of the blessing on the heels of the last prophetic vision, the reader is quickly brought out of the ecstatic trance and back to the reality of life.

In both instances, the blessing begs the question, "What are we supposed to do as a result of reading the book of Revelation?" For if we are to receive the blessing, then we must obey its message. And if we are to obey its message, then we must know what the book is telling us to do. It is this question I would like to explore in the last part of this book.

Hear the Words
ΑΩ

The Importance of Hearing

The first exhortation that we want to consider is embedded in the blessing itself. Revelation 1:3 says, "Blessed is the one who reads aloud the words of this prophecy, and blessed are those who hear, and who keep what is written in it, for the time is near." If we are to receive the blessing of Revelation, then we must hear its message.

The importance of hearing is mentioned throughout the book of Revelation. The blessing requires hearing (Rev. 1:3). In every message to the seven churches, Jesus calls the person who has ears to "*hear* what the Spirit says to the churches" (Rev. 2:7, 11, 17, 29; 3:6, 13, 22, italics mine). Jesus tells the church in Sardis to "remember...what you received and *heard*" (Rev. 3:3, italics mine). Jesus declares to the church in Laodicea that he stands at the door and knocks; and "if anyone *hears* my voice and opens the door, I will come in to him and eat with him, and he with me" (Rev. 3:20, italics mine). Halfway through the book of Revelation, Jesus proclaims again, "If anyone has an ear, let him *hear*" (Rev. 13:9, italics mine). Multiple times, the apostle John is said to have heard (Rev. 1:10; 4:1; 5:11, 13; 6:1, 3, 5, 6, 7; 7:4; 8:13; 9:13, 16; 10:4, 8; 12:10; 14:2, 13; 16:1, 5, 7; 18:4; 19:1, 6; 21:3; 22:8). In contrast, the idols of gold and silver and bronze that the inhabitants of the earth worship cannot hear (Rev. 9:20). As the book of Revelation draws to a close, the one who hears invites the one who is thirsty to come and take the water of life without price (Rev. 22:17). And, the apostle John warns "everyone who *hears* the words of the prophecy of this book" not to add to it or to take away from it (Rev. 22:18-19, italics mine).

Clearly, the book of Revelation emphasizes the importance of hearing. But, what does "hearing" mean? Having looked at the importance of hearing, let us now consider the meaning of hearing.

The Meaning of Hearing

What does it mean "to hear" the book of Revelation? There are three aspects to hearing: reading, accepting, and doing. Let's look at each of these in turn.

To Hear Is To Read

To hear the book of Revelation is to read the book of Revelation.

The book of Revelation is a book (Rev. 1:11; 22:7, 8-9, 10, 18-19). The apostle John wrote down what he had seen on a papyrus scroll (Rev. 1:10-11, 19; 2:1, 8, 12, 18; 3:1, 7, 14; 10:4; 14:13; 19:9; 21:5). This book was then painstakingly copied and sent by courier to each of the seven churches (Rev. 1:4, 10-11; 22:16). Upon arrival, a church leader would stand up and read the book, and the rest of the congregation would sit and listen. Notice that "the one who reads" is singular and "those who hear" is plural in the blessing found in Revelation 1:3. Thus, to hear includes the physical act of reading with one's eyes and hearing with one's ears.

In the first century, to read the book of Revelation was a challenge. It was a challenge, first of all, because access to the book of Revelation was limited. Books at that time had to be copied by hand: The printing press had not yet been invented; the digital age had not yet dawned. Copies of any book, let alone the book of Revelation, were few and far between. Consequently, there were not many copies of Revelation available to be read. Secondly, it was a challenge because not everyone could read. While the literacy rate in the nation of Israel is 91.8% today,[36] most people believe it was much lower during the first century. In his paper entitled, "Illiteracy in the Land of Israel in the First Centuries C.E.," Meir Bar-Ilan concluded that the literacy rate in the land of Israel was less than 3% in the first centuries.[37] No wonder the apostle John calls the one who is able to read and those who were able to hear blessed, for they were a small and privileged group of people.

Times have certainly changed.

Access to the Word of God is not a problem in the United States. Most people in America "not only have access to the Bible, but they also own a Bible. Nearly nine in 10 American households report having at least one Bible, with the average household owning four copies."[38] We have multiple translations from which to choose (KJV, NIV, ESV, NLT, etc.). We have different formats to suit our liking (large print, compact, wide margin, loose leaf, etc.). We have editions tailored specifically to us (men's, women's, children's, teens', etc.) and others that serve particular purposes (study, apologetics, archaeology, application, etc.). And this is just the print medium. We also have immediate access to hundreds of electronic versions via the internet and mobile devices.

Yet, the challenge to read the book of Revelation still remains.

Our challenge is not that we *cannot* read the book of Revelation, but that we *do not* read the book of Revelation. The problem is not access to the Word of God but the overabundance of the Word of God. When access to the Word of God is limited, we treasure it. We hold onto any scrap of material that has even a portion of the Bible written on it. We wrap it in a protective covering and store it in a special place so that it will not get damaged. We get it out often and handle it carefully. We read it over and over. We meditate on it. We memorize it. We copy it. We offer it to others. But when the Bible is as accessible as the air we breathe, we take it for granted. We assume that it will always be there.

There are a number of reasons why we do not read the book of Revelation. We think it is too difficult to understand, or that we have it all figured out, or that it only stirs up controversies. We are terrified by the events described in its pages. We do not understand how the book applies to our lives. We confuse accessibility to the book of Revelation with the acquisition of its content. We are absorbed by the cares of this world—movies to watch, songs to download, books to read, games to play—and subject to the tyranny of the urgent—calls to make, texts to tweet, e-mails to write, posts to check, etc. We are too busy and have no time.

The apostle John wrote, "Blessed is the one who reads." Do we believe these words?

Let us accept the challenge before us and read the book of Revelation. This means recognizing the value of Revelation. This means making the reading of Revelation a top priority. This means setting other demands aside and dedicating time to the task. This means unplugging from the world around us and tuning into the message before us. This means pulling the Bible off the shelf, dusting it off, and cracking the cover. This means not being content with owning a copy of Revelation but pressing to know what the book of Revelation is all about. This means struggling to understand it and entering into controversies about it. This means taking the seat of a student and being willing to be instructed by it. This means abandoning our fears and trusting the Father no matter what may lie in the future.

A parishioner once asked his pastor, "What is the right translation of the Bible?" The wise pastor gave this simple reply, "The one that is read." That must be our response. To hear the book of Revelation means we must read the book of Revelation.

To Hear Is To Accept

To hear the book of Revelation is to accept what it says.

In Revelation 22:18-19, the apostle John pronounced this warning:

> "I warn everyone who hears the words of the prophecy of this book: if anyone adds to them, God will add to him the plagues described in this book, and if anyone takes away from the words of the book of this prophecy, God will take away his share in the tree of life and in the holy city, which are described in this book." Rev. 22:18-19

Clearly, it is not our place to sit in judgment of the book of Revelation or, worse yet, to alter its message. We are not to come along and say, "This is good, and this is bad. And, oh, you forgot a paragraph here." Rather, we are to accept the message as it is, the Word of God. We must not talk back to God. We must recognize the authority of our Creator and humbly accept our status as a creature. We must be quick to listen, slow to speak, and slow to become angry.

This warning obviously applies to other religions and cults that have added to the book of Revelation. For instance, Islam has added the Koran, and the church of Jesus Christ of Latter-day Saints has added the Book of Mormon. It likewise applies to other religions and heresies that take away from the book of Revelation. For instance, Judaism denies that Jesus is the Christ and liberal theology denies the supernatural. These all leave people in a precarious position before God.

But this warning also applies to believers who unwittingly discount the clear teaching of Scripture. Consider, for instance, the apostle Peter. After Simon Peter declared, "You are the Christ, the Son of the living God," Jesus began to show his disciples that he must go to Jerusalem, suffer many things from the religious establishment, be killed, and on the third day be raised (Matt. 16:16, 21). Despite the clear teaching of Jesus, Peter took him aside and began to rebuke him, saying, "Far be it from you, Lord! This shall never happen to you" (Matt. 16:22). Because of his preconceived notions of the Christ, Peter could not reconcile a suffering servant with his theology and consequently denied the possibility.

I fear that we too have adopted a theology that prevents us from seeing and accepting the clear teaching of Revelation. We have adopted a rigid version of dispensationalism. This view of Scripture draws a sharp distinction between Israel and the church, which tells us that the book of Revelation does not apply to us but Israel. So, when Jesus writes a book to, for, and about the church to prepare us for things to come, we do not see it. We cannot see it. Our theology will not permit it. We stand with Peter and make statements that ought not to be said. We blatantly contradict the express purpose of the book.

To hear the book of Revelation means we must accept what it says, even if we cannot get our minds around it.

To Hear Is To Do

To hear the book of Revelation is to obey what it says. It is not enough to read the book of Revelation and accept what it says. We must also do what it commands, for the apostle John twice connected the blessing to obedience: first in Revelation 1:3, when he wrote, "Blessed are those who hear, *and who keep* what is written in it, for the time is near" (italics mine); and again, in Revelation 22:7, when he wrote, "Blessed is *the one who keeps* the words of the prophecy of this book" (italics mine).

Such obedience is mentioned throughout the book of Revelation.

> The one who conquers *and who keeps* my works until the end, to him I will give authority over the nations. Rev. 2:26 (italics mine)
>
> Remember, then, what you received and heard. *Keep it,* and repent. If you will not wake up, I will come like a thief, and you will not know at what hour I will come against you. Rev. 3:3 (italics mine)
>
> Then the dragon became furious with the woman and went off to make war on the rest of her offspring, on *those who keep* the commandments of God and hold to the testimony of Jesus. Rev. 12:17 (italics mine)
>
> Here is a call for the endurance of the saints, *those who keep* the commandments of God and their faith in Jesus. Rev. 14:12 (italics mine)
>
> I fell down to worship at the feet of the angel who showed [these things] to me, but he said to me, "You must not do that! I am a fellow servant with you and your brothers the prophets, and with *those who keep* the words of this book." Rev. 22:8-9 (italics mine)

The apostle John gave us the reason why the blessing accompanies obedience when he added the short prepositional phrase, "for the time is near." These prophetic events about which John wrote would soon take place, and the book of Revelation would prepare its readers for things to come. What the readers do with this prophecy could significantly change how they respond to the events as they begin to unfold. They could take no action and be overwhelmed by the pressure coming against them, or they could prepare themselves and be confident as the world is in upheaval all around them. This does not mean it will be an easy road for them, but they will know their ultimate destiny and how to successfully navigate their lives to get there.

During his earthly life, Jesus similarly told his disciples about things to come so that they might be prepared for the future. For instance, Jesus told his disciples about the opposition they would face after his departure. Jesus said:

> "I have said all these things to you to keep you from falling away. They will put you out of the synagogues. Indeed, the hour is coming when whoever kills you will think he is offering service to God. And they will do these things because they have not known the Father, nor me. But I have said these things to you, that when their hour comes you may remember that I told them to you." John 16:1-4

While Jesus informed his disciples about this future opposition, he explained to his disciples why he was telling them in advance. He wanted his disciples to know so that, when the opposition came, they would not be caught off-guard and fall away. Instead, they would be able to remember his words and stand firm.

As Jesus told his disciples about things to come so that they might be prepared, Jesus tells his church about things to come so that she might be prepared. This is all in keeping with the character of Jesus who calls his disciples "friends." Jesus declared, "You are my friends if you do what I command you. No longer do I call you servants, for the servant does not know what his master is doing; but I have called you friends, for all that I have heard from my Father I have made known to you" (John 15:14-15).

In the book of Revelation, Jesus has revealed to us what he is doing now and what he is about to do in the future. He has been given the seven-sealed scroll and the right to open it, and he has revealed its contents to us. We have the opportunity to be one step ahead of the world. If we obey what has been commanded, then we will be well-prepared for things to come and consequently blessed. But, if we do not obey what has been commanded, then we have not even heard the book of Revelation, and we certainly cannot claim its promise.

Summary

If we are to receive the blessing of Revelation, then we must "hear" the book of Revelation. To "hear" the book of Revelation requires three actions. First, we must physically read the book of Revelation. Second, we must accept its message without argumentation or adulteration. And, third, we must do what it says. This we will do, Lord willing, in the pages ahead.

Believe in Jesus Christ
ΑΩ

We live in a world where acceptance is laudable, multiculturalism is fashionable, and tolerance is a moral. We plaster "Love Wins" bumper stickers on our cars. We ask the rhetorical question, "Can't we all just get along?" We write laws against discrimination based on race, color, religion, gender identity, and sexual orientation. We live in a global community where we work together to tackle the world's problems of climate change, terrorism, poverty, and disease. And we spell the word "Peace" and "Coexist" using symbols from different world religions.

For better or worse, these same values are finding their way into the church. We embrace the apostle Paul's declaration, "There is neither Jew nor Greek, there is neither slave nor free, there is no male and female, for you are all one in Christ Jesus" (Gal. 3:28). We celebrate the eschatological community that Christ is making, a people "from every tribe and language and people and nation" (Rev. 5:9). We elevate our unity in Christ above all other doctrinal and moral distinctions. We attribute gender differences to the curse of sin and ordain female pastors. We attribute sexual orientation to genetics and accept homosexual behavior as an acceptable lifestyle.

In a culture that wants to accept everyone, we must make clear distinctions. There is a world of difference between accepting everyone as created in the image of God, enslaved to sin, and in need of a Savior, and indiscriminately accepting the beliefs and behaviors of everyone. While we may not like to hear it, the book of Revelation distinguishes between two groups of people. There are those who are "in" and those who are "out." There are those who are on God's side and those who are not. Not everyone is the same.

There are Two Sides

The book of Revelation puts all people on one of two sides: those who belong to Christ and his kingdom, and those who belong to the Antichrist and his kingdom.

These two sides have opposing allegiances. The Antichrist and his followers have given themselves over to Satan to do his bidding (Rev. 13:2; 20:1-3, 7-10), while Christ and his followers have submitted their will to the One seated on the throne in heaven (Rev. 4:1-11; 7:9-17; 22:3-5).

These two sides have conflicting purposes. The Antichrist and his followers seek to overthrow the rule of God and his Christ (Rev. 17:12-14), while Christ and his followers seek to crush the rebellion and bring everything under the head of him who rules forever (Rev. 19:11-16).

These two sides are all inclusive: no one is exempt. Everyone will have to make a decision as it relates the Antichrist, his image, and his mark, for the False Prophet will force the issue (Rev. 13:11-14). Anyone who refuses to worship the Antichrist and his image will be slain (Rev. 13:15); and anyone who refuses to accept his mark will be unable to engage in business transactions (Rev. 13:16-17). People will have to make a choice. No one is exempt. There is no middle ground.

These two sides are mutually exclusive: we cannot be on one side without being excluded from the other side. If we refuse to worship the Antichrist and his image, then we will incur the wrath of the Antichrist (Rev. 13:7-8; cf. Rev. 12:14-15, 17). On the other hand, if we choose to worship the Antichrist and his image, then we will incur the wrath of the Lamb.

The third angel flying overhead makes this point very clear:

> "If anyone worships the beast and its image and receives a mark on his forehead or on his hand, he also will drink the wine of God's wrath, poured full strength into the cup of his anger, and he will be tormented with fire and sulfur in the presence of the holy angels and in the presence of the Lamb. And the smoke of their torment goes up forever and ever, and they have no rest, day or night, these worshipers of the beast and its image, and whoever receives the mark of its name." Rev. 14:9-11

And these two sides have contrasting destinies. The Antichrist and his followers will face the wrath of God and ultimately be thrown into the lake of fire (Rev. 16; 19:17-21; 20:7-10, 11-15; 21:8, 27; 22:3, 14-15), while Christ and his followers will live in the new heaven and the new earth where they will live and reign forever (Rev. 21:1-22:5).

A Description of the Two Sides

Listen to how the book of Revelation describes the two sides.

There are those who have been loved by God (Rev. 1:5) and those who have not. There are those who have been freed from their sin (Rev. 1:5) and those who have not. There are those who have been made kings and priests (Rev. 1:6; 5:9-10; 20:6) and those who have not. There are those who welcome the coming of Christ (Rev. 1:7; 22:17, 20) and those who do not. There are those who have been redeemed from the earth (Rev. 5:9; 14:3-4) and those who could care less about the earth (Rev. 11:18). There are those whose citizenship is in heaven (Rev. 12:12; 13:6) and those who dwell on earth (Rev. 3:10; 6:10; 8:13; 11:10, 18; 12:12; 13:8, 12, 14; 14:6; 17:2, 8). There are those who have washed their robes in the blood of the Lamb (Rev. 7:14; 19:7-8; 22:14) and those who have not. There are those who have the seal of God on their forehead (Rev. 7:1-8; 14:1; 22:3-4) and those who do not (Rev. 9:4).

There are those who conquer (Rev. 2:7, 11, 17, 26; 3:5, 12, 21; 12:11; 15:2; 21:7) and those who do not (Rev. 21:8). There are those who keep the commandments of God (Rev. 12:17; 14:12; 22:14) and those who do not (Rev. 9:20-21; 16:8-9, 21). There are those who hold to the testimony of Jesus (Rev. 6:9; 12:17; 19:10; 20:4) and those who do not. There are those who fear God and give him glory (Rev. 14:6-7; 15:3-4; 22:3) and those who do not (Rev. 9:20; 21:8; 22:15). There are those who refuse to worship the Beast and its image (Rev. 13:15; 20:4) and those who do not (Rev. 13:4, 8, 12; 14:9, 11; 16:2; 19:20). There are those who reject the mark of the Beast (Rev. 20:4) and those who do not (Rev. 13:16-17; 14:9; 16:2, 10-11; 19:20). There are those who heed the call for wisdom (Rev. 13:18; 17:9) and conquer the Beast (Rev. 12:11; 15:2; 21:7), albeit through death (Rev. 11:7; 13:7), and those who do not but are deceived by the dragon, the Antichrist, and the False Prophet (Rev. 12:9; 13:13-14; 18:23; 19:20; 20:3, 7-8, 9-10).

There are those whose names are written in the Lamb's Book of Life (Rev. 3:5; 21:27) and those whose names are not (Rev. 13:8; 17:8; 20:13, 15). There are those who will be invited to the marriage supper of the Lamb (Rev. 19:9) and those who will not receive any such invitation. There are those who will participate in the first resurrection (Rev. 20:6) and those who will be raised later (Rev. 20:5; 11-15). There are those who will dwell on the new earth (Rev. 21:7) and those who will not (Rev. 21:8). There are those who will live in the New Jerusalem (Rev. 21:24-26; 22:14) and those who will not (Rev. 21:27; 22:15). There are those who will eat from the Tree of Life (Rev. 22:1-2, 14) and those who will not (Rev. 22:15). There are those whose thirst will be quenched (Rev. 22:17) and those who have no such thirst. There are those who will rest from their labors (Rev. 14:13) and those who will never find rest (Rev. 14:11).

There are those who hear and obey the message of Revelation (Rev. 1:3; 22:7) and those who ignore or alter the message of Revelation (Rev. 22:18-19). There are those who know the grace of the Lord Jesus (Rev. 1:4; 22:21) and those who will never know his grace.

Two Practical Questions

The book of Revelation clearly teaches that all people are on one of two sides, and that these two sides are all-inclusive, mutually exclusive, and diametrically opposed to one another. This raises a couple of practical questions, specifically, "Whose side am I on?" and "How can I change sides, if I so choose?" Our children got it right when they sang:

> One door and only one,
>   and yet its sides are two;
> Inside and outside,
>   on which side are you?

> One door and only one,
> > and yet its sides are two;
> I'm on the inside,
> > on which side are you?

For the remainder of this chapter, we would like to address these two questions.

The Primary Audience

The book of Revelation, having been written to the seven churches that are in Asia, presumes that its readers are on the side of Christ. It serves the primary purpose of building up the body of Christ. Consequently, the book of Revelation does not focus on how to choose one's side but how to live as one who is on Christ's side. To find out how to choose our side or, more specifically, how to choose Christ's side, we have to turn back to John's gospel, which is evangelistic in nature.

The gospel of John was written with the express purpose of bringing people to faith in Jesus Christ. John wrote, "these [things] are written so that you may believe that Jesus is the Christ, the Son of God, and that by believing you may have life in his name" (John 20:31).

In the gospel of John, we hear of God's love for humanity, "God so loved the world, that he gave his only Son, that whoever believes in him should not perish but have eternal life" (John 3:16). God sent his Son to take the punishment that we deserve, so that we might be ransomed from our sins. Thus, when the crowd asked Jesus, "What must we do, to be doing the works of God? (John 6:28). Jesus did not reply with a litany of commands but with an invitation to believe. "This is the work of God, that you believe in him whom he has sent" (John 6:29). In other words, if we put our trust in Jesus Christ, he will do the rest. He will deliver us from the coming wrath and usher us safely into the paradise of God described in the book of Revelation.

While this salvation is generous and its receipt simple, people still refuse it. Why? John explained in the third chapter of his gospel. Although Jesus came to seek and to save the lost, people do not want to approach Jesus because he is absolutely pure and they are thoroughly wicked (John 3:17-20). People know that if they approach

Jesus for salvation, the brilliance of his holy character will expose the depths of their depravity. Such exposure terrifies them and drives them away from Christ. Rather than embracing his love, they despise his sacrificial death and life-giving resurrection. Instead of loving Christ, they hate him. Nonetheless, the offer stands. To all who receive him, he gives the right to become children of God (John 1:12).

John 3:36 summarizes the spiritual state in which people find themselves: "Whoever believes in the Son has eternal life; whoever does not obey the Son shall not see life, but the wrath of God remains on him." The question remains, "Have we believed in Jesus?" If we have placed our faith in Jesus Christ, then we will escape the wrath that is coming against those who do not believe; but, if we have not yet called out to Jesus, then we are aligning ourselves with those who hate the Son, that is, those who will incur his wrath at his coming.

The Secondary Audience

Although the primary audience of Revelation is the church, the book also serves a secondary audience, the unbelieving world. As such, it calls people to faith in Jesus Christ. It calls unbelievers to turn away from the path that leads to destruction and to take a path that leads to life. Implicit in a prophet's message of doom is a message of hope, for God is allowing people to see the outcome of their ways and granting them an opportunity to change. For God does not delight in the death of the wicked, but that he should turn from his way and live (Ezek. 18:23).

The prophet Ezekiel taught the nation of Israel that the Lord wants the wicked to turn from their rebellious way and live. In Ezekiel 18, the prophet confronted the erroneous proverb: "The fathers have eaten sour grapes, and the children's teeth are set on edge" and introduced his own corrective proverb: "The soul who sins shall die." The children of Israel had basically adopted an attitude of "Que sera, sera" ("Whatever will be, will be"). In other words, Israel believed they were being punished for the sins of their ancestors, and there was no way out. Ezekiel interjected that Israel was being punished for their own sins, and their future rested in their own hands.

Ezekiel put forward several scenarios to illustrate his point. I will repeat two of his scenarios here. First, Ezekiel spoke about a righteous son born to a wicked father. In this case, the righteous son sees all the sins that his father has done and does not follow in the footsteps of his father but instead walks according to the law of the Lord. Ezekiel declared that such a man will live (Ezek. 18:14-18). Second, Ezekiel spoke about a wicked person who turns to righteousness. In this case, the wicked man comes to his senses and turns from all the sins he has committed and walks according to the law of the Lord. Ezekiel declared that such a man will live (Ezek. 18:21-23). In both cases, the Lord's compassion triumphed over his judgment. The Lord did not hold the former sins of the people against them.

The life of the prophet Jonah historically validated the truth that the Lord wants the wicked to turn from their rebellious way and live. The prophet Jonah was called by the Lord to go to Nineveh and preach a message of judgment: "Yet forty days, and Nineveh shall be overthrown!" (Jonah 3:4). Jonah refused to accept the mission, not because he was afraid to convey a message of judgment, but because he did not want to offer a message of hope. The Lord was granting the citizens of Nineveh an opportunity to repent. Jonah did not want the Lord to show compassion to Israel's worst enemies, the Assyrians.

When his fears were realized, Jonah confessed:

> "O Lord, is not this what I said when I was yet in my country? That is why I made haste to flee to Tarshish; for I knew that you are a gracious God and merciful, slow to anger and abounding in steadfast love, and relenting from disaster. Therefore now, O Lord, please take my life from me, for it is better for me to die than to live." Jonah 4:2-3

Although the Lord took unusual measures to soften Jonah's heart, we never hear whether Jonah's attitude changed. For all we know, Jonah is still sitting under a scorched plant, with a migraine headache, waiting for Nineveh's destruction or his own death. What we do know is that God does not delight in the death of the wicked, but that he should turn from his way and live (Ezek. 18:23; cf. Ezek. 33:1-20).

Like the preaching of Jonah, the book of Revelation includes a message of judgment. It speaks about the devastating judgment that God is about to unleash upon the world. Anyone who hears this message of judgment has the opportunity to repent and to escape the coming wrath.

When cosmic disturbances signal the end of the world, people of all stations in life hide themselves in the caves of the mountains and cry out in sheer terror, "Who is able to stand the day of God's wrath?" (Rev. 6:15-16). The question they raise is a rhetorical one. No one is able to pass a thorough examination administered by a holy God who knows the thoughts that occupy our mind and the desires that intrigue our heart. No one is able to withstand the just punishment that ensues from such a perfectly administered, accurate evaluation of our lives. Our sin and idolatries make us the object of God's wrath, and our refusal to repent and to believe only seals our fate.

In Revelation 8 and 9, the apostle John detailed the judgments that will accompany the blasts of the seven trumpets. The first trumpet burns up a third part of the earth. The second trumpet turns the sea into blood, kills a third of the sea creatures, and destroys a third of the ships. The third trumpet makes the fresh water bitter. The fourth trumpet darkens the sun, moon, and stars. The fifth trumpet releases scorpions from the bottomless pit, which torment the inhabitants of the earth for five months. The sixth trumpet kills a third of humanity through plagues of fire, smoke, and sulfur. And the seventh trumpet declares the reign of the Lord and the destruction of the earth.

Significantly, the apostle John pointed out that these judgments are specifically directed against those who refuse to repent.

> The rest of mankind, who were not killed by these plagues, *did not repent* of the works of their hands *nor give up* worshiping demons and idols of gold and silver and bronze and stone and wood, which cannot see or hear or walk, *nor did they repent* of their murders or their sorceries or their sexual immorality or their thefts. Rev. 9:20-21 (italics mine)

Evidently, those who did repent have been delivered, for they are not mentioned in this passage.

In Revelation 16, the apostle John detailed the bowls of wrath that God will pour out on the kingdom of the Antichrist. The first bowl causes sores to come upon those who worshiped the Beast and received his mark. The second bowl turns the salt water into blood. The third bowl turns the fresh water into blood. The fourth bowl causes the sun to scorch people with fire. The fifth bowl plunges the kingdom of the Antichrist into darkness. The sixth bowl prepares the way for the kings of earth to assemble for the final battle. And the seventh bowl declares the completion of God's wrath

Again, the apostle John pointed out that these judgments are specifically directed against those who refuse to repent. Listen to the fourth and fifth judgment.

> The fourth angel poured out his bowl on the sun, and it was allowed to scorch people with fire. They were scorched by the fierce heat, and they *cursed the name of God* who had power over these plagues. They *did not repent* and give him glory. Rev. 16:8-9 (italics mine)

> The fifth angel poured out his bowl on the throne of the Beast, and its kingdom was plunged into darkness. People gnawed their tongues in anguish and cursed the God of heaven for their pain and sores. They *did not repent* of their deeds. Rev. 16:17-21 (italics mine)

Moreover, the apostle John heightened the rebellion of the people in the description of the last judgment.

> The seventh angel poured out his bowl into the air, and a loud voice came out of the temple, from the throne, saying, "It is done!"....And great hailstones, about one hundred pounds each, fell from heaven on people; and they *cursed God* for the plague of the hail, because the plague was so severe. Rev. 16:17, 21 (italics mine)

Not only did the people refuse to repent, but they went so far as to curse God for all the woes they were experiencing. In their minds, they were not at fault for all the wrong in this world, rather God was the culprit. No wonder the angel in charge of the waters said:

> "Just are you, O Holy One, who is and who was,
>   for you brought these judgments.
> For they have shed the blood of saints and prophets,
>   and you have given them blood to drink.
> It is what they deserve!" Rev. 16:5-6

As much as these descriptions of God's wrath assure believers of their ultimate victory, they also serve as a measure of grace to unbelievers. These descriptions warn unbelievers of what is in store for them if they do not turn from their sin and call out for mercy. Implicit in a prophet's message of doom is a message of hope, for God is offering an opportunity to repent. For God does not delight in the death of the wicked, but that they should turn from their rebellious way and live.

A Call to Repent

What is implicit in a prophet's message of judgment is made explicit in Revelation 14:6-7. In these verses, an angel flies overhead and commands the inhabitants of the earth to repent. With a loud voice, the angel says, "*Fear God and give him glory*, because the hour of his judgment has come, and worship him who made heaven and earth, the sea and the springs of water" (Rev. 14:6-7, italics mine).

The coming judgment of God should drive the inhabitants of the earth to "fear God and give him glory." Through the proclamation of the angel, unbelievers are encouraged to cross enemy lines and to align themselves with Christ.

There is a path of sin that leads to destruction, and there is a path of righteousness that leads to life. To unbelievers who recognize their damnable condition and desire God's mercy, Jesus offers forgiveness and newness of life. In Revelation 22:17, Jesus says, "And let the one who is thirsty [for righteousness] come; let the one who desires take the water of life without price."

The Nature of Redemption

Lest we think that our repentance saves us, we are often reminded throughout the book of Revelation that Christ saved us by his death, burial, and resurrection. We did not save ourselves; rather, we are a redeemed community.

In Revelation 1:5, Jesus Christ is described as "him who loves us and has freed us from our sins by his blood and made us a kingdom, priests to his God and Father, to him be glory and dominion forever and ever." In Revelation 5:9-10, we hear the twenty-four elders declare the worthiness of the Lamb: "For you were slain, and by your blood you ransomed people for God from every tribe and language and people and nation, and you have made them a kingdom and priests to our God, and they shall reign on the earth." In Revelation 14:4, the 144,000 people who have the name of the Lamb and his Father's name written on their forehead are described as those who "have been redeemed from mankind as firstfruits for God and the Lamb." And Revelation 19:8 says that the bride of the Lamb was given fine linen, bright and pure, with which to clothe herself.

Repentance, though necessary, is insufficient. While repentance results in a change in future behavior, it does not remove the penalty for sins previously committed. Without Christ's redemption, we are still accountable for those sins. Moreover, even after we repent of our sins, we still find ourselves sinning. Thus, the apostle John calls the person who says he does not sin a liar and exhorts us to confess our sins (1 John 1:8-10). What we need is salvation, and this may only be secured in Christ. Jesus Christ took our punishment so that we might go free. Jesus Christ, not our repentance, is the basis of our salvation.

No wonder why the great multitude stood before the throne and before the Lamb, with palm branches in their hands, and cried out with a loud voice, "Salvation belongs to our God who sits on the throne, and to the Lamb!" (Rev. 7:9-10).

Two Questions Answered

This brings us back to the two practical questions that we raised earlier in this chapter.

"Whose side am I on?" we asked. In our natural condition, our wickedness puts us on the side of the Antichrist.

"How can I change sides, if I so choose?" The book of John and the book of Revelation answer with a singular voice, "Believe on the Lord Jesus Christ!"

By believing in Jesus we may have life in his name and be saved from the coming wrath.

Separate Yourselves
AΩ

The book of Revelation commands us to separate ourselves from the world. In Revelation 18, we read about the fall of Babylon, the capital city of the Antichrist's kingdom. The apostle John writes:

> After this I saw another angel coming down from heaven, having great authority, and the earth was made bright with his glory. And he called out with a mighty voice, "Fallen, fallen is Babylon the great! She has become a dwelling place for demons, a haunt for every unclean spirit, a haunt for every unclean bird, a haunt for every unclean and detestable beast." Rev. 18:1-2

In this chapter, John recorded the call to God's people to separate themselves from Babylon, the great prostitute:

> Then I heard another voice from heaven saying, "Come out of her, my people, lest you take part in her sins, lest you share in her plagues; for her sins are heaped high as heaven, and God has remembered her iniquities." Rev. 18:4-5

God calls his people to separate themselves from the world so that they will not share in the punishment due her sins.

Not a Physical Separation

When God commanded his people to come out of Babylon, he was not speaking about a physical separation, for some Christians will suffer persecution at the hands of the world. Christians cling to the Lord's promise to the church in Philadelphia: "I will keep you from the hour of trial that is coming on the whole earth" (Rev. 3:10). But

Christians ignore the Lord's warning to the church in Smyrna: "Do not fear what you are about to suffer. Behold, the devil is about to throw some of you into prison, that you may be tested, and for ten days you will have tribulation. Be faithful unto death, and I will give you the crown of life" (Rev. 2:10). Though the Christians in Smyrna would love to separate themselves physically from the world, they will not be able to do so. God has called them to go through persecution.

Similarly, the souls under the altar were not able to separate themselves physically from the world. They did not leave the world except through death. They bore witness to the word of God and, consequently, were slain for the witness they had borne (Rev. 6:9-10). Likewise, the two witnesses were called to prophesy for 1,260 days until they were killed by the Beast that rises from the bottomless pit (Rev. 11:1-3). Moreover, when the Beast of the sea makes war on the saints, they will not be able to hide but will be killed by him (Rev. 13:7). Thus, the third angel flying overhead pronounces a blessing on those "who die in the Lord from now on...that they may rest from their labors" (Rev. 14:13). The phrase "their labors" does not refer to their efforts to elude the Beast but their efforts to remain faithful to Christ, even in such difficult times.

A Moral Separation

When God commanded his people to come out of Babylon, he was not speaking about a physical separation, for the blood of prophets and saints was found in Babylon (Rev. 18:24). Did the prophets and saints die because they were physically in the city of Babylon? Did the prophets and saints die because they failed to obey God when he commanded them to flee? Did the prophets and saints die because they were in the wrong place when God unleased his judgment against the city? No, God did not sweep away the righteous with the wicked. Rather, the great prostitute had killed the saints and prophets prior to the judgment of God.

When God commanded his people to come out of Babylon, he was speaking about a moral separation, for he stated, "lest you take part in *her sins*" (Rev. 18:4, italics mine). And, he pointed out that "*her sins* are heaped high as heaven, and God has remembered *her iniquities*" (Rev. 18:5, italics mine). Although the prophets and saints mentioned in

Revelation 18:24 were physically in Babylon, they had long before separated themselves morally from the city. They had lived a righteous life in a sinful city. We need to follow their example. We need to separate ourselves from Babylon. We need to live differently from the world around us.

Separation in Practice

The book of Revelation most often talks about this separation in general terms. It talks about doing good works (Rev. 2:2, 19; 14:13; 19:8), loving others (Rev. 2:19), and serving God (Rev. 2:19; 7:15). It talks about avoiding evil and doing what is right (Rev. 22:11). It talks about being holy (Rev. 22:11) and living so as to be rewarded (Rev. 11:18; 18:6; 20:12, 13; 22:12). It talks about buying white garments from Christ (Rev. 3:18) and keeping our garments on (Rev. 16:15). It talks about not soiling our garments (Rev. 3:4; 22:11) but rather washing them in the blood of the Lamb (Rev. 7:14; 22:14). And it talks about having a godly thirst for righteousness and satisfying that thirst with the water of life (Rev. 22:17).

However, there are three passages that help us understand this separation in specific terms.

The first passage is found in the context of the seven trumpets. After describing the destruction that accompanies the sixth trumpet, the apostle John noted:

> The rest of mankind, who were not killed by these plagues, did not repent of the works of their hands nor give up *worshiping demons and idols* of gold and silver and bronze and stone and wood, which cannot see or hear or walk, nor did they repent of their *murders* or their *sorceries* or their *sexual immorality* or their *thefts*. Rev. 9:20-21 (italics mine)

From this passage, we hear the sins for which God is sending his judgment upon the world: idolatry, murder, sorcery, sexual immorality, and theft. These sins not only characterize the world's actions; they also characterize the world's heart. When confronted for these sins, the world refuses to give them up.

The second passage is found in the context of the new heaven and the new earth. After declaring that the dwelling place of God is with man, the One seated on the throne qualifies his statement:

> But as for the cowardly, the faithless, the detestable, as for *murderers, the sexually immoral, sorcerers, idolaters,* and *all liars*, their portion will be in the lake that burns with fire and sulfur, which is the second death. Rev. 21:8 (italics mine)

From this passage, we hear the sins for which God is excluding people from the new creation: murder, sexual immorality, sorcery, idolatry, and falsehood. People who commit such sins will be assigned a place in the lake of fire.

The third passage is found in the epilogue.

> Blessed are those who wash their robes, so that they may have the right to the tree of life and that they may enter the city by the gates. Outside are the dogs and *sorcerers* and *the sexually immoral* and *murderers* and *idolaters*, and *everyone who loves and practices falsehood*. Rev. 22:14-15 (italics mine)

From this passage, we hear the sins for which God is excluding people from the New Jerusalem: sorcery, sexual immorality, murder, idolatry, and falsehood. People who commit such sins will not have access to the Tree of Life; rather, they will only see the New Jerusalem from the outside. Such will be their state forever, for John noted: "Nothing unclean will *ever* enter it, nor anyone who does what is detestable or false, but only those who are written in the Lamb's book of life" (Rev. 21:27, italics mine).

Each of these passages specifies a number of sins, and there is considerable overlap in the sins that these passages mention. These passages do not claim to provide a comprehensive list of all sins; rather, these sins show the bent of people's hearts. As in the days of Noah, the wickedness of man will be great on the earth, and every intention of the thoughts of man's heart will be only evil continually (Gen. 6:5). At the same time, God, through the inspiration of Scripture, has intentionally drawn special attention to these sins.

Let us consider why God has chosen to focus on these specific sins.

The Future of Society

These sins—idolatry, murder, sorcery, sexual immorality, theft, and falsehood—will increasingly describe the society in which we live as we approach the end of time.

Idolatry

People will turn away from the One who is seated on the throne and from the Lamb that was slain, and they will worship gods of their own imagination. They will worship objects made by their own hands; idols of gold, silver, bronze, stone, and wood; figures which cannot see, hear, or walk but may be empowered by demons (Rev. 9:20-21).

Murder

Because of the increase of lawlessness, the love of many will grow cold (Matt. 24:12). People will be more concerned about self-preservation and personal advancement than the sanctity of human life or the bonds of family relationships. Many will fall away and betray one another and hate one another (Matt. 24:10). Brother will deliver brother over to death, and the father his child, and children will rise against parents and have them put to death (Matt. 10:21). A person's enemies will be those of his own household (Matt. 10:36).

Sorcery

Having rejected God as the ultimate authority in the universe, people will turn to other sources for divine guidance and supernatural power. They will seek divine knowledge from the deceased, and they will obtain supernatural power from demons. The ultimate source of this knowledge and power is not God but his archenemy, that ancient serpent, who is called the devil and Satan, the deceiver of the whole world. Interest in the occult will grow as people seek to harness these malignant powers—powers which they should only fear—resulting in their own enslavement and destruction.

Sexual immorality

Worshiping and serving the creature instead of the Creator, people will forsake all sensibility and give themselves over to dishonorable passions. Men and women will exchange natural relations for those that are contrary to nature. Men will commit shameless sexual acts with other men, and women with women. Premarital sex, adultery, pornography, homosexuality, incest, bestiality, etc. will permeate society.

Theft

Comparing themselves to others, people will grow discontent in what God has provided them, and they will allow envy to take hold of their heart. They will envy their neighbor's job; they will envy their neighbor's spouse; they will envy their neighbor's children; they will envy their neighbor's house; they will envy their neighbor's possessions. Feeling slighted by God, people will throw off all restraint, and they will kill and destroy to get what their heart desires.

Falsehood

Having rejected the God of truth, people will believe the Father of Lies. People will not only tell lies but they will entertain lies (Rev. 22:15). They will want to be deceived. They will want to hear anything other than the Truth.

The Kingdom of the Antichrist

These sins—idolatry, murder, sorcery, sexual immorality, theft, and falsehood—will characterize the manner by which the Antichrist administrates his kingdom in the last days.

Idolatry

There are two forms of idolatry: People can worship other gods (Ex. 20:3), and people can worship physical representations of God (Ex. 20:4-6). Both forms of idolatry will be prominent in the kingdom of the Antichrist. First, the Antichrist himself will claim to be God (Rev. 13:5-6) and demand that people worship him as God (Rev. 13:7-8). Second, the False Prophet will erect an image to the Beast and will demand that people worship this image (Rev. 13:13-15).

Murder

The Antichrist will seek out, arrest, and put to death anyone who identifies himself with the One seated on the throne. He will put to death the brothers of the souls under the altar (Rev. 6:9-11). He will put to death the two witnesses who prophesy in the Holy City for

1,260 days (Rev. 11:7-8). He will pursue so as to put to death those who keep the commandments of God and hold to the testimony of Jesus (Rev. 12:17). He will declare war on the saints, those whose names are written in the Lamb's Book of Life, and put them to death (Rev. 13:7-8). He will put to death those who labor against him and usher them into eternal rest (Rev. 14:13). Because of her insatiable appetite for the blood of the prophets and the saints, the capital city of the Antichrist will be destroyed in a single hour (Rev. 6:9-10; 16:5-6; 17:6; 18:24; 19:1-2).

Sorcery

The kingdom of the Antichrist will be undergirded by Satan himself. Satan will give the Antichrist "his power and his throne and great authority" (Rev. 13:2). Satan will enable the Antichrist to recover from a mortal wound (Rev. 13:3-4). Satan will give the Antichrist the audacity to speak "haughty and blasphemous words" and to utter "blasphemies against God, blaspheming his name and his dwelling" (Rev. 13:5-6). Satan will incite the Antichrist "to make war on the saints and to conquer them" (Rev. 13:7). And Satan will enable the False Prophet to perform miraculous signs so as to deceive the world into following the Beast (Rev. 13:11-14).

Sexual immorality

Throughout the Bible, sexual immorality serves as a word picture for spiritual apostasy. In this sense, the book of Revelation describes Babylon as, "the great prostitute who is seated on many waters, with whom the kings of the earth have committed sexual immorality, and with the wine of whose sexual immorality the dwellers on earth have become drunk" (Rev. 17:1-2). She will lure the kings of the earth and those who dwell on the earth into a spiritual union with her, and they will be smitten by her enticement (Rev. 14:8; 17:4-5; 18:2-3, 9; 19:1-2). They will all be of one mind and purpose, to make war on the Lamb and to defeat the One seated on the throne (Rev. 17:12-14).

Theft

The great prostitute is condemned for her shameless pride founded upon her economic prosperity. She has stripped the nations of their wealth—gold, silver, jewels, pearls, fine linen, purple cloth, silk, scarlet cloth, all kinds of scented wood, all kinds of articles of ivory, all kinds of articles of costly wood, bronze, iron and marble, cinnamon, spice, incense, myrrh, frankincense, wine, oil, fine flour, wheat, cattle and sheep, horses and chariots, and slaves—and acquired it for herself (Rev. 18:11-13). She has achieved her financial success not by honest employment but by misdeeds to others (Rev. 18:4-6), the enslavement of mankind (Rev. 13:16-17; 18:11-13), and the coldblooded murder of the saints (Rev. 6:9-10; 16:5-6; 17:6; 18:24; 19:1-2).

Falsehood

The kingdom of the Antichrist will be built upon lies. First, he will lie about his identity. He will masquerade as the Christ, the one who was alive, and died, and lives forever (compare Rev. 13:3-4, 12, 14 with Rev. 1:17-18; 2:8). With this lie, he will demand that everyone worship him (Rev. 13:13-15). Secondly, he will lie about the source of people's troubles. He will blame the world's ills on the One who is seated on the throne (Rev. 11:10; 13:5-6; 16:8-9, 10-11, 21). With this lie, he will incite the world against God, his Christ, and his people (Rev. 11:7-8; 13:7-8; 16:12-14; 17:12-14; 19:19; 20:7-10).

The Lives of Christians

These sins—idolatry, murder, sorcery, sexual immorality, theft, and falsehood—will specify how Christians will differentiate (or separate) themselves from the world around them. Each of these sins may be turned around so as to describe what Christians should look like in contrast to the rest of humanity.

Idolatry

Whereas the world will worship the Beast and receive his mark, Christians will worship the One seated on the throne and the Lamb that was slain. When Jesus was asked what the greatest commandment is in the Law, he replied, "You shall love the Lord your God with all your heart and with all your soul and with all your mind. This is the great and first commandment" (Matt. 22:37-38). Moreover, when Jesus was tempted to worship Satan, Jesus said, "Be gone, Satan! For it is written, 'You shall worship the Lord your God and him only shall you serve'" (Matt. 4:10). Christians will recognize that God and God alone is the sole object of our worship.

Murder

Whereas the world will allow anger to give way to murder, Christians will protect human life and take extraordinary measures to bring peace. Jesus said, "You have heard that it was said to those of old, 'You shall not murder; and whoever murders will be liable to judgment.' But I say to you that everyone who is angry with his brother will be liable to judgment; whoever insults his brother will be liable to the council; and whoever says, 'You fool!' will be liable to the hell of fire. So if you are offering your gift at the altar and there remember that your brother has something against you, leave your gift there before the altar and go. First be reconciled to your brother, and then come and offer your gift" (Matt. 5:21-24; cf. Matt. 5:38-42).

Sorcery

Whereas the world will turn to other sources for divine guidance and supernatural power, Christians will humble themselves before the Lord and wait for God to speak and to act. Toward the end of his life, Moses had warned the children of Israel not to follow the abominable practices of the nations—which sought divine knowledge from sorcerers, diviners, fortune-tellers, and necromancers, and the like—but to wait for God to raise up a prophet like himself (Deut. 18:9-22). God identified this prophet when he pulled back the heavens and spoke at Jesus' baptism, and again at his transfiguration, "This is my beloved Son, with whom I am well pleased; listen to him" (Matt. 17:5; cf. Matt. 3:17). As Christians, we wait for God to act. God has assured us that Christ will ride into history and overthrow the kingdom of the Antichrist (Rev. 19:11-21).

Sexual immorality

Whereas the world will allow lust to give way to all kinds of sexual perversion, Christians will uphold the marriage covenant and keep the marriage bed undefiled. Jesus said, "You have heard that it was said, 'You shall not commit adultery.' But I say to you that everyone who looks at a woman with lustful intent has already committed adultery with her in his heart. If your right eye causes you to sin, tear it out and throw it away. For it is better that you lose one of your members than that your whole body be thrown into hell....It was also said, 'Whoever divorces his wife, let him give her a certificate of divorce.' But I say to you that everyone who divorces his wife, except on the ground of sexual immorality, makes her commit adultery, and whoever marries a divorced woman commits adultery" (Matt. 5:27-29, 31-32).

Theft

Whereas the world will allow envy to give way to stealing and destruction, Christians will uphold the right to private property and use their own goods to make friends in heavenly places. Jesus said, "Do not lay up for yourselves treasures on earth, where moth and rust destroy and where thieves break in and steal, but lay up for yourselves treasures in heaven, where neither moth nor rust destroys and where thieves do not break in and steal...Therefore I tell you, do not be anxious about your life, what you will eat or what you will drink, nor about your body, what you will put on. Is not life more than food, and the body more than clothing? ...But seek first the kingdom of God and his righteousness, and all these things will be added to you" (Matt. 6:19-20, 25, 33).

Falsehood

Whereas the world will lie and say what people want to hear, Christians will see the world from God's perspective and speak the truth in love. Jesus said, "Again you have heard that it was said to those of old, 'You shall not swear falsely, but shall perform to the Lord what you have sworn.' But I say to you, Do not take an oath at all, either by heaven, for it is the throne of God, or by the earth, for it is his footstool, or by Jerusalem, for it is the city of the great King. And do not take an oath by your head, for you cannot make one hair white or black. Let what you say be simply 'Yes' or 'No'; anything more than this comes from evil" (Matt. 5:33-37).

Summary

Christians are called to separate themselves from the world. This separation is not a physical separation; it is a moral separation. Whereas the world will be bent on idolatry, murder, sorcery, sexual immorality, theft, and falsehood, Christians will have nothing to do with these vices. In contrast to the world, Christians will pursue God with all of their heart, pursue peace and protect life, wait for God to speak and act, uphold the marriage covenant, protect the right of private property, use their resources to further God's kingdom, and speak the truth in love. Although Christians will be *in* the world, Christians will not be *of* this world. They belong to another kingdom. They belong to God's kingdom.

Worship God
ΑΩ

Proper Worship

The heavenly scene gives us a proper perspective of worship: God is at the center, and everything emanates from him.

In John's vision of heaven, God was sitting on a throne (Rev. 4:2). *Around the throne* was a rainbow that had the appearance of an emerald (Rev. 4:3). *Around the throne* were twenty-four thrones, on which were seated twenty-four elders (Rev. 4:4). *From the throne* came flashes of lightning, and rumblings and peals of thunder (Rev. 4:5). *Before the throne* were burning seven torches of fire, which are the seven spirits of God (Rev. 4:5). *Before the throne* was a sea of glass, like crystal (Rev. 4:6a). *Around the throne* and *on each side of the throne* were four living creatures, full of eyes in front and behind, and ever crying out "Holy, holy, holy!" (Rev. 4:6b-8, italics mine).

From this heavenly scene, we can see that proper worship centers on God and God alone.

Reasons for Worship

The heavenly scene gives us many reasons why God is worthy of our praise.

God Is Eternal

God ought to be worshiped because he is eternal. The four living creatures never cease to say, "Holy, holy, holy, is the Lord God Almighty, who was and is and is to come!" (Rev. 4:8).

The eternal nature of God places him in a category all his own. God is eternal, and we are temporal. God is infinite, and we are finite. God is transcendent, and we are insignificant. God is self-existent, and we are dependent on him. Indeed, God is "the Alpha and the Omega, the first and the last, the beginning and the end" (Rev. 22:13; cf. Rev. 1:8, 17; 2:8; 21:6).

May we worship this being who is so other than ourselves!

God Has Created All Things

God ought to be worshiped because he has created all things. The twenty-four elders cast their crowns before the throne, saying, "Worthy are you, our Lord and God, to receive glory and honor and power, for you created all things, and by your will they existed and were created" (Rev. 4:10-11). When the book of Revelation says "all things," it means everything—the heavens, the earth, and everything in them. Since we live on the earth, this includes us. We owe our existence to him.

God created everything *by his will*. God did not need us. God was not incomplete without us. Rather, God chose to bring creation into existence simply because he wanted to. We owe our existence to God. Not simply our coming into existence but our continuing existence. If God were to forget about us but for a moment, we would cease to exist. We continually draw our existence from God. Whereas God is self-existent and dependent upon no one, we continually draw our existence from God and are completely dependent upon him. God is the source of our life and being.

God created everything *for himself*. God created everything to bring him glory and honor and power. This is our purpose in life. We are most fulfilled when we are glorifying God, and we are most frustrated when we are not. In the book of Revelation, those who worship God are able to recognize the Beast for who he is, foil his schemes, and ultimately eat from the Tree of Life; but the inhabitants of the earth are deceived by the Antichrist, fight against the Lamb, and are ultimately cast into the lake of fire.

May we acknowledge the One who created us and fulfill the purpose for which we were created!

God Has Redeemed Us

God ought to be worshiped because he has redeemed us from our sins. The four living creatures and the twenty-four elders sang a new song, saying, "Worthy are you to take the scroll and to open its seals, for you were slain, and by your blood you ransomed people for God from every tribe and language and people and nation, and you have made them a kingdom and priests to our God, and they shall reign on the earth" (Rev. 5:9-10).

While our sins condemn us, Christ's blood acquits us. While we were caught up in the sins of this world—idolatry, murder, sorcery, sexual immorality, theft, and falsehood—Christ broke these bonds that enslaved us and made us priests to God. While we were worthy of the judgment described in the pages of Revelation—the seals, the trumpets, and the bowls of wrath—God has exempted us from these judgments and extended to us the citizenship of his kingdom.

May we often remember what we were saved *from* that we may remember what we were saved *to!* We were saved to bring grateful, heartfelt worship to God.

God Will Judge the Earth

God ought to be worshiped because he will judge the earth. An angel flew directly overhead and proclaimed an eternal gospel to every nation and tribe and language and people: "Fear God and give him glory, because the hour of his judgment has come" (Rev. 14:6-7).

God will judge the earth because of its refusal to worship him. The inhabitants of the earth will be subjected to the seven bowls of God's wrath because "they did not repent and give him glory" (Rev. 16:9; cf. Rev. 16:10-11, 21). The great prostitute will be destroyed in a single day because "she glorified herself and lived in luxury" (Rev. 18:7). The Beast and the False Prophet will be thrown alive into the lake of fire because they deceived the world into worshiping the Beast (Rev. 19:20). Moreover, all idolaters—those who directed their worship to anyone or anything but God—will find their final resting place, outside of the New Jerusalem, in the lake that burns with fire and sulfur (Rev. 21:8; 22:15).

God will not share his glory with another, and God will not tolerate those who divert the glory that is due his name. This is why, when the apostle John bowed before his angelic guide, the angel corrected John: "You must not do that! I am a fellow servant with you and your brothers who hold to the testimony of Jesus. Worship God" (Rev. 19:10; cf. Rev. 22:8-9).

May we render to God what rightfully belongs to God!

God Will Triumph Victoriously

God ought to be worshiped because he will triumph victoriously. Though the Antichrist will wield incredible power for a time, his reign will be short (Rev. 12:12) and his end, sure (Rev. 20:1-2, 10).

Christ will ride into history, mounted on a white horse, eyes burning with fire, head crowned with diadems, body clothed in a blood-stained robe, the armies of heaven following, and a sword emerging from his mouth (Rev. 19:11-16). He will strike down the nations (Rev. 19:15). He will tread the winepress of the fury of the wrath of God the Almighty (Rev. 14:19-20; 19:15). And he will destroy the kingdom of the Antichrist in a single day (Rev. 18). Then, he will establish his own kingdom where righteousness and justice will prevail (Rev. 11:15-18; 20:4).

No matter how disorderly society may get, we have this assurance from Scripture: The Lord our God the Almighty reigns.

Thus, the voice of a great multitude in heaven will cry out, "Hallelujah! Salvation and glory and power belong to our God, for his judgments are true and just; for he has judged the great prostitute who corrupted the earth with her immorality, and has avenged on her the blood of his servants" (Rev. 19:1-2).

Thus, the great multitude will cry out again, "Hallelujah! The smoke from her goes up forever and ever" (Rev. 19:3).

Thus, the twenty-four elders and the four living creatures will voice their agreement, "Amen. Hallelujah!" (Rev. 19:4).

Thus, a voice from the throne will say, "Praise our God, all you his servants, you who fear him, small and great" (Rev. 19:5).

Thus, the great multitude will conclude, "Hallelujah! For the Lord our God the Almighty reigns" (Rev. 19:6).

While the benefit of worshiping God may not be apparent or pleasant now, particularly in light of the coming tribulation, we have this assurance: God will triumph victoriously. The kingdom of this world will become the kingdom of our Lord and of his Christ (Rev. 11:15).

May our vision be far-sighted, may we see the final outcome, and may we voice our congratulations to the ultimate Victor!

The Worship of the Lamb

God will not share his glory with another, nor will he tolerate those who divert the glory that is due his name; yet, a remarkable incident is recorded in the fifth chapter of Revelation. A Lamb enters the heavenly scene and stands at the center of the throne room without any opposition from the court, without any confusion as to the object of heaven's worship, and without any diminution of the glory due to him who is seated on the throne. There, the Lamb stands in the front of the heavenly congregation, between the throne and the four living creatures and among the elders (Rev. 5:6).

This Lamb did not wander in by mistake, but his arrival was announced to the court. A strong angel asks the heavenly court, "Who is worthy to open the scroll and break its seals?" (Rev. 5:2). When no one in heaven, on earth, or under the earth is found, the apostle John begins to weep. Then one of the elders announces the arrival of the Lamb: "Weep no more; behold, the Lion of the tribe of Judah, the Root of David, has conquered, so that he can open the scroll and its seven seals" (Rev. 5:5). When John looks up, he sees the Lamb standing, front and center. A mistake might be excusable, but this incident was intentional.

Moreover, the Lamb is not simply standing there; he becomes the object of heaven's praise. Myriads of myriads and thousands of thousands of angels are all around, shouting in one voice, "Worthy is *the Lamb* who was slain, to receive power and wealth and wisdom and might and honor and glory and blessing!" (Rev. 5:11-12, italics mine). The whole cosmos erupts in praise: "To him who sits on the throne *and to the Lamb* be blessing and honor and glory and might forever and ever!" (Rev. 5:13, italics mine). And the four living creatures echo, "Amen!" and the twenty-four elders fall down and worship (Rev. 5:14).

Wow! He who sits on the throne, he who does not tolerate the worship of any other, approves of the worship of the Lamb. Such acceptance by the heavenly court affirms the divine nature of the Lamb.

Two Divine Persons

The One seated on the throne and the Lamb that was slain are both divine. For this reason, the book of Revelation will often categorize them together.

Consider the following references:

> Then the kings of the earth and the great ones and the generals and the rich and the powerful, and everyone, slave and free, hid themselves in the caves and among the rocks of the mountains, calling to the mountains and rocks, "Fall on us and hide us *from the face of him who is seated on the throne, and from the wrath of the Lamb*, for the great day of their wrath has come, and who can stand?" Rev. 6:15-17 (italics mine)

> After this I looked, and behold, a great multitude that no one could number, from every nation, from all tribes and peoples and languages, standing *before the throne and before the Lamb*, clothed in white robes, with palm branches in their hands, and crying out with a loud voice, "Salvation belongs *to our God who sits on the throne, and to the Lamb!*" Rev. 7:9-10 (italics mine)

> [The 144,000 servants] have been redeemed from mankind as firstfruits *for God and the Lamb*, and in their mouth no lie was found, for they are blameless. Rev. 14:4-5 (italics mine)

> And I saw no temple in the city, for its temple is *the Lord God the Almighty and the Lamb*. And the city has no need of sun or moon to shine on it, for *the glory of God gives it light, and its lamp is the Lamb*. Rev. 21:22-23 (italics mine)

> No longer will there be anything accursed, but *the throne of God and of the Lamb* will be in it, and his servants will worship him. Rev. 22:3 (italics mine)

For this same reason, Jesus the Lamb of God accepts worship from the apostle John. Whereas the angelic guide deflects the worship of John and instructs him to "Worship God" (Rev. 19:10; 22:8-9), Jesus exercises his divine authority and extends his arm to the awestruck apostle. The apostle John wrote, "When I saw him, I fell at his feet as though dead. But he laid his right hand on me, saying, 'Fear not, I am the first and the last, and the living one. I died, and behold I am alive forevermore, and I have the keys of Death and Hades'" (Rev. 1:17-18).

One Divine Essence

Lest we think there are two gods—the One seated on the throne and the Lamb that was slain—the book of Revelation makes it clear that there is only one God.

Consider the following verses that all speak of a singular God who is to be worshiped:

> And [the angel flying overhead] said with a loud voice, "Fear God [singular noun] and give him glory, because the hour of his judgment has come, and worship him who made heaven and earth, the sea and the springs of water." Rev. 14:7

> And from the throne came a voice saying, "Praise our God [singular noun], all you his servants, you who fear him small and great." Rev. 19:5

> Then I [the apostle John] fell down at his feet to worship [the angel], but he said to me, "You must not do that! I am a fellow servant with you and your brothers who hold to the testimony of Jesus. Worship God [singular noun]." Rev. 19:10

Other verses to note include Revelation 7:11-12; 11:16-17; 15:3-4; 19:1-2, 4-5; 22:8-9.

This heavenly picture of the One seated on a throne and of the Lamb that was slain teaches us that there is a plurality of persons within the one divine being. There is but one God, and he alone is to be worshiped forever. The One seated on the throne is assumed to be divine, and the Lamb that was slain is depicted as divine. The divine nature of the Lamb in no way diminishes the glory of the One seated on the throne; rather, it prompts even more praise for God's redemptive work. Every creature in heaven and on earth and under the earth proclaim, "To him who sits on the throne and to the Lamb be blessing and honor and glory and might forever and ever!" (Rev. 5:13).

Implications for Worship

That the Lamb is divine has significant implications as it relates to the command to worship God.

The command to worship God is not a call to worship some generic god acceptable to any man's religion or imagination. Rather, the command to worship God is a call to worship Jesus Christ in particular. For this reason, the Jews of the first century, despite the fact that they were monotheistic and shared the same religious heritage as Christians, are called "a synagogue of Satan" (Rev. 2:9). Although they claimed to be Jews and, by birth, they were Jews, Jesus calls them "liars" because they had rejected him as the Christ (Rev. 3:9).

Lest we think any belief in a divine being fulfills the command to worship God, let us be reminded that only the worship of Jesus Christ, the Lamb of God, as revealed in Scripture is acceptable in God's eyes. Jesus Christ needs to be at the center of our worship.

Take Your Stand
ΑΩ

Although everyone is commanded to worship God, not everyone will worship God.

The inhabitants of the earth will not worship God. Rather than worship the true and living God, the inhabitants of the earth will worship demons and objects of gold, silver, bronze, stone, and wood, figures which cannot see, hear, or walk. For this reason, God will pour out his righteous judgment. Even under the judgment of God, people will still choose to curse rather than glorify God (Rev. 9:20-21; 16:9, 21).

The Antichrist will not worship God. The Antichrist will rise out of the sea and challenge rather than submit to God's authority. He will speak haughty and blasphemous words. He will defy God's commands, and he will curse God's people. He will imitate Christ's death and resurrection, and he will proclaim himself to be God (Rev. 13:1, 5-6; cf. 2 Thess. 2:3-4).

The False Prophet will not worship God. The False Prophet will rise out of the earth and redirect people's devotion away from God and to the Antichrist (Rev. 13:11-14). His activity is not arbitrary but deliberate. He will use miraculous signs to deceive the earth, so that people will not worship God but fall under the judgment of God (Rev. 19:20).

The great prostitute will not worship God. The great prostitute who rides on the scarlet beast does not glorify God but herself. She proudly boasts, "I sit as a queen, I am no widow, and mourning I shall never see" (Rev. 18:7). Refusing to acknowledge her dependence upon God, she commits all kinds of abominations against him (Rev. 17:4-5).

And, of course, Satan will not worship God. Satan has been opposed to God's plans from the beginning (Gen. 3). He is the one who sought to kill Jesus (Rev. 12:3-4). He is the one who sought to kill Jesus' mother (Rev. 12:13-14). He is the one who seeks to kill Jesus' brothers and sisters (Rev. 12:17; cf. Rev. 2:9, 13; 3:9). He is the source of power behind the strength of the Antichrist (Rev. 13:2), and he is the mastermind behind the deception of the False Prophet (Rev. 20:2-3, 7-8, 10). For his rebellion, Satan will be cast into the lake of fire. There, he will be tormented day and night forever and ever (Rev. 20:10).

The Demand of the Antichrist

The Antichrist will demand that everyone worship him instead of God. Empowered by Satan, the Antichrist will wield great authority over the earth (Rev. 13:1-2). When he is opposed and dealt a mortal wound, he will miraculously recover to the amazement of the world. People will think that he is indestructible, if not immortal (Rev. 13:3-4). Riding on the elation of the people, the Antichrist will become haughty and speak blasphemous words. He will proclaim himself to be God and utter blasphemies against God and those who follow him (Rev. 13:5-6). He will demand that everyone worship him, and he will pursue and kill anyone who does not (Rev. 13:7-8).

The False Prophet will erect an image of the Antichrist and demand that everyone worship it. Exercising all the authority of the Antichrist, the False Prophet will support the Antichrist in his initiatives and command the inhabitants of the earth to worship the Antichrist (Rev. 13:11-12). Performing miraculous signs, even making fire come down from heaven to earth, the False Prophet will deceive the inhabitants of the earth and compel them to erect an image of the Antichrist (Rev. 13:13-14). He will breathe life into this image so that it can talk and put to death those who refuse to worship the Antichrist (Rev. 13:15).

The False Prophet will require that everyone accept a mark on their right hand or forehead, without which they cannot buy or sell (Rev. 13:16-17). This mark does not simply serve as a convenient means for conducting financial transactions, but it serves as a distinguishing mark of those who worship the Antichrist (Rev. 13:18). This mark will force everyone to make a decision as to whose side they are on. People will no longer be able to keep their personal faith private but will have to declare it publicly. Christians will no longer be able to live a quiet and peaceable life, but they will be singled out and/or forced to go into hiding.

Refuse the Mark

Although the Antichrist will demand that we worship him, the book of Revelation commands us not to worship the Beast, to bow down to his image, or to receive his mark. No matter the pressure, we must continue to worship God and him alone. The warning is clear: to worship the Antichrist is to forfeit our soul.

Revelation 13:8 declares that everyone whose name has not been written in the Lamb's Book of Life will worship the Beast. In other words, all unbelievers will worship the Beast. Only believers will refuse to worship the Beast. Thus, this verse gives assurance of salvation only to those who do not worship the Antichrist. This is a firm admonition to us not to worship the Antichrist.

Revelation 13:18 instructs us to calculate the number of the Beast. To calculate the number of the Beast means to identify the Antichrist when he comes. This instruction is not without reason. We are to identify the Antichrist, so that we do not worship him.

Revelation 14:9-11 tells us that anyone who worships the Beast, bows down to its image, or receives its mark will drink the wine of God's wrath. Such a person will be tormented with fire and sulfur in the presence of God, and the smoke of their torment will continually go up forever. They will have no rest day or night, but they will feel the horror of the torment every moment. This foresight into the future state of the unbeliever is another admonition to us not to worship the Beast.

Revelation 20:4-6 teaches us the fate of those who *chose* to worship the Beast and the fate of those who *refused* to worship the Beast. Those who *refused* to worship the Beast will come to life and reign with Christ for a thousand years (Rev. 20:4). In contrast, the rest of the dead—those who *chose* to worship the Beast—will be raised to life a thousand years later, face the great white throne judgment, and be thrown into the lake of fire (Rev. 20:5, 12, 15). Thus, the author declares, "Blessed and holy is the one who shares in the first resurrection! Over such the second death has no power, but they will be priests of God and of Christ" (Rev. 20:6).

Revelation 21:8 teaches us that the cowardly and the faithless will be excluded from the new earth. While being fearful and faithless may not seem like big sins to us (we may not even consider these characteristics to be "sins"), these two sins are given the prominent place on the list. The cowardly and faithless are those who recognized right from wrong but were too afraid to do anything about it. They may have initially opposed the wrong; but, as the intensity of the persecution increased, wavered in their faith and gave up.

Who Is the Beast?

The command not to worship the Beast begs the question, "Who is the Beast?"

There are two dangers when reading the book of Revelation: ignoring the book altogether because we think it cannot be understood, or obsessing over the details because we think we can figure it all out. As I answer this question, I hope to walk the fine line between these two dangers. I will focus on what the Scripture says about the Antichrist and refuse to speculate about what the Scripture does not say about the same. Such parameters will help us filter out a lot of nonsense that takes place in the name of biblical prophecy.

The book of Revelation does not identify the Antichrist by name; rather, it focuses on the characteristics that will help us identify the Antichrist when he comes. Since we cannot positively identify the Antichrist, we should steer clear of anyone who exhibits these characteristics. The reality is that there are many antichrists who will arise throughout the course of history. All of these antichrists anticipate and lead up to the one final eschatological Antichrist described in the book of Revelation (1 John 2:18, 22; 4:2-3; 2 John 1:7). We need to avoid them all.

Worldwide Authority

The Beast will possess worldwide authority. Empowered by Satan, the Antichrist will wield great authority over the earth. He will be as quick as a leopard, strong as a bear, and ferocious as a lion (Rev. 13:2). Amazed by his authority and awestruck by his indestructibility, the whole world will follow him (Rev. 13:3-4). Though he will directly rule over a federation of ten countries, his influence and authority will extend to every nation on earth. All the leaders of the world will be in league with him.

Divine Proclamation

The Beast will proclaim himself to be God. During his rise to power, the Antichrist will be opposed and dealt a mortal wound. To the amazement of the world, he will miraculously recover. Having survived certain death, the Antichrist will come to think of himself as not simply indestructible but immortal, if not divine (Rev. 13:3-4). In his pride and arrogance, he will square off with God and utter all kinds of blasphemies, even proclaiming himself to be God (Rev. 13:5-6). And God will grant him this freedom for a time.

Systematic Persecution

The Beast will seek out, arrest, and kill Christians (Rev. 13:7-8). Christians will be hated for two reasons.

First, Christians will be hated because they bear the name of Christ. Because the Antichrist is diametrically opposed to the Lamb of God, the Antichrist will pursue anyone who associates with the Lamb. Thrown out of heaven and unable to touch the woman or her son, the dragon "went off to make war on the rest of her offspring, on those who keep the commandments of God and hold to the testimony of Jesus" (Rev. 12:17).

Second, Christians will be hated because they refuse to worship the Antichrist or bow down to his image. Infuriated by the insubordination of Christians, he will launch a coordinated attack against Christians and seek to destroy them (Rev. 13:7-8, 13-15); and, for a time, he will succeed. The book of Revelation attests to the martyrdom of the saints (Rev. 6:9-11; 11:7-8; 12:17; 13:7-8, 15; 14:13; 16:5-6; 17:6; 18:24; 19:1-2).

Unrestrained Lawlessness

The Beast will be characterized by lawlessness. Having been thrown out of heaven and knowing his time is short, the dragon will hold nothing back and use any means to accomplish his purposes (Rev. 12:9, 12). The Antichrist will care nothing for the kingdom of God or his righteousness, for he has thrown off the rightful authority of the One seated on the throne of heaven. The kingdom of the Antichrist will be marked by idolatry, murder, sorcery, sexual immorality, theft, falsehood, to name a few. For this reason, the apostle Paul calls the Antichrist, "the man of lawlessness" (2 Thess. 2:3-4).

Unyielding Demand

The Beast will demand that everyone worship him. The Antichrist will settle for nothing less than single-hearted allegiance to himself, and he will threaten with death anyone who refuses to give him such allegiance (Rev. 13:7-8). Through the False Prophet, he will erect an image of himself and demand that everyone bow down to it (Rev. 13:13-15). And he will fashion a mark that will publicly identify a person with his regime, and he will require everyone to receive this mark (Rev. 13:16-17).

Sovereign Control

The Beast will rule over a totalitarian state. The Antichrist will not care about the rights of the individual; rather, the Antichrist will be engrossed in his own success and preservation. He will control all aspects of life, including who people worship and what people can buy and sell. Through the False Prophet, the Antichrist will require everyone to receive a mark on the right hand or forehead that will enable him to manage the individual affairs of everyone (Rev. 13:16-17). People will be but a pawn in his match against God.

What Is the Mark?

The command not to receive the mark of the Beast begs the question, "What is the mark?"

Many Christians have sought to identify the mark of the Beast. Some believe the mark will be some type of universal identification system, similar to the social security system in the United States. Others believe it refers to the cashless society to which we are moving, where all of our money is stored digitally. Still others point to biochip implants that may be used to conduct business transactions or store medical records. While all these suggestions may accomplish the function of the mark as described in the book of Revelation, they fail to accomplish the purpose of the mark.

The purpose of the mark is to identify a person with the Antichrist and his kingdom. We would be better served if we thought of the mark as a sign, symbol, or emblem that represents the ideology of the Antichrist. The mark is more akin to a flag, banner, or pennant that publicly displays one's allegiance to a political party, state, or country. There is nothing hidden or private about it. It is an open show of one's support and loyalty.

The secondary purpose of the mark is to call people to make a decision about the Antichrist. When people are offered the mark, they will know what the mark is and what it stands for. They will understand that receiving the mark means aligning oneself with the Antichrist. People will have to make a choice. They will have to decide whether or not to support the Antichrist. No one, in this sense, will be deceived. People will not receive the mark by mistake.

In short, "the mark of the beast will be a *recognizable* sign of those who have *voluntarily* chosen to follow the Antichrist."[39]

Some Practical Advice

Our private faith will one day have public ramifications. We will no longer have the freedom to worship as our conscience would dictate. We will be forced to make a decision. Do we violate our conscience and worship the Beast, or do we violate public policy and worship God? For some, this will be a difficult decision, for they have never taken a public stand to this point. For others, this will be an easy decision, for it has been the pattern of their lives. As we prepare for the future, allow me to offer some practical advice.

First, take a stand now while the stakes are low. When I was a child and earned my first dollar, I gave a tithe of ten cents to the Lord and did not think much of it. Ten cents, though significant to the Lord, did not cost me much. As I grew older, this tithe grew with my income. Today, I do not think much about the amount of money I give away. Why? Because giving has been the pattern of my life. If, however, I had not started giving as a child, this story would be much different. If I were asked to give a tithe of my income as an adult, I would be challenged. That's a lot of money. Thus, Jesus said to his disciples, "only with difficulty will a rich person enter the kingdom of heaven" (Matt. 19:23).

Take Your Stand

Similarly, I challenge you to take a stand now while the stakes are low. While we may experience some resistance now, it will be nothing compared to the opposition we will face during the tribulation. As Christians living in the United States, we can escape most forms of persecution by keeping a low profile. For many of us, verbal ridicule is about the extent of the persecution that we will face. If we take a stand today against some of the ills, philosophies, and unbelief in our generation, we will be better equipped to handle persecution later when more is at stake.

Second, take a stand now while the potential for impact is high. In the United States, Christians have a great opportunity to impact our world for Christ. As citizens, we have many freedoms guaranteed to us in the First Amendment of the Constitution. We have the freedom of speech, the freedom of the press, the right to peaceably assemble, and the right to petition our government.

Furthermore, we live in a culture that predominately declares itself to be Christian. Seventy-seven percent of the population professes to be Christian, at least in name. Fifty-one percent is Protestant, twenty-four percent is Roman Catholic, and two percent is other Christian.[40] The opportunity is great. The question is, "Do we take advantage of it?"

On January 6, 1946, Martin Niemöller spoke to the representatives of the Confessing Church in Frankfurt, Germany. In his speech, he challenged the Confessing Church to speak out against the atrocities of the Nazi regime:

> First they came for the Jews and I did not speak out because I was not a Jew. Then they came for the Communists and I did not speak out because I was not a Communist. Then they came for the trade unionists and I did not speak out because I was not a trade unionist. Then they came for me and there was no one left to speak out for me.[41]

Let us accept Niemöller's challenge and learn from his experience. Let us speak up while we have the freedoms to support us, and let us speak out while we have others to encourage us. We may not always have these benefits.

Third, keep an eye out for anyone who exhibits the characteristics of the Antichrist and oppose him. Similarly, watch out for anything that exhibits the characteristics of his mark and refuse it. Though we may have to suffer for such a stand, the eternal reward will far exceed the cost.

Hold to the Testimony
ΑΩ

The book of Revelation describes Christians as those who hold to the testimony of Jesus. The apostle John was exiled to the island of Patmos because he held to the testimony of Jesus (Rev. 1:9). The souls under the altar had been slain because of the testimony to which they held (Rev. 6:9). The two prophetic witnesses were killed because of the testimony which they bore (Rev. 11:7-8). The brothers of those in heaven overcame the accuser by the word of their testimony (Rev. 12:10-11). The children of the woman clothed with the sun were pursued by the dragon because they held to the testimony of Jesus (Rev. 12:17). The spiritual brothers of the apostle John are described as those who hold to the testimony of Jesus (Rev. 19:10). And the souls that reign with Christ for a thousand years had been beheaded because they held to the testimony of Jesus (Rev. 20:4).

If Christians are described as those who hold to the testimony of Jesus, then we as Christians should hold to the testimony of Jesus. Before we can *hold* to the testimony of Jesus, we must *understand* what the testimony of Jesus is. Let us consider for a moment this question: "What *is* the testimony of Jesus?"

The Testimony of Jesus

The phrase "the testimony of Jesus" may be understood grammatically in one of two ways. First, "Jesus" may be understood as the subject of "the testimony." As such, the phrase could be translated "the testimony which Jesus bore." Second, "Jesus" may be understood as the object of "the testimony." As such, the phrase could be translated "the testimony that others bore about Jesus." To help us decide which of these two options is meant, we must look for clues given in the text.

There are at least three clues that suggest that Jesus should be considered the subject of the phrase "the testimony of Jesus." First, Jesus is portrayed as the witness of God's revelation. He is the revelatory agent through whom God has made known the things that are to come (Rev. 1:1-2, 5; 3:14; 22:16, 20). Second, the phrase "the testimony of Jesus" is used in parallel with the phrases "the word of God" (Rev. 1:2, 9; 6:9; 20:4) and "the commandments of God" (Rev. 12:17). As God is the subject of his word and the giver of his commands, so Jesus is the bearer of his testimony. Lastly, the apostle John uses a similar phrase in 1 John 5:9 where he contrasts "the testimony of God" with "the testimony of man." In this verse, God is clearly the subject of the testimony.

These clues lead us to the conclusion that Jesus is the subject, not the object, of the testimony. As such, the testimony of Jesus refers to the testimony that Jesus bore. This leads us to another question: "If the testimony of Jesus refers to the testimony that Jesus bore, what is the testimony that Jesus bore?"

The Testimony That Jesus Bore

The testimony that Jesus bore sometimes refers to the book of Revelation. From the prologue, we read that God gave this message to Jesus so that he might deliver it to his servants (Rev. 1:1-2). Jesus, in turn, passed on this message to John through his angel (Rev. 22:16, 20). John completed the transmission of the message by bearing witness to all that he saw, that is, the testimony of Jesus (Rev. 1:1-2). In this sense, Jesus is a faithful witness to the prophetic word of God as given in the book of Revelation (Rev. 1:4-5; 3:14).

The testimony that Jesus bore refers more broadly to everything to which Jesus testified. We know this from those occasions in which "the testimony of Jesus" is used in parallel with "the word of God" (Rev. 1:1-2, 9; 6:9; 20:4) and with "the commandments of God" (Rev. 12:17). As the word of God and the commandments of God encompass more than what is contained in the book of Revelation, so the testimony of Jesus goes beyond what he has revealed in the book of Revelation.

Furthermore, the apostle John was exiled to the island of Patmos because of "the testimony of Jesus," yet he wrote the book of Revelation from the island of Patmos (Rev. 1:9). Obviously, John could not have been referring to the book itself. The same might be said of the souls under the altar (Rev. 6:9), those who are pursued by the dragon (Rev. 12:17), and those who had been beheaded (Rev. 20:4). They were afflicted because of their commitment, not to the book of Revelation specifically, but to everything to which Jesus testified.

To find out the extent of the testimony of Jesus, we must turn back to the Gospels and listen to his teaching.

The Teaching of Jesus

The testimony of Jesus refers to everything to which Jesus testified. From the Gospels, we can learn the extent of the testimony of Jesus.

Jesus testified that he was the Christ, the Son of the living God. Jesus began his public ministry by going to the synagogue, reading from the scroll of Isaiah about the redemptive work of the Messiah (the Messiah would bring sight to the blind, freedom to the oppressed, and good news to the poor), and declaring publicly, "Today this Scripture has been fulfilled in your hearing" (Luke 4:21). When John the Baptist (who had denied that he himself was the Messiah but pointed to Jesus as the Messiah) doubted, he sent an envoy to Jesus to ask if he really was the Messiah. Jesus responded, "Go and tell John what you have seen and heard: The blind receive their sight, the lame walk, lepers are cleansed, and the deaf hear, the dead are raised up, the poor have good news preached to them" (Luke 7:22). When Jesus asked his disciples, "Who do you say that I am?" and Peter responded, "You are the Christ, the Son of the living God," Jesus stated that God had revealed this truth to Peter (Matt. 16:16-17). And when Caiaphas the high priest demanded Jesus to say in court whether he was the Christ, Jesus declared boldly that, the next time Caiaphas saw him, Jesus would be sitting at the right hand of God and riding on the clouds of heaven (Matt. 26:64).

Jesus testified that the Christ must first suffer many hardships and then enter into his glory. Once the disciples understood that Jesus was the Christ, Jesus began to correct their misconceptions about the role of the Messiah. Jesus began to show his disciples that he must go to

Jerusalem and suffer many hardships from the elders and chief priests and scribes, and be killed, and on the third day be raised (Matt. 16:21). As they were gathering in Galilee, Jesus said to them, "The Son of Man is about to be delivered into the hands of men, and they will kill him, and he will be raised on the third day" (Matt. 17:22-23). And again, as they were going up to Jerusalem, Jesus said to them, "See, we are going up to Jerusalem. And the Son of Man will be delivered over to the chief priests and scribes, and they will condemn him to death and deliver him over to the Gentiles to be mocked and flogged and crucified, and he will be raised on the third day" (Matt. 20:17-19).

Jesus testified that repentance and forgiveness of sins would be proclaimed in his name. Although Jesus had prepared his disciples for his suffering and death, they were disillusioned when it happened. They still did not understand. Their grief was expressed in the words of the two disciples on the road to Emmaus: "We had hoped that he was the one to redeem Israel" (Luke 24:21). Patiently, Jesus once again walked them through the pages of Scripture and explained to them why it was necessary for the Christ to suffer these things and then enter into his glory (Luke 24:25-27). The Messiah endured this suffering so that the Scriptures might be fulfilled and "repentance and forgiveness of sins should be proclaimed in his name to all nations, beginning from Jerusalem" (Luke 24:46-47).

To summarize, Jesus testified that he was the Christ, the Son of the living God. As the Christ, Jesus testified that he must suffer many hardships and then enter into his glory. After he rose from the dead, Jesus testified that repentance and faith would be proclaimed in his name. In short, the testimony of Jesus refers to the gospel of Jesus Christ. This is the testimony of Jesus.

The Testimony of Others

The testimony of Jesus is the testimony that others confirmed.

While Jesus was on earth, he understood that his testimony was insufficient by itself (John 5:31). Although he knew his testimony was true, the law required multiple witnesses to confirm the truth (Deut. 19:15; John 8:14-18). With this in mind, Jesus brought forward others who could testify that his own testimony was true.

John the Baptist bore witness to Jesus. Jesus said, "You sent to John, and he has borne witness to the truth. Not that the testimony that I receive is from man, but I say these things so that you may be saved. He was a burning and shining lamp, and you were willing to rejoice for a while in his light" (John 5:33-35). When John was baptizing in the Jordan and saw Jesus, he shouted out, "Behold, the Lamb of God, who takes away the sin of the world! This is he of whom I said, 'After me comes a man who ranks before me, because he was before me.' I myself did not know him, but for this purpose I came baptizing with water, that he might be revealed to Israel...And I have seen and have borne witness that this is the Son of God" (John 1:29-31, 34, cf. John 3:25-30).

Jesus' miraculous works bore witness to Jesus. Jesus said, "But the testimony that I have is greater than that of John. For the works that the Father has given me to accomplish, the very works that I am doing, bear witness about me that the Father has sent me" (John 5:36; cf. John 2:11; 20:30-31). The man whose blind eyes Jesus had healed recognized this witness. To the Pharisees, he declared, "Whether [Jesus] is a sinner I do not know. One thing I do know, that though I was blind, now I see" (John 9:25).

God the Father bore witness to Jesus. Jesus said, "And the Father who sent me has himself borne witness about me. His voice you have never heard, his form you have never seen, and you do not have his word abiding in you, for you do not believe the one whom he has sent" (John 5:37-38). On at least two occasions, God the Father spoke from heaven confirming his Son: once, at the baptism of Jesus; and again, at his transfiguration. God said, "This is my beloved Son, with whom I am well pleased" (Matt. 3:16-17; 17:5).

The Scriptures bore witness to Jesus. Jesus said, "You search the Scriptures because you think that in them you have eternal life; and it is they that bear witness about me, yet you refuse to come to me that you may have life" (John 5:39-40). Jesus went on to say, "Do not think that I will accuse you to the Father. There is one who accuses you: Moses, on whom you have set your hope. For if you believed Moses, you would believe me; for he wrote of me" (John 5:45-46; cf. Luke 16:19-31, esp. vv. 29-31).

The Spirit bore witness to Jesus. Jesus said, "But when the Helper comes, whom I will send to you from the Father, the Spirit of truth, who proceeds from the Father, he will bear witness about me" (John 15:26; cf. John 14:25-26; 16:12-14). This was apparent at Pentecost, when the Spirit took the form of a rushing wind and tongues of fire, and he filled the disciples, and they spoke about the mighty works of God in foreign languages (Acts 2:1-4).

And the disciples bore witness to Jesus. Speaking to his disciples, Jesus said, "And you also will bear witness, because you have been with me from the beginning" (John 15:27; cf. Matt. 28:16-20; Mark 16:14-16; Luke 24:44-49, esp. v. 48).

The Testimony of the Apostles

The testimony of Jesus is the testimony that the apostles proclaimed.

The apostles confessed that Jesus is the Christ. At Pentecost, Peter stood up and confessed before a crowd of religious Jews and Gentile proselytes that God showed Jesus, whom they had crucified, both Lord and Christ (Acts 2:36). As Paul traveled from city to city, it was his custom to go to the synagogue each Sabbath and reason with the Jews from the Scriptures that Jesus was the Christ (Acts 17:2-3; 18:5). And the apostle John wrote his gospel with the express purpose that "you may believe that Jesus is the Christ, the Son of God, and that by believing you may have life in his name" (John 20:30-31).

The apostles bore witness to the historical reality of the death, burial, and resurrection of Jesus the Christ. After Jesus' ascension, Peter advised the rest of the disciples that they should select someone to replace Judas who had betrayed Jesus. This person had to have accompanied them since the baptism of John until Jesus' ascension, so that he might also become a witness to his resurrection (Acts 1:21-22). In his letter to the Corinthians, Paul provided a litany of people who had seen the resurrected Christ and completed his list by stating, "Last of all, as to one untimely born, he appeared also to me" (1 Cor. 15:8). And the apostle John began his first letter with these words: "That which was from the beginning, which we have heard, which we have seen with our eyes, which we looked upon and have touched with our hands...we proclaim also to you" (1 John 1:1, 3).

The apostles proclaimed the theological significance of the death, burial, and resurrection of Jesus Christ. When the Jews and proselytes recognized their mistake in killing Christ, they asked Peter what they should do. Peter responded, "Repent and be baptized every one of you in the name of Jesus Christ for the forgiveness of your sins, and you will receive the gift of the Holy Spirit" (Acts 2:38). In his letter to the Romans, Paul wrote, "If you confess with your mouth that Jesus is Lord and believe in your heart that God raised him from the dead, you will be saved. For with the heart one believes and is justified, and with the mouth one confesses and is saved" (Rom. 10:9-10). And the apostle John penned that most beloved verse: "For God so loved the world, that he gave his only Son, that whoever believes in him should not perish but have eternal life" (John 3:16).

The Testimony We Have Received

The testimony of Jesus is the testimony that we have received.

The testimony to which Jesus bore witness, that others confirmed, and that the apostles proclaimed, we have received. The apostle Paul wrote, "Now I would remind you, brothers, of the gospel I preached to you, which you received, in which you stand, and by which you are being saved, if you hold fast to the word I preached to you—unless you believed in vain" (1 Cor. 15:1-2; cf. Gal. 1:6-9). Thus, Jesus exhorted the church in Sardis, "Remember, then, what you received and heard. Keep it, and repent" (Rev. 3:3).

The testimony of Jesus is the testimony to which we must hold. The book of Revelation exhorts us to hold to the testimony of Jesus. The basic meaning of the Greek word (ἔχω) that lays behind this exhortation is "to have, to hold." As it relates to physical objects, the word takes on the nuances of getting (acquisition), possessing (ownership), enjoying (freedom of use), and keeping (maintenance, protection). As it relates to immaterial objects, such as, the testimony of Jesus, it does not convey the idea of possession; rather, it indicates close association. In other words, we do not own the gospel message. Quite the opposite is true; it owns us (1 Cor. 6:19-20).

An apt analogy is the marriage covenant. In marriage, a man pledges himself to one woman for life and is privileged "to have and to hold" her from that day forward. A man is commanded to "leave his father and his mother and hold fast to his wife" (Gen. 2:24). The bond formed between a man and his wife is so tight that God no longer sees them as two people but one (Gen. 2:24). Moreover, Jesus declares, "What therefore God has joined together, let not man separate" (Matt. 19:6).

Similarly, we are to have and to hold the gospel of Jesus Christ. To take hold of the testimony of Jesus means to accept the historical fact of Christ's death, burial, and resurrection; to believe in the redemptive meaning of the historical facts—that Jesus died for our sins and was raised for our justification; and to live in the divine reality of these truths. Since we have taken hold of the gospel, we may embrace its benefits and must guard against losing it. To hold is to embrace and not let go.

Dangerous Threats

There are many dangers that threaten our hold of the testimony. Some of these dangers include false teaching, apathy/neglect, arrogance/pride, deception, temptation, and persecution.

False Teaching

The testimony of Jesus includes certain propositional truths that must be accepted. In a day that devalues theology, we must remember that what we believe affects how we live. Bad theology will lead us away from Christ and his testimony. Christ's exhortations to the churches make this point evident.

To the church in Pergamum, Jesus said:

> But I have a few things against you: you have some there *who hold the teaching of Balaam*, who taught Balak to put a stumbling block before the sons of Israel, so that they might eat food sacrificed to idols and practice sexual immorality. So also you have some *who hold the teaching of the Nicolaitans*. Therefore repent. If not, I will come to you soon and war against them with the sword of my mouth. Revelation 2:14-16 (italics mine)

And to the church in Thyatira, Jesus said:

> But I have this against you, that you *tolerate that woman Jezebel, who calls herself a prophetess and is teaching and seducing my servants to practice sexual immorality and to eat food sacrificed to idols.* I gave her time to repent, but she refuses to repent of her sexual immorality. Behold, I will throw her onto a sickbed, and those who commit adultery with her I will throw into great tribulation, unless they repent of her works, and I will strike her children dead. Revelation 2:20-22 (italics mine)

Apathy/Neglect

The testimony of Jesus must be kept alive. Neglect and apathy will cause us to loosen our grip on the testimony. Again, this is evident in the messages given to the churches.

To the church in Ephesus, Jesus said:

> But I have this against you, that *you have abandoned the love you had at first.* Remember therefore from where you have fallen; repent, and do the works you did at first. If not, I will come to you and remove your lampstand from its place, unless you repent. Revelation 2:4-5 (italics mine)

To the church in Sardis, Jesus said:

> I know your works. *You have the reputation of being alive, but you are dead.* Wake up, and strengthen what remains and is about to die, for I have not found your works complete in the sight of my God....If you will not wake up, I will come like a thief, and you will not know at what hour I will come against you. Revelation 3:1-3 (italics mine)

And to the church in Laodicea, Jesus said:

> I know your works: *you are neither cold nor hot.* Would that you were either cold or hot! So, because you are lukewarm, and neither hot nor cold, I will spit you out of my mouth....Those whom I love, I reprove and discipline, so be zealous and repent. Revelation 3:15-16, 19 (italics mine)

Arrogance/Pride

The testimony of Jesus must be accepted as it is, the word of God. We should not be so proud or arrogant to think we can selectively decide what we want to hear and/or add what we think is missing.

Jesus gives this stern warning in the epilogue of Revelation:

> I warn everyone who hears the words of the prophecy of this book: *if anyone adds to them*, God will add to him the plagues described in this book, and *if anyone takes away from the words of the book of this prophecy*, God will take away his share in the tree of life and in the holy city, which are described in this book. Revelation 22:18-19 (italics mine)

Deception

As we approach the end of time, lies and deception will abound. The Antichrist will make all kinds of arrogant claims and blasphemous statements. He will claim to be God, and he will blame the world's ills on Christ and his followers. Because of his unrestrained authority and apparent success, the world will flock after him (Rev. 13:5-8). Moreover, the False Prophet will perform such miraculous signs that, if it were possible, even the elect would be deceived. He will call fire down from heaven and breathe life into inanimate objects (Rev. 13:13-15).

In a world in which the testimony of Jesus will be intentionally ambiguous, distorted, or outright contradicted, Christians must be clear. This is the testimony to which we hold: Jesus died for our sins, was buried, and rose again; and by believing, you may have life in his name. Christians must know the One that they follow and follow no other. Christians must know that the Bible is our only infallible rule for faith and practice, and they must immerse themselves in its truths.

Temptation

Whereas deception will be from without, temptation will be from within. The Antichrist will rise, rule over the nations for forty-two months, and succeed in all that he does. He will pursue those who follow the Lamb and put them to death. He will amass for himself the wealth of the nations, and the merchants of the earth will grow rich from his business. He will sit arrayed in scarlet and purple, and he will be adorned with gold and jewels and pearls. As he pampers himself in his luxury, he will say in his heart, "I sit as a queen, I am no widow, and mourning I shall never see" (Rev. 18:7). And no one will be able to stand against him.

The temptation will be to loosen our grip on the testimony of Jesus. Dejected and alone, Christians will see the wicked prosper and the righteous suffer. They will question whether there is justice in the world. Seeing none, they will be tempted to let go of the testimony of Jesus. Nonetheless, we as Christians must not give up hope; we must remain strong. We must see the end from the present. We must remember that one day the kingdom of the Antichrist will come crashing down, never to rise again. The kingdom of the world will become the kingdom of our Lord and of his Christ, and he will reign forever and ever.

Persecution

As outlined in the previous chapter, the testimony of Jesus will be challenged. The Antichrist will rise and demand that everyone worship him, and we will be forced to make a decision. Which will we choose? Worshiping the Beast may bring temporal relief but will result in eternal damnation. Defying the Beast will bring temporal hardship but will pay eternal dividends.

To the church in Sardis, Jesus said:

> I know your tribulation and your poverty (but you are rich) and the slander of those who say that they are Jews and are not, but are a synagogue of Satan. Do not fear what you are about to suffer. Behold, the devil is about to throw some of you into prison, that you may be tested, and for ten days you will have tribulation. Be faithful unto death, and I will give you the crown of life. Rev. 2:9-10

And to the church in Philadelphia, Jesus said:

> I know that you have but little power, and yet you have kept my word and have not denied my name. Behold, I will make those of the synagogue of Satan who say that they are Jews and are not, but lie—behold, I will make

them come and bow down before your feet, and they will learn that I have loved you. Because you have kept my word about patient endurance, I will keep you from the hour of trial that is coming on the whole world, to try those who dwell on the earth. Rev. 3:8-10

Summary

The book of Revelation describes Christians as those who hold to the testimony of Jesus. Since we are Christians, we should be among those who hold to the testimony of Jesus.

The testimony of Jesus refers to everything to which Jesus testified about himself. During his life on earth, Jesus testified that he was the Christ. He testified that he would suffer, die, and rise again. And he testified that repentance and forgiveness of sins would be proclaimed in his name.

In short, the testimony of Jesus refers to the gospel of Jesus Christ. This testimony was confirmed by others, proclaimed by the apostles, and received by us.

Although many dangers threaten our hold of the testimony, we must hold firmly to the testimony and not let go.

Endure to the End
ΑΩ

It is not enough to have taken hold of the confession of Christ sometime in the past, nor is it enough to be holding the confession of Christ right now. What ultimately counts is that we are holding the confession of Christ at the end of our lives. No matter what obstacles or hardships we face, we must persist in our faith in Christ until he comes back or calls us home. Such endurance is a dominant theme throughout the book of Revelation.

The Seven Churches

In his messages to the churches in Asia, Jesus encourages each of them to conquer. The Greek word for "conquer" (νικάω) means to win the battle or to gain the victory. In Revelation 11:7, it is used to describe the Beast which fights against the two faithful witnesses. The Beast eventually gains the upper hand and successfully puts them to death. In Revelation 13:7, the word "conquer" is again used to describe the Beast which makes war on the saints and is able to put them to death. And, in Revelation 17:14, the word "conquer" is used to describe Christ who breaks into history with his heavenly armies, wars against the great prostitute, and triumphs over her, for "he is Lord of lords and King of kings." All this to say, to conquer means to go to war with the enemy, to endure a grueling fight for faith and righteousness, and to come out on top, that is, to be still holding our confession of faith.

The church in Ephesus was waging a war that was threatening their faith. Jesus commended them because they had "tested those who call themselves apostles and are not, and have found them to be false" (Rev. 2:2). They also had fought hard against "the works of the

Nicolaitans, which I also hate" (Rev. 2:6). In this context, Jesus commended their "toil" and "patient endurance" (Rev. 2:2), for "you are enduring patiently and bearing up for my name's sake, and you have not grown weary" (Rev. 2:3). And he promised, "To the one who conquers I will grant to eat of the tree of life, which is in the paradise of God" (Rev. 2:7).

The church in Smyrna was waging a war that was threatening their faith. Jesus acknowledged the tribulation, poverty, and slander they were facing because of their faith. They were facing "those who say they are Jews and are not" (Rev. 2:9). These Jews were, in fact, "a synagogue of Satan," for they refused to acknowledge Jesus as the Christ and had ostracized his followers. And life was not going to get better; rather, some of the Christians would be thrown into prison and even put to death. In this context, Jesus encouraged them, "Be faithful unto death, and I will give you the crown of life" (Rev. 2:10). And he promised, "The one who conquers will not be hurt by the second death" (Rev. 2:11).

The church in Pergamum was waging a war that was threatening their faith. Jesus commended them that they had not denied the faith in spite of the fact that one of their own members had been killed for his faithful witness (Rev. 2:13). Still, Jesus warned them of another threat: Some of them held "the teaching of Balaam," which leads to idolatry and sexual immorality (Rev. 2:15); and others held "the teaching of the Nicolaitans" (Rev. 2:14). From these teachings, Jesus told them that they needed to repent; otherwise, he himself would fight against them (Rev. 2:16). In this context, Jesus promised, "To the one who conquers I will give some of the hidden manna, and I will give him a white stone, with a new name written on the stone that no one knows except the one who receives it" (Rev. 2:17).

The church in Thyatira was waging a war that was threatening their faith. Jesus commended their "love and faith and service and patient endurance" (Rev. 2:19). Nonetheless, they were facing false teaching. They tolerated "that woman Jezebel, who calls herself a prophetess and is teaching and seducing my servants to practice sexual immorality and to eat food sacrificed to idols" (Rev. 2:20). Some of them had even taken hold of this teaching and had "learned what some call the deep things of Satan" (Rev. 2:24). In this context,

Jesus encouraged the rest of the believers to "hold fast what you have" (Rev. 2:25). And he promised, "The one who conquers and who keeps my works until the end, to him I will give authority over the nations, and he will rule them with a rod of iron" (Rev. 2:26-27).

The church in Sardis was waging a war that was threatening their faith. Jesus reminded them that they were their own worst enemies. Though they had a reputation of life, they were dead. Though they thought they were awake, they were in fact asleep. Though they were to clothe themselves in white, many of them had soiled their garments with unrighteousness. In this context, Jesus urged them to "Wake up, and strengthen what remains" (Rev. 3:2). And he promised, "The one who conquers will be clothed thus in white garments, and I will never blot his name out of the book of life" (Rev. 3:5).

The church in Philadelphia was waging a war that was threatening their faith. Jesus knew that they had been struggling for some time and only had a little strength left. Like the church in Smyrna, they were facing "those of the synagogue of Satan who say they are Jews and are not" (Rev. 3:9). In this context, Jesus commended their "patient endurance" and promised to keep them from "the hour of trial that is coming on the whole world" (Rev. 3:10). Still, he told them to "hold fast what you have [their faith in Christ], so that no may seize your crown" (Rev. 3:11). And he promised, "The one who conquers, I will make him a pillar in the temple of my God….and I will write on him the name of my God" (Rev. 3:12).

The church in Laodicea was waging a war that was threatening their faith. Jesus knew about their pathetic condition. They were neither hot nor cold, and he wished that they were one or the other. Because of their wretched condition, Jesus counseled the believers in Laodicea to buy from him gold, so that they might be rich; garments, so that they might be clothed; and ointment, so that they might be healed. In this context, Jesus promised, "The one who conquers, I will grant him to sit with me on my throne, as I also conquered and sat down with my Father on his throne" (Rev. 3:21).

This encouragement to conquer is not limited to the seven churches in Asia, but it is applied to all Christians in Revelation 21:7. After speaking about the blessings of the new heaven and the new earth, Jesus declared, "The one who conquers will have this heritage, and I will be his God and he will be my son. But as for the cowardly, the faithless, [those who do not conquer]...their portion will be in the lake that burns with fire and sulfur, which is the second death" (Rev. 21:7-8). May we hear the encouragement of Christ, and may we be found among those who conquer!

Victory Comes with a Fight

As we seek to be among those who conquer, remember that this victory does not come easily. Victory comes with a fight.

In Revelation 13:1-8, we read about the Antichrist who will rise and rule over the earth for three and a half years. During which time, he will incur a mortal wound and recover. As a result, the world will flock after him and think he is invincible, if not divine. He will make great boasts and even utter blasphemies against God. He will demand that everyone worship him and put to death those who do not. Those whose names are written in the Lamb's book of life will not worship the Beast.

In this context, we hear these words:

> If anyone has an ear, let him hear: If anyone is to be taken captive, to captivity he goes; if anyone is to be slain with the sword, with the sword must he be slain. Here is a call for the endurance and faith of the saints. Rev. 13:9-10

In Revelation 14:9-11, we hear about the demands of the False Prophet. He will require everyone to worship the image of the Beast and to receive a mark on their forehead or hand. But the angel flying overhead warns that, if anyone gives in, "he also will drink the wine of God's wrath, poured full strength into the cup of his anger, and he will be tormented with fire and sulfur in the presence of the holy angels and in the presence of the Lamb" (Rev. 14:10).

Again, we hear this encouragement:

> Here is a call for the endurance of the saints, those who keep the commandments of God and their faith in Jesus. Rev. 14:12

Victory Comes in Death

As we seek to be among those who conquer, remember that this victory may not necessarily come through life. Victory may come in death.

To conquer the Beast does not mean that we will be able to remove the Antichrist from power or put him to death. Quite the opposite is true. Twice we hear that the Antichrist will conquer the saints and put them to death (Rev. 11:7; 13:7). To conquer the Beast means that we will resist all of his efforts to destroy our faith. We will endure to the end. Though the Antichrist may be said to conquer us by killing us, we will in fact conquer him by holding firmly to our faith.

For this reason, heaven declares,

> "And [the brothers] have conquered him by the blood of the Lamb and by the word of their testimony, for they loved not their lives even unto death." Rev. 12:11

Jesus, the Faithful Witness

The book of Revelation contains many examples of people who have conquered through death. They include Antipas, God's faithful witness in Pergamum (Rev. 2:13); the souls under the altar who had been slain for the word of God (Rev. 6:9); the innumerable multitude standing before the throne (Rev. 7:9, 13-14); the two witnesses who prophesied in Jerusalem (Rev. 11:3, 7-11); those who were slain by the Beast, killed by his image, and/or conquered in their resistance (Rev. 13:7-10, 13-15; 14:9-13); the saints whose blood was shed by the great prostitute (Rev. 16:5-6; 17:6; 18:24; 19:1-2); and the souls who were beheaded for the testimony of Jesus (Rev. 20:4).

But our chief example is Jesus Christ who, in the face of opposition, did not swerve from the mission he was given; rather, he was "obedient to the point of death, even death on a cross" (Phil. 2:8). Peter wrote, "When he was reviled, he did not revile in return; when he suffered, he did not threaten, but continued entrusting himself to him who judges justly" (1 Peter 2:23). For this reason, Jesus is called "the faithful witness, the firstborn of the dead, and the ruler of kings on earth" (Rev. 1:5). He is "the Amen, the faithful and true witness, the beginning of God's creation" (Rev. 3:14; cf. 19:11).

Jesus Christ is the Lion of Judah, the Root of David, who has conquered sin and death; and so he is worthy to open the scroll and bring history to its rightful conclusion (Rev. 5:5). He is the Lamb that was slain. By his blood he has ransomed people for God and has made them a kingdom to our God (Rev. 5:6, 9-10). For this reason, we cry out, "To him who loves us and has freed us from our sins by his blood and made us a kingdom, priests to his God and Father, to him be glory and dominion forever and ever " (Rev. 1:5).

Let us follow the example of "Jesus, the founder and perfecter of our faith, who for the joy that was set before him endured the cross, despising the shame, and is seated at the right hand of the throne of God" (Heb. 12:2). May we hold fast to our confession, no matter what our cross may be, and gain the victory through our Lord and Savior Jesus Christ!

Glory in the Cross
ΑΩ

When Christians think about things to come, they respond in different ways and adopt different courses of action. In this final chapter, I want to advise against three courses of action that Christians sometimes take but are misguided, if not wrong. By so doing, I hope to focus our attention on the heart of the matter and to direct us to a more appropriate course of action.

Trust in God, Not in Politics

Some Christians who anticipate things to come respond by endearing themselves to a political candidate or party, as if our choices in the polls will prevent or, at least, delay the coming of the tribulation. The problem with this course of action is that the coming of the Antichrist is inevitable. God has declared the end from the beginning. These events are all part of his masterful plan to bring all creation under one head, Christ. To think that we can change what God has declared by how we vote is foolishness, if not Satanic.

Peter made this mistake during Christ's first coming. Although Jesus had clearly revealed that "he must go to Jerusalem and suffer many things...and be killed, and on the third day be raised" (Matt. 16:21), Peter took Jesus aside and began to rebuke him: "Far be it from you, Lord! This shall never happen to you" (Matt. 16:22). To which Jesus spoke the harsh words to Peter: "Get behind me, Satan!" (Matt. 16:23). Jesus went on to explain to Peter, "For you are not setting your mind on the things of God, but on the things of man" (Matt. 16:23).

Christ's crucifixion, the greatest travesty of justice the world will ever see, did not take God by surprise. God had delivered Jesus up to be crucified according to his predetermined and perfect plan (Acts

2:22-24). Through Christ's death, God demonstrated his greatest act of love for humanity (1 John 4:10) and his unwavering commitment to justice (Rom. 3:25-26). Through the greatest act of human injustice, God upheld his perfect standard of justice. Now, as a result of God's plan in this world, people may repent and receive forgiveness of sins (Luke 24:46-47).

As Jesus revealed to his disciples that he "must" go to Jerusalem and suffer many things, Jesus has similarly revealed to the church "the things that must soon take place" (Rev. 1:1; cf. Rev. 22:6). The book of Revelation does not describe the things that may be, but the things that will be. These things "must" take place. They must take place to bring history to its rightful conclusion.

When that day comes, our political clout will not matter. Christians will be in the minority; the whole world will be following the Beast (Rev. 13:3-4, 8). The voice of Christians, if heard at all, will only be despised by the world and silenced by the Antichrist (Rev. 13:6-7). Furthermore, the Antichrist will be given his authority from God (Rev. 13:5). Yes, Satan is the immediate source of his authority (Rev. 13:2); however, let us remember that even Satan does not have any authority apart from God (Rev. 12:7-12). While we may not understand the purposes for such a despot in history, we must recognize that God is the one who causes leaders to rise and to fall.

While Christians should use their sphere of influence to change the world around them, we must also recognize that there will be times when our political efforts will be futile. If changing society through politics is our spiritual goal, then we will surely lose. We don't want to tie our success to a political candidate or party. Rather, we want to tie our success to the ultimate victor, Jesus Christ, who will rule over the kingdoms of this world.

Let us remember that, when it comes to the end of time, it is not a political battle. It is a spiritual battle.

Trust in God, Not in Strength

Some Christians who anticipate things to come respond by taking up arms, joining a militia and/or preparing for combat, as if they will be able to fight against the Antichrist and win. The problem with this course of action is that the Antichrist will be given authority "to make war on the saints and to conquer them" (Rev. 13:7). These are not idle words: the book of Revelation is soaked in the blood of believers who die at the hands of the Antichrist (see chapter entitled "Endure to the End" in Part Four).

Again, let us learn from the negative example of Peter. When Jesus was about to be arrested, Peter drew his sword to prevent Jesus' arrest. Jesus responded to Peter, "Put your sword back into its place. For all who take the sword will perish by the sword" (Matt. 26:52). The book of Revelation similarly states, "If anyone is to be taken captive, to captivity he goes; if anyone is to be slain with the sword, with the sword must he be slain" (Rev. 13:10).

Jesus went on to say to Peter, "Do you think that I cannot appeal to my Father, and he will at once send me more than twelve legions of angels? But how then should the Scriptures be fulfilled, that it must be so?" (Matt. 26:53-54). Jesus had to go to the cross. To fight against this plan was not to fight against man but God who had ordained it (Matt. 16:22-23). In the book of Revelation, Jesus has similarly declared "the things that must soon take place" (Rev. 1:1). To fight against what must soon take place is not to fight against man but God who has ordained it.

While we should love God with all of our strength, the Bible consistently warns against trusting in our strength, for the flesh of men will fail us. The psalmist declares, "The king is not saved by his great army; a warrior is not delivered by his great strength. The war horse is a false hope for salvation, and by its great might it cannot rescue" (Psalm 33:16-17). The prophet Isaiah wrote, "Woe to those who go down to Egypt for help and rely on horses, who trust in chariots because they are many and in horsemen because they are very strong, but do not look to the Holy One of Israel or consult the Lord!" (Isaiah 31:1). And Jeremiah added, "Cursed is the man who trusts in man and makes flesh his strength, whose heart turns away from the Lord. He is like a shrub in the desert, and shall not see any good come" (Jer. 17:5-6).

Instead, Psalm 44:1-8 should reflect the attitude of our heart:

> O God, we have heard with our ears,
>   our fathers have told us,
> what deeds you performed in their days,
>   in the days of old:
> you with your own hand drove out the nations,
>   but them you planted;
> you afflicted the peoples,
>   but them you set free;
> for not by their own sword did they win the land,
>   nor did their own arm save them,
> but your right hand and your arm,
>   and the light of your face,
>   for you delighted in them.
> You are my King, O God;
>   ordain salvation for Jacob!
> Through you we push down our foes;
>   through your name we tread down those who rise up against us.
> For not in my bow do I trust,
>   nor can my sword save me.
> But you have saved us from our foes
>   and have put to shame those who hate us.
> In God we have boasted continually,
>   and we will give thanks to your name forever. Selah

Let us remember that, when it comes to the end of time, it is not a physical battle. It is a spiritual battle.

Trust in God, Not in Riches

Some Christians who anticipate things to come respond by purchasing parcels of land, investing in gold rather than stocks, and stockpiling supplies as if they will be able to weather the tribulation and come out relatively unscathed. The problem with this course of action is that they fail to recognize the intensity and duration of the tribulation. The Antichrist will control the marketplace, and Christians will not be able to buy or sell (Rev. 13:16-17). In addition, Christians will be hunted down, arrested, and killed. They will not be able to hide away. Their property will be confiscated and given to the state (Rev. 13:7).

While we should use our monetary resources to support godly causes, the Bible consistently warns against trusting in riches, for they are fleeting. The book of Proverbs declares, "Whoever trusts in his riches will fall, but the righteous will flourish like a green leaf" (Prov. 11:28). The apostle Paul instructed Timothy to charge those who are rich "not to be haughty, nor to set their hopes on the uncertainty of riches, but on God, who richly provides us with everything to enjoy" (1 Tim. 6:17). And, James told the twelve tribes in the diaspora, "Let the lowly brother boast in his exaltation, and the rich in his humiliation, because like a flower of the grass he will pass away" (James 1:9-10).

Instead, Jesus exhorts us to focus our time and energy on the kingdom of God and his righteousness:

> Therefore do not be anxious, saying, "What shall we eat?" or "What shall we drink?" or "What shall we wear?" For the Gentiles seek after all these things, and your heavenly Father knows that you need them all. But seek first the kingdom of God and his righteousness, and all these things will be added to you. Therefore do not be anxious about tomorrow, for tomorrow will be anxious for itself. Sufficient for the day is its own trouble. Matt. 6:31-34

Let us remember that, when it comes to the end of time, it is not a financial battle. It is a spiritual battle.

Trust in God and in His Christ

The book of Revelation describes a battle to come. It is not a political battle, so let us not trust in the wisdom of man. It is not a physical battle, so let us not trust in the strength of man. It is not a financial battle, so let us not trust in the riches of man. It is a spiritual battle, so let us trust in God and in his Christ.

The prophet Jeremiah summarized the heart of the matter in this passage:

> Let not the wise man boast in his wisdom, let not the mighty man boast in his might, let not the rich man boast in his riches, but let him who boasts boast in this, that he understands and knows me, that I am the Lord who practices steadfast love, justice, and righteousness in the earth. For in these things I delight, declares the Lord. Jer. 9:23-24

The book of Revelation describes a battle between God and Satan over the souls of men. To whom will we belong? To whom will we swear our allegiance? Having freed us from our sins, Jesus Christ is fighting for us. He has given us the book of Revelation to prepare us for things to come. Having been thrown out of heaven and knowing his time is short, Satan is fighting against us and seeking to destroy our faith. On which side will we fight? The one who conquers will have this as his heritage: God will be his Father, and he will be his son (Rev. 21:7).

Knowing the nature of the battle and the promise set before us, let us trust in God and in his Christ, as the following song so beautifully captures in its lyrics.

Let It Be Said of Us[42]

Let it be said of us that the Lord was our passion.
That with gladness we bore every cross we were given;
That we fought the good fight, that we finished the course,
Knowing within us the power of the risen Lord.

Let the cross be our glory and the Lord be our song;
By mercy made holy, by the Spirit made strong.
Let the cross be our glory and the Lord be our song
'Til the likeness of Jesus be through us made known.
Let the cross be our glory and the Lord be our song.

Notes
AΩ

The Whole Church

[1] John McRay, *Archaelology and the New Testament* (Grand Rapids, Mich: Baker, 1991), 243-44.

[2] Galyn Wiemers, "Lesson 22 of 50 - The Book of Acts (part four of four)," *Generation Word:* http://www.generationword.com/bible_school_notes/22.html (March 5, 2016).

[3] Robert H. Mounce, *The New International Commentary on the New Testament: The Book of Revelation* (Grand Rapids, Mich: Eerdmans, 1998), 56.

Purpose of Revelation

[4] George Eldon Ladd, *A Commentary on the Revelation of John* (Grand Rapids, Mich: Eerdmans, 1972), 41.

All Things New (Rev. 21-22:5)

[5] Saint Augustine, *Confessions* (London: Penguin Books, 1961), 21.

Exegetical Weakness

[6] *The Bible Knowledge Commentary: An Exposition of the Scriptures by Dallas Seminary Faculty*, eds. John F. Walvoord and Roy B. Zuck, 2 vols. (Wheaton: Victor Books, 1983) 2: 938.

[7] Robert H. Gundry, *The Church and the Tribulation* (Grand Rapids, Mich: Zondervan, 1973), 69.

Hermeneutical Weakness

[8] *Creeds of the Churches: A Reader in Christian Doctrine from the Bible to Present*, ed. John H. Leith, 3rd ed. (Louisville: John Knox, 1982), 196.

[9] Edward J. Young, *The Prophecy of Daniel: A Commentary* (Grand Rapids, Mich: Eerdmans, 1949), 191.

[10] *The Bible Knowledge Commentary: An Exposition of the Scriptures by Dallas Seminary Faculty*, eds. John F. Walvoord and Roy B. Zuck, 2 vols. (Wheaton: Victor Books, 1983) 2: 926.

Structural Weakness

[11] *The Bible Knowledge Commentary: An Exposition of the Scriptures by Dallas Seminary Faculty*, eds. John F. Walvoord and Roy B. Zuck, 2 vols. (Wheaton: Victor Books, 1983) 2: 980.

[12] Ibid., 2: 975.

Historical Weakness

[13] Gleason L. Archer Jr., Paul D. Feinberg, Douglas J. Moo, and Richard R. Reiter. *Three Views on the Rapture: Pre-, Mid-, or Post-tribulational?* (Grand Rapids, Mich: Zondervan, 1996), 11-24.

[14] "The Didache - The Complete Text," trans. Tony Jones, *Paraclete Press:* http://www.paracletepress.com/didache.html (March 5, 2016).

[15] *Creeds of the Churches: A Reader in Christian Doctrine from the Bible to Present*, ed. John H. Leith, 3rd ed. (Louisville: John Knox, 1982), 339.

Second Chances

[16] Tim LaHaye and Jerry B. Jenkins, *Left Behind: A Novel of the Earth's Last Days* (Wheaton: Tyndale House, 1995), 102, italics mine.

[17] Ibid., 212, italics mine.

[18] Ibid., 214, italics mine.

[19] Ibid., 299, italics mine.

[20] Leon J. Wood, *The Bible & Future Events: An Introductory Survey of Last-Day Events* (Grand Rapids, Mich: Academie Books, 1973), 72.

Purgatory

[21] Tim LaHaye and Jerry B. Jenkins, *Left Behind: A Novel of the Earth's Last Days* (Wheaton: Tyndale House, 1995), 213, italics mine.

[22] Ibid., 215, italics mine.

Escapism

[23] Tim LaHaye and Jerry B. Jenkins, *Left Behind: A Novel of the Earth's Last Days* (Wheaton: Tyndale House, 1995), 202.

[24] Robert H. Mounce, *The New International Commentary on the New Testament: The Book of Revelation* (Grand Rapids, Mich: Eerdmans, 1998), 147.

Impersonal Gospel Agents

[25] Leon J. Wood, *The Bible & Future Events: An Introductory Survey of Last-Day Events* (Grand Rapids, Mich: Academie Books, 1973), 71.

[26] Tim LaHaye and Jerry B. Jenkins, *Left Behind: A Novel of the Earth's Last Days* (Wheaton: Tyndale House, 1995), 121.

[27] Ibid., 155.

Abandoned Christians

[28] Tim LaHaye and Jerry B. Jenkins, *Left Behind: A Novel of the Earth's Last Days* (Wheaton: Tyndale House, 1995), 200.

[29] Ibid., 201.

[30] Ibid., 216.

[31] Ibid., 221.

Israel and the Church

[32] Hale Lindsey, *The Late Great Planet Earth* (Grand Rapids, Mich: Zondervan, 1970), 142.

Logical Weakness

[33] *The Bible Knowledge Commentary: An Exposition of the Scriptures by Dallas Seminary Faculty*, eds. John F. Walvoord and Roy B. Zuck, 2 vols. (Wheaton: Victor Books, 1983) 2: 990.

Literary Weakness

[34] Hollis Summers, "Literature," *The World Book Encyclopedia*, 22 vols. (Chicago: World Book, 2005) 12: 353.

[35] Stephen Motyer, "Apocalyptic," *Evangelical Dictionary of Biblical Theology*, ed. Walter A. Elwell (Grand Rapids, Mich: Baker, 1996), 28.

Hear the Words

[36] *The World Almanac and Book of Facts 2010*, ed. Sarah Janseen (New York: World Almanac Books, 2010), 793.

[37] Meir Bar-Ilan, "Illiteracy in the Land of Israel in the First Centuries C.E.," *Essays in the Social Scientific Study of Judaism and Jewish Society*, eds. S. Fishbane, S. Schoenfeld, and A. Goldschlaeger (New York: Ktav, 1992), 46-61. Last updated May 27, 1997. *https://faculty.biu.ac.il/~barilm/illitera.html* (March 5, 2016).

[38] "Americans' Perceptions of the Bible's Global Reach," *Research Releases in Culture & Media*. Published April 7, 2015. Barna Group: https://www.barna.org/barna-update/culture/715-americans-perception-of-the-bible-s-reach-globally#.VtjthSjSljo (March 5, 2016).

Take Your Stand

[39] Jack Zavada, "Mark of the Beast: What Is the Mark of the Beast?" *End Times - Topical Bible Study*. Last updated December 15, 2014. *About Religion:* http://christianity.about.com/od/endtimestopicalstudy/a/Mark-Of-The-Beast.htm (March 5, 2016), italics mine.

[40] *The World Almanac and Book of Facts 2010*, ed. Sarah Janseen (New York: World Almanac Books, 2010), 851.

[41] "Martin Niemöller," Last updated February 25, 2016. *Wikiquote:* https://en.wikiquote.org/wiki/Martin_Niem%C3%B6ller (March 5, 2016).

Glory in the Cross

[42] Steve Fry, "Let It Be Said of Us," Maranatha Praise, Inc. (Admin. by Maranatha! Music) Word Music, LLC (a div. of Word Music Group, Inc.), 1999.